Theory for Economic Efficiency:
Essays in Honor of
Abba P. Lerner

Abba P. Lerner

Edited by
Harry I. Greenfield
Albert M. Levenson
William Hamovitch
Eugene Rotwein

Theory for Economic Efficiency:
Essays in Honor of
Abba P. Lerner

The MIT Press
Cambridge, Massachusetts,
and London, England

Copyright © 1979 by
The Massachusetts Institute of Technology

This book was printed and bound by The Murray Printing Company in the
United States of America

Library of Congress Cataloging in Publication Data

Main entry under title:

Theory for economic efficiency.

"Selected bibliography of Abba P. Lerner": p.
Includes bibliographical references and index.
CONTENTS: Arrow, K. J. The trade-off between growth and equity.—
Bergson, A. Consumer's and producer's surplus and general equilibrium.—
Fellner, W. Neo-Keynesianism, monetarism, and the short and the long run.
[etc.]

1. Economics—Addresses, essays, lectures. 2. Efficiency, Industrial—
Addresses, essays, lectures. 3. Lerner, Abba Ptachya, 1903–   I.
Lerner, Abba Ptachya, 1903–   II. Greenfield, Harry I., 1922–
HB34.T52   330.1   78-13391
ISBN 0-262-07074-X

Contents

Preface   vii

1 The Trade-Off Between Growth and Equity
Kenneth J. Arrow   1

2 Consumer's and Producer's Surplus and General Equilibrium
Abram Bergson   12

3 Neo-Keynesianism, Monetarism, and the Short and the Long Run
William Fellner   24

4 A Skeptical Look at the "Natural Rate" Hypothesis
R. A. Gordon   47

5 Is Symmetry Possible in International Money?
Charles P. Kindleberger   63

6 Political Aspects of Economic Control
L. R. Klein   76

7 The Effects of Fiscal Policy and the Choice of Definitions
Fritz Machlup   92

8 Efficient Organizational Design
Jacob Marschak   110

9 Does Perfect Competition in Mining Produce an Optimal Rate of Exploitation?
Ezra J. Mishan   120

10 Abba Lerner and the Theory of Foreign Trade
Robert A. Mundell   144

11 The Development of Keynes's Policy Thinking
Don Patinkin   151

12 Land and the Rate of Interest
Paul A. Samuelson

167

13 Environmental Factors in Project Analysis: A Conceptual Note
Hans W. Singer

186

14 Changing Factor Shares and the Translog Production Function
Jan Tinbergen

195

15 Deficit Spending and Crowding Out in Shorter and Longer Runs
James Tobin

217

A Selected Bibliography: Abba P. Lerner

237

Preface

This festschrift is dedicated to our colleague and friend, Abba P. Lerner, on the occasion of his seventy-fifth birthday. The volume has been assembled by his colleagues at Queens College as a tribute to a great economist who has made significant and long-lasting contributions to many fields of economic theory and policy.

The quality of the contributions in this volume and the eminence of the contributors to it are fitting tribute to the esteem with which Abba Lerner is regarded in the economics profession. In a piece written on the occasion of Abba Lerner's sixtieth birthday, Professor Paul Samuelson noted: "Abba Lerner has been a great theoretical economist in a vintage epoch for theorists. This last third of a century he has poured out one brilliant paper after another—in micro theory and macro, in pure thought, and in the realms of policy. At every public gathering of the field, it is his dynamic wit that brings up the house, and at any age he is still the glorious wunderkind of our guild."[1]

Professor Milton Friedman, in an extensive review of Lerner's *Economics of Control*, while generally critical of the book, nevertheless had this to say: "The book throughout reveals Lerner's very considerable gifts—his acuteness as a theorist and dialectician, his skill and patience in exposition, his flexibility of mind, his profound interest in social welfare, and his willingness to accept and courage to state what seems to him right social policy, regardless of precedent or accepted opinion."[2]

Lerner's work and activities over the past fifteen years (which include his election in 1974 as a Fellow of the National Academy of Sciences) demonstrate a continuity of the same characteristics noted by the two Laureates. It remains as true as ever that "the drum beat Abba Lerner answers to is that of science, and when he plays his pipe we economists of all ages become like the little children of Hamlin."[3]

This volume is not intended to serve as an assessment of Lerner's place in economic theory. Rather it is an outpouring of creativity from his friends and colleagues, perhaps the greatest birthday celebration one can receive from one's peers.

For making this volume possible, our most sincere thanks go first to the contributors. Their enthusiastic support and cooperation was most gratifying. We are sorry to note here that Harry G. Johnson died before he could complete a piece for this volume, but we know from Professor Jacob Frenkel, a close colleague of his, that Johnson had completed parts of the essay—undoubtedly one of his last creative efforts. We regret also to note that Professor Jacob Marschak died about two weeks after sending his essay to us, making this piece one of his last works. Another sad note must be added here: Robert Aaron Gordon died about one month after submitting his essay.

Our thanks are due to colleagues in our department who read some of the essays—Michael Dohan, Hugo Kaufmann, and Michael Edelstein. Michael Intriligator was kind enough to proofread Marschak's paper.

Our acknowledgments would be incomplete if we did not mention the invaluable administrative help of our college assistant, Beatrice Schwartz.

The editors of this volume apologize to Dr. Lerner's many friends who could not be asked, because of space limitations, to contribute to it. We are confident, however, that they join with his colleagues at Queens College and the eminent contributors to this volume in wishing Abba Lerner a happy birthday and in expressing to him our joint thanks, along with that of economists everywhere, for his monumental contributions to the solution of so many of the important problems of our discipline.

The traditional birthday greeting in Hebrew is *Ad Mea Essrim*—"may you live to be one-hundred and twenty"—to which the modern Israelis have added, "plus 8 percent for value added tax." Amen.

The Publications Committee
Harry I. Greenfield, chairman
Albert M. Levenson
William Hamovitch
Eugene Rotwein

Queens College, City University of New York
December 1977

Notes

1. Paul A. Samuelson, "A. P. Lerner at Sixty," *Review of Economic Studies* 31, No. 3 (1965): 169.

2. Milton Friedman, *Essays in Positive Economics* (Chicago: University of Chicago Press, 1953), p. 319. The original article appeared in *Journal of Political Economy* 22 (October 1947).

3. Samuelson, "A. P. Lerner," p. 178.

Theory for Economic Efficiency:
Essays in Honor of
Abba P. Lerner

Chapter 1

Kenneth J. Arrow

The Trade-off Between Growth and Equity

The goals of economic policy are many and varied. Some of them are drawn from outside the economic sphere: national security and power, the achievement of a broad range of social goals (such as the aesthetic improvement of urban life, social communication, health, and internal order and personal security), or the better development of individuals and of the modes of social interaction. Even within what might loosely be regarded as the endogenous goals of economic policy (perhaps defined as those for which the market is or could be used as a detailed allocative instrument), there is a considerable variety. But perhaps all or virtually all can be reduced in one way or another to three: economic stability, allocative efficiency, and distributive equity.

Where does the goal of economic growth appear in this short list? In some ways, economic growth has been a recurrent theme of economic analysis since the days of Adam Smith. But perhaps the period since World War II has seen more emphasis than ever before. This is not surprising since this period has also seen a more rapid rate of economic growth than anything achieved in the past. This period may be drawing to a close. I have no more belief in the existence of the Kondratiev cycle now than I did when my professors ridiculed the idea, but it still may be true that high productivity growth is due to random and unpredictable causes; we may just have had a run of good luck, aided by an arrears of technological development resulting from the Great Depression and World War II. Further the exaggerated views of the limits-of-growth proponents do contain a genuine if tautological truth: there are resources, land and minerals, whose total stock is fixed, and continued use must eventually lead to their exhaustion. If these limited resources are indeed essential, growth must become negative.

But resource scarcities are not, in my judgment, a problem that will restrict growth seriously within the next twenty-five to fifty years; and I think it by no means unlikely that the rapid growth of scientifically inspired technology will lead to a resumption of growth of factor productivity. So growth, the attitudes toward it, and the policies that can achieve it or at least prevent its cessation are still major issues. But growth is not an elementary goal; it is one derived from the goals of efficiency and equity as applied to choices over time. Specifically just as we are concerned with possible conflicts between efficiency and equity in resource allocation at a moment of time, so we are also concerned with possible conflicts between efficiency and equity in allocating resources among individuals at different points of time.

From the viewpoint of values, this is what the problem of optimal growth policy amounts to. There is also the descriptive problem: identifying both the different policies that can affect the distribution of income or that can affect the future evolution of the economy and the effects of egalitarian policies on growth and of growth-promoting policies on equality of distribution.

Let us start with a review of the problems of reconciling efficiency and equity in a static context. First there is the conceptual question of what is meant by efficiency and what by equity. The answers to both question have been (and doubtless always will be) matters of dispute as long as humanity, with its inevitable tension between the demands of the individual and those of society, exists. I confine myself to a few observations, to set the basis for subsequent discussion.

Efficiency and equity are both judgments, statements of preference. In the context of economics, the judgments or preferences are about allocations of resources. By an allocation in the full sense, I mean a statement of the inputs and outputs of every production process, of the assignments of final goods to individuals or households, and of the productive resources, labor and property, required of each individual or household.

Interest is clearly confined to feasible allocations. An allocation that requires the use of more of a primary resource than is available or that calls for the distribution of final consumers of more of a commodity than is produced cannot be considered. Further, the outputs required of any production process must in fact be obtainable from the inputs; the allocation has to be consistent with the available technological knowledge.

Modern economic analysis has begun to emphasize that there are restrictions on feasibility, in addition to those of resource availability and technology. The very nature of our economic institutions prevents us from achieving any allocation we wish. In an economy based on private property

and free sale of labor services, the initial distribution of skills and ownership of property determines the distribution of income, which in turn
determines the allocation of consumers' goods. Thus not all technically
feasible allocations can be realized. To be sure, the market allocation can
be modified by government actions, either by directly allocating goods or
by modifying the distribution of income through taxation, but the possibilities for reallocation in this manner are limited.

A socialist economy might, in theory, achieve a wider set of allocations,
but it is also subject to limitations. If it relies heavily on the market and its
incentives, then its outcome is similar to that of a capitalist economy. If it
tends more toward direct allocation, then it is apt to be mechanically
egalitarian and give the same bundle of goods to individuals of varying
needs and tastes, not merely for ideological reasons but also for lack of
information to make finer differentiations. Thus the concept of feasibility
takes account not merely of resource limitations and technology but also
of institutional constraints.

Of efficiency and equity, efficiency is the simpler concept. The usual
definition in economics was first clearly formulated by Vilfredo Pareto:
an allocation of resources is efficient if there is no other feasible allocation
that will make everyone better off. The only ambiguity in this definition,
is the meaning of "better off." I will confine myself to the individualistic
interpretation: each individual is to be the judge of when he or she is
better off, so that we respect individual decisions in the market and in
voting.[1]

Even in a static world, equity is an elusive concept. There is no need to
enlarge on the rival concepts that have always held the field. The differences among the utilitarian viewpoint, Rawls's principle of benefiting
the worst off, and Nozick's view that any distribution arrived at by free
contracting is just, sufficiently illustrate the variety of views. I will assume
simply that equity means as much equality of income as is possible, that
the only reason that can be raised against policies leading to equalization
of income is that they impair efficiency (or other desirable aims not
considered in this article). I have stated this in an extreme fashion for
simplicity. All that is really needed for my purposes is that the desirable
income distribution is more nearly equal than would be yielded by the
natural workings of the system.

To some extent, economic theory can be used to argue that the goals of
efficiency and equity can be separated, that any distribution deemed equitable can be achieved without loss of efficiency. The argument is based on
important properties of the competitive price system. There are two pro-

positions here: any resource allocation achieved by a competitive price system is efficient; and for any efficient resource allocation, there is a redistribution of initial assets such that the competitive system will, after the redistribution, come to rest at the given resource allocation. These conclusions are valid only under some significant conditions, but for the moment let us assume that the conditions are met. Then the policy implication is that equity should be achieved by redistributing initial assets and then letting the market operate freely to determine production and consumption. In the extreme case, an equal division of initial holdings of primary resources would be called for.

It is important that the redistribution of assets not be made dependent on the individual's subsequent actions in the market, for that would amount to a tax on the sales of certain goods, which will impair efficiency. The most important case is that of labor skills, which cannot be redistributed. An alternative would be to redistribute the income arising from their sale, but this amounts to a tax on the sale of skilled labor, as in the case of an ordinary income tax. Since an individual always has the power to reduce his or her offering of labor, the efficiency of allocation is reduced. In short, under a system in which individuals have some control over the total amounts or the particular kinds of labor services they will offer, arbitrary redistributions of income are not feasible. Hence there is a trade-off between equity and efficiency.

One important qualification to this last statement must be registered: the undisturbed market system leads to efficiency only under the assumption of perfect competition, but competition is far from perfect. It is therefore conceivable that steps that interfere with the market might improve both efficiency and equity. Antimonopoly policy is a case in point. To the extent that monopolies increase the inequality of income, breaking them up may be a policy in which the efficiency-equity conflict is absent. But one cannot generalize. If antimonopoly policy includes policy against labor monopolies, the effect may be to decrease equity. It is, however, in the context of time that imperfections of competition are most relevant to the efficiency-equity issue.

In considering the relations between efficiency and equity over time, I will simplify the discussion by ignoring problems of equity within a generation and assume provisionally that all individuals in a given generation are alike.

In the context of allocation over time, there is a new kind of redistribution of resources as compared with the static case: resources can be distributed from the present to the future. This typically takes the form of investment, a sacrifice of current consumption to increase future products. Refraining from consumption of exhaustible resources can be thought of as a special case of investment.

The condition for efficiency in this context is well known; it is the requirement that all investments yield the same rate of return in any given time period. However, among the efficient allocations, there is a distinction between the concept of growth and the concept of equity. If, for the moment, we assume that growth basically results from capital accumulation, then the greater the capital accumulation, the faster the rate of growth. (It is generally recognized that this process cannot continue indefinitely, eventually the rate of growth is conditioned by labor and other fixed factors. But clearly an increase in capital accumulation can increase growth for a period which may be rather long.) But indefinitely high growth is not necessarily good. Quite apart from problems of exhaustible resources, there is no particular reason why the present generation should sacrifice large amounts of consumption indefinitely to achieve higher rates of growth and higher rates of consumption for its successors. Justice requires a balance between competing values of the current and future generations.

Redistributions in time differ from redistributions at a given moment of time in one important aspect. Usually we think of the latter as reducing total product by reducing incentives. Redistribution from the present to the future, however, is typically productive: we expect such an allocation to yield a return over and above the initial resources invested. In terms of goods, the recipient gains more than the donor loses. Whatever one's exact form of ethics, this clearly is a powerful argument for benefiting the future.

There are, however, two offsetting considerations. One is that present investments tend to make future individuals better off than present ones, so the redistribution is from the present poor to the future rich. To minimize this adverse redistribution, the rate of return required on investments for the future should be higher, the higher is the rate of growth. A second— more disputed—consideration is that there is an intrinsic tendency to discounting the future. No individual living today can really regard individuals living in the future, particularly the far future, as being equivalent to himself. Indeed, if benefits for all future generations were counted equally, the value of the present would dwindle into insignificance. If we consistently refuse to discount the future, then a current generation should reduce itself to subsistence levels if there is any positive return on investment, no matter how small.

Thus a rough consensus is that a future investment ought to be made if and only if the productivity of the investment is at least as great as the sum of two countervailing effects, the pure futurity or discount effect and an allowance for the greater income of future generations. I will call this statement the Investment Criterion.

I have spoken so far, for simplicity, as if growth were entirely due to large capital accumulation. In fact a large fraction of growth in modern society is a result of technological advances that are to a considerable extent at least independent of the usual form of capital accumulation. Hence the future generations may well be richer even if no investment were made today. To that extent the argument for restricting redistribution to the future is strengthened.

Economists typically argue that public investment should be governed by the Investment Criterion. But actual public investments are not necessarily made in accordance with them. The question may also rise whether private investments are made this way. Indeed if concern for the future is considered social rather than individual in nature—that is, an expression of justice or of concern for the perpetuation of humanity—then we would expect individuals to save and invest less than the Investment Criterion requires.

The situation in practice is more complicated than the simple model I have assumed thus far because individuals live over time and because they are concerned about the futures of their families. Hence individuals as well as society have some reason to save or invest for the future. Their behavior in this regard is indeed parallel to that of the social sector, and they may come up with a rather similar criterion.

To the extent that this is true, we may suppose that the market will lead to something like a just and efficient allocation of resources over time. The theoretical argument might suggest some underinvestment in the future; optimal investment might be more than would be sustained by the preferences of individuals for their own future and for that of their children.

But I think a more serious question may be one of imperfections of the capital market. In a world of uncertainty, borrowing cannot necessarily reach the optimal levels. In particular, borrowing for human capital formation, as in education or for development of new technologies, is likely to be restricted, and the government intervention for these purposes has been well argued; in the case of education, the need is essentially fully accepted by most nations, possibly even overaccepted.

Today there is a widely dispersed distribution of income. Individuals and institutions, through their decisions, allocate their resources between current consumption and investment and saving for the future. Capital markets, to the extent that they operate, direct the desired saving into different forms of specific investment. The economy of the future is generated from all these decisions, together with the outside forces that also influence growth. The result, as experience has shown, is a restructuring of an economy, generally at a higher average income level but again with a widely dispersed distribution of income.

What, then, is the effect of classical redistributive policy through the tax system on efficiency and growth? There are both positive and negative effects. To start with the latter, the first, and perhaps most important, point is the reduced efficiency of the economic system. This has consequences for growth. The loss in income compared with what might have been means both that there is less available for capital accumulation and that the capital accumulated is used less efficiently. Hence the economy is on a permanently lower level, and perhaps the growth rate is lowered.

A second problem arises out of the redistribution itself, apart from the efficiency problems arising from the taxes to pay for the redistribution. It appears that savings by individuals is likely to rise more than proportionately with income. Hence total personal savings will fall as a result of redistribution. Further, to the extent that redistributive taxes fall on the business institutions that form such a large part of the saving mechanism, there may again be a reduction in saving. The income, concentrated in one place and therefore easier to use for saving, is now scattered. In a world of perfect capital markets, this redistribution from firms to individuals would make no difference, but internal financing by firms is to a large extent precisely a compensation for imperfect capital markets.

For these reasons, the aggregate volume of capital formation may fall as a consequence of redistribution. There are compensating factors, however. The recipients of the redistributed income may now have better access to capital markets—for example, through mutual funds or even through savings banks. Their incomes may rise to the point where saving becomes worthwhile.

More important is the increased ability of lower-income individuals to engage in forms of capital formation not handled well through the market.

I am thinking especially of human capital formation. More schooling may become financially possible. The poor may have a greater chance to choose among jobs the ones for which they are best fitted. Improved conditions in the home are an important, though informal, type of capital formation. Because human capital formation among the poor will not be financed through capital markets, there is special reason to believe it will have an unusually high rate of return.

Taking everything together, taxation-financed redistribution will probably lower aggregate saving, though possibly redirecting part of it into higher-return activities. But such a policy will have in general a positive effect in reducing the future inequality of income. On the high-income side, the taxes will have the effect of reducing the concentration of wealth. The rich allocate their resources between current consumption and wealth accumulation for themselves and their heirs. If they are taxed, they will in general reduce both. Hence to the extent that income inequality is perpetuated by inheritance, the same policies that redistribute wealth today will reduce inequality tomorrow. On the low-income side, the subsidies will be used for human capital formation, which is largely devoted to affecting income tomorrow. While inheritance can make no significant contribution to improving the income of the next generation of poor, improvement in the household and more schooling can.

Different types of taxes can be used to finance redistribution. Although the ordinary income tax has many merits, it also has some defects. It distorts the choice between labor and leisure, but this is probably unavoidable in any tax system. It imposes a double taxation on saving by taxing both saved income and the return to that saving. How serious the resulting distortion is not known, but it might be considerable. It can be avoided by shifting to progressive taxes on total consumption. This will have the additional virtue, from the redistributionist point of view, of taxing consumption derived from gifts and inheritances, which are effectively taxed at much lower rates.

It will still be necessary to have annual taxes on wealth, as in Sweden today, to prevent a concentration of wealth by those who consume relatively little out of high incomes. The rate can be low enough to minimize disincentives to save by those who are saving for the purpose of future consumption, while the annual repetition of the tax over a long period of time will fall on those who are accumulating wealth for its own sake or for the sake of the power it conveys.

A policy of income redistribution through taxes and transfers does involve a risk of efficiency losses both at a moment of time and over time. On the other hand, there are some gains in efficiency if the income of lower groups is raised sufficiently to enable them to engage in some rational planning. On the whole redistribution within a single generation tends to have some positive effect toward equality in the future.

Earlier I singled out the imperfection of the capital markets as the largest element of inefficiency in allocation over time. This raises the question of whether it is possible to counteract these distortions and at the same time decrease inequality. It is clear that the imperfection of the capital market weighs most heavily upon the poor in their human capital formation, and this suggests the proper course of action.

A great part of redistribution should take the form of social capital formation of a kind that will raise the productivity of the poor. The negative income tax will allow the poor the right to choose their own consumption patterns, for example. But I think that it is fairly clear that many kinds of capital formation that will benefit them cannot be carried out at all or at least cannot be carried out efficiently on an individual level.

The most obvious example of social capital formation is education. It may be objected reasonably that this activity is already largely socialized and that there is little possibility of further gains in highly educated countries like the United States and Japan. However this obvious lesson has not been learned by many—perhaps even most—developing countries. They have not realized that education provides a means of achieving both high-productivity investment and income equalization.

Even in advanced countries, there is room for improvement. I would judge that the biggest lack is technical education. This becomes especially important in a technologically advancing world where skills have not only to be acquired but also changed. Mid-career shifts should be facilitated by suitable education, as well as updating in the same line of work. The facilities provided are inadequate in most countries. There is another problem. For an individual capable of earning an income, even an adolescent going to the university, the sacrifice of income is a larger investment than the cost of providing the educational facility. This situation illustrates an imperfection of the capital market; ideally the individual should be able to borrow against future earnings but cannot.

Providing technical education and financing students is both equalizing and socially efficient in producing appropriate growth. It would be desirable, in my view, that the beneficiary ultimately be responsible for the costs incurred. The best way would be a repayment dependent upon future income. In this way the risks and uncertainties of the benefits are borne by the state, which is an ideal insurer, rather than by the individual. If such a repayment scheme is considered too difficult to achieve, however, I would rather have free tuition and scholarships than no system of technical education or one paid for out of current income.

Similarly government subsidy to facilitate labor mobility across occupations and across regions would seem an appropriate form of social investment, aimed simultaneously at intertemporal efficiency and equity.

A more speculative idea is subsidizing investment by the poor. Currently in most advanced countries, subsidized housing is provided for lower-income groups. In the United States, the program has not worked, possibly for reasons peculiar to the country. This program is investment on behalf of the poor but not by them. An alternative possibility is to enable the poor to own their own homes by subsidizing the investment— for example, by interest-free or low-interest loans. This will constitute a transfer of wealth, not merely of income. In addition to giving the poor a greater stake in the maintenance of their housing, it offers a chance to make more equal the future distribution of income.

Finally I urge that the government take a much greater role in the development of civilian technology, particularly in the basic steps. It is a familiar argument of economists that in a competitive world, a firm's incentives to innovate will be limited if the innovation will become everyone's property. Patent rights protect only a limited range of innovations. Government addition to the supply of innovative effort will therefore improve efficiency.

The policy of government development of civilian technology will also contribute to equality. In the absence of markets to achieve efficient risk bearing, the resources for technological development come from those already wealthy, and hence technical progress on the whole reinforces the existing distribution of income. If the supply of new technologies comes from the government and is freely available to all newcomers, there is likely to be greater opportunity for equalization of wealth through competition.

I take very seriously the moral obligation to achieve equity in income, now and in the future. This obligation does have to be properly balanced against the requirements of efficient allocation at a given moment of time and over time. No simplistic solution is possible, but recognizing the intrinsic imperfections of competition in a capitalist system affords opportunities to reconcile the two aims.

Note

1. In the context of time, which is discussed later, this viewpoint may not be en-

tirely admissible. In education and in other social institutions, we do seek to influence what kind of individuals will emerge, not merely accept whatever emerges.

Chapter 2

Abram Bergson

Consumer's and Producer's Surplus and General Equilibrium

In a recent essay (1973), I challenged a widely held view as to the negligible impact on welfare of monopoly pricing distortions. In the process I also elaborated on consumer's surplus analysis. As formulated, for example, in Hicks (1956), that analysis is essentially of a partial equilibrium sort. My concern was to reformulate the theory in a general equilibrium context that seemed appropriate to the measurement of monopoly welfare losses. The result also appeared to provide further perspective on pre-Hicksian, that is Marshallian consumer's surplus.

In this essay I propose to extend the analysis somewhat further. Previously I assumed a linear production possibilities schedule. For the sake of generality, I now refer to curvilinear production possibilities. The analysis will also permit a reinterpretation of pre-Hicksian consumer's surplus analysis with more explicit attention than was possible before to producer's surplus, or at least to one outstanding facet of that rather complex phenomenon.

Consumer's surplus analysis is often formulated in more or less general terms and without reference to any particular application. That might be possible here, but the analysis seems facilitated if I refer again to monopoly pricing.[1]

What is in question is the welfare loss suffered because monopolistic firms charge prices that, rather than being equal to marginal costs as under perfect competition, tend systematically to be above that level. Attention has usually been focused on monopoly pricing for final, rather than intermediate, goods. I consider here, therefore, an economy in which only consumers' goods are produced. The losses in question might fall unevenly among different income groups and so pose a question of equity, but the concern generally has been with efficiency. I will accordingly adopt the familiar device of addressing an economy in which there is but a single household that behaves as a perfect competitor in purchasing consumer's goods.

Although, consumer's surplus may be represented variously, I focus on the "compensating variation": the compensatory change in income needed to ensure that a household's utility is unaffected by a change in price (Hicks 1956, pp. 61ff, 69ff). Hicks refers, however, to the hypothetical variation from an otherwise constant money income. Such a variation is properly taken to measure a welfare loss or gain if income is actually constant. Where the concern is with the welfare loss resulting from monopoly pricing, however, attention—at least tacitly—has been focused on a particular sort of misallocation, one that occurs without any concomitant unemployment. In other words, the supposition is that any resources excluded from monopolistic industries by monopolistic pricing there are employed instead in competitive industries. In equilibrium, in the consumers' goods economy in question, the corollary is that the community fuly realizes its production possibilities both with and without monopolistic pricing in the monopolistic industries.[2] That is not apt to be possible unless our household's income changes along with prices in the monopolistic industries. At least it is apt not to be possible if, for convenience, one or another price in the competitive sector is taken as numeraire.

Consider the two-commodity economy shown in figure 2.1. Let x_1 represent the output and consumption of a monopolistic good and x_2 the output and consumption of a competitive good. The latter is the numeraire. Also shown are PP', the community's production possibility schedule, and U', U'', U''', and U'''', four of the household's indifference curves. With perfect competition in the economy generally, prices in equilibrium must equal marginal costs and are also proportional to the household's marginal utilities. The household then consumes x, and output corresponds to that budget point.

At x the household's budget constraint DK is tangent to both PP' and to one of the household's indifference curves, here shown as U''''. Furthermore, at that budget point, the price ratio, the household's marginal rate of substitution, and the community's marginal rate of transformation are all equal.

With a monopoly price charged for x_1, however, and with household income constant in terms of x_2, the good that is still produced competitively, output and consumption will be at x'. There the household's new budget constraint, DE, is again tangent to an indifference curve –in this case U'—but the economy, except by coincidence, will no longer be realizing its production possibilities. It follows that Hicks's compensating varia-

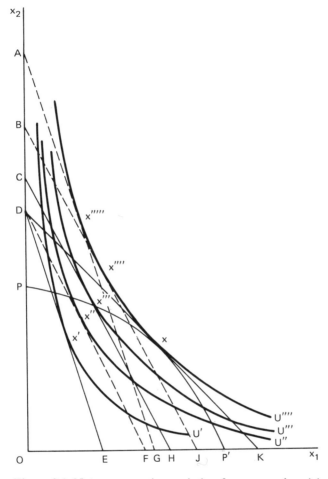

Figure 2.1 Net compensating variation for monopoly pricing.

tion, if construed as it usually is, is AD in the figure and measures the loss due to not only the misallocation occurring when production possibilities are realized but a shortfall from those possibilities. The loss due to the misallocation is alone of interest here.[3] In sum if we are to use Hicks's compensating variation, we must recast it in a way that allows the community to remain on its production possibilities schedule when prices are monopolistically instead of competitively determined. I did that in my previous article, and it was chiefly on that account that the resulting measure of loss seemed properly viewed as of a general equilibrium nature, and so to contrast with Hicks's compensating variation. The latter evidently relates to partial equilibrium. The procedure adopted before may also serve here, but, as indicated, reference previously was to a community where production possibilities are linear. With production possibilities curvilinear as in figure 2.1, the analysis must be restated.

To continue with the community shown in the figure, the measure of loss that is of interest is BC. With monopolistic pricing for x_1, we suppose that the household's income has been increased from OD to OC. On that basis the household's consumption shifts to x''', where the new budget constraint CH is tangent to another indifference curve, U'''. At x''', moreover, production possibilities are again fully realized. In other words at x''', the household's marginal rate of substitution differs from the marginal rate of transformation by just an amount corresponding to the monopolistic divergence of the price of x_1 from its marginal cost. BC, then, represents the further increment of income that would still have to be made available to the household to restore it to the initial indifference curve, U''''. With a monopolistic price charged for x_1, that would occur with the household's consumption shifting to x''''. True x'''' is beyond the range of production possibilities, but BC still can serve as a measure of the relevant loss.

I will designate the money income needed to ensure realization of production possibilities at any given prices as a 'full-employment' money income. With monopoly pricing for x_1 and income at a full-employment level, the price of x_1 (in terms of the numeraire) might conceivably be the same as when income fails to ensure that production possibilities are realized. But more likely, it would not be, and I have drawn figure 2.1 accordingly. Thus the slope of the budget constraint through x''' differs from that through x'. Recall that x' represents consumption when the household's income is as it was initially at x, but a monopoly price is charged for x_1.

Although BC is the desired measure of loss, it is obtainable as the difference between two further increments in income, BD and CD. Consider the market basket x''. It represents the household's consumption if income were as it was at x and a monopoly price were charged for x_1, but now there is a monopoly price corresponding to a full-employment income rather than the monopoly price that actually would be charged if income remained as at x. At x'' the household experiences a level of utility U''. BD, then, is the increment of income needed to raise the consumption to x'''', where the household is once more experiencing its initial utility U''''. And that increment is again Hicks's compensating variation, though now what is compensated for is a change in the price of x_1 from the competitive level to the monopolistic one that finally will prevail when production possibilities are reattained. As for CD, that is simply the increment of money income needed to ensure that production possibilities are in fact reattained.

More generally, let us designate Hicks's compensating variation as the *gross compensating variation* (GCV) but on the understanding that the income variation in question is now that needed to compensate for a change from a competitive price to the monopolistic one that would prevail when income remains at a full-employment level. The increment of income needed to assure reattainment of production possibilities when that monopolistic price is charged is referred to as the *money income adjustment* (MIA), and the desired measure of loss is the *net compensation variation* (NCV):

$$NCV = GCV - MIA. \tag{2.1}$$

Producer's surplus has diverse manifestations, but my concern is only with one of them, though clearly it is a principal one. Suppose, for convenience, that our monopolistic product is produced by a single firm whose marginal cost schedule is as shown in figure 2.2. Since we are interested only in monopoly power that the firm exercises over the price of its product, I assume that prices of factor inputs do not vary as the firm varies its employment of them. Indeed for the moment it is just as well to assume that there is but a single variable factor employed—labor—, that the supply of labor available to the economy generally is fixed, and that in our competitive industry the marginal and average productivity of labor are constant. Hence in terms of the numeraire, the wage rate must indeed be constant.

In these circumstance, if our monopolistic producer charged a price equal to marginal cost (p^c in figure 2.2), he evidently would be earning an

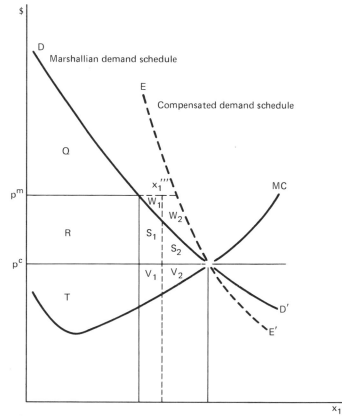

Figure 2.2 Marshallian surpluses under monopoly pricing

income in excess of his total variable costs corresponding to the area $(T + V)$, where $V = V_1 + V_2$. Such excess income is usually called *producer's economic rent*. Such rent seems always to have been understood as a form of producer's surplus, and under our assumptions it will be agreed that it is the only form that would materialize in the economy considered if the monopolist charged a price equal to marginal cost.

Suppose now that the monopolist appropriately exploits his monopoly power and charges a price above marginal cost, say p^m. Here perhaps usage in respect of the concept of economic rent varies. Such rent, it is always understood, falls by an amount equivalent to V, but some would probably hold producer's rent to rise concomitantly by the amount represented as R in the figure. That, of course, corresponds to the profit the monopolist reaps by charging a price above marginal costs. As for producer's surplus, usage here too is perhaps not fully settled, but the most usual convention clearly decrees that it still be taken to correspond to producer's economic rent, though in the inclusive sense that now embraces monopoly profits.[4] Hence producer's surplus is properly seen now as corresponding to $(R + T)$ and so as increasing by $(R - V)$.

We are interested not in producer's surplus in itself but in the welfare loss resulting from monopoly pricing. To represent that, we must also consider consumer's surplus, though now in the Marshallian way: with the monopoly's price at marginal cost, the area $(Q + R + S)$, where $S = S_1 + S_2$, and with the monopoly's charging a monopolistic price, the area Q. That means that consumer's surplus is reduced by $R + S$. In order to obtain the indicated loss of welfare—the *net surplus variation* (NSV)—we must deduct from the fall in consumer's surplus, the increase in producer's surplus:

$$\text{NSV} = (R + S) - (R - V) \tag{2.2}$$

or

$$\text{NSV} = S + V. \tag{2.3}$$

In this way we arrive at the proverbial textbook representation of the loss of welfare as a quasi-triangle such as that indicated in the figure. Here again, of course, the analysis is of a partial equilibrium sort, though now pre-Hicksian.

How does NSV compare with NCV as given by equation (2.1)? That is the chief question that remains to be considered, but on one further condition, the answer is simply that the two coincide. The condition is the famous one that the income elasticity of demand for the product in question be zero. In that case the budget points x'', x''' and x'''' in figure 2.1 all include the same x_1 and differ only in respect of x_2. Also the GCV in (2.1), or BD in figure 2.1, corresponds to the reduction in consumers' surplus as represented by the area $(R + S)$ in figure 2.2, for there are no income effects that might distort the relation between those two aspects (see Hicks 1956, pp. 68ff).

It also follows that MIA, or CD in figure 2.1, corresponds to the increase in producer's surplus as represented by the area $(R - V)$ in figure 2.2, for if there is still to be full employment, our household must be able to pay for the reduced output of the monopolist an amount that now includes the monopolist's profit R. The contraction of output, however, obviates the need for purchasing power by an amount V, representing the excess in the value of that output decrement over earnings of the concomitantly released labor. The latter earnings are represented geometrically by the relevant area under the marginal cost schedule. Hence V is the excess of the value of the output decrement over the value of the additional output that the released labor will produce in the competitive industry, and we have

$$NCV = (R + S) - (R - V) = NSV. \tag{2.4}$$

In short the reduction in consumer's surplus in its pre-Hicksian version comes to the same thing as our GCV. The increase in producer's surplus corresponds to MIA. The NSV that is obtained as the difference between the changes in consumer's and producer's surplus is properly viewed as the pre-Hicksian measure of welfare loss. That loss then comes to the same thing as NCV, which is obtained as the difference between GCV and MIA.

In calculating NSV, when there were no income effects, I had to consider only one demand schedule, the Marshallian one shown in figure 2.2. That schedule obtains no matter what the level of the household's income. With income effects, NSV might be calculated from either of two such schedules, one relating to a full-employment income when prices in both industries considered are at competitive levels and one relating to a full-employment income when our monopolist charges a monopoly price for his product. Although the texts are rarely explicit on the matter, NSV seems usually envisaged as reflecting a demand schedule of the latter sort, but it facilitates discussion here to refer instead to that where a full-employment income prevails with competitive pricing for the monopoly good. What has to be said about the alternative computation will be evident.

The precise correspondence of GCV and the reduction in consumer's surplus, as represented by $(R + S)$, reflects the fact that, without income effects, the Marshallian demand schedule corresponds to a compensated one associated with the initial equilibrium consumption of x_1. With income effects, those two schedules no longer coincide, and for GCV we now have

$$GCV = R + S + W, \tag{2.5}$$

where $W = W_1 + W_2$. When the Marshallian and the compensated schedules differ, as Hicks brought out, the compensating variation must be computed from the compensated schedule, and that is also true of GCV. I refer here to the compensated schedule in figure 2.2; for illustration, I assume that the monopoly good is a normal or superior one. Hence if we continue to compute the reduction in consumer's surplus as $(R + S)$, we must consider that that sum falls short of GCV by the amount W.

We must also consider, however, that the x_1 in the budget position x''' (figure 2.1) now exceeds the x_1 in the budget position x'', though it falls short of that in the budget position x''''. The indicated magnitude of x_1 is shown in figure 2.2 as x_1'''. In that case, we have

$$\text{MIA} = R + W_1 + S_1 - V_2. \tag{2.6}$$

Should the increase in producer's surplus still be taken as $(R - V)$, then, MIA exceeds that sum by $(W_1 + S_1 + V_1)$. For NCV we have

$$\text{NCV} = S_2 + W_2 + V_2, \tag{2.7}$$

and NSV, as given by (2.3), now diverges from that measure:

$$\text{NSV} = \text{NCV} + (S_1 + V_1 - W_2). \tag{2.8}$$

If we accept the Hicksian conception of consumer's surplus as reformulated here, that divergence must also be viewed as an error in NSV as a measure of welfare loss. The error, as long understood, originates in income effects. But usually attention has been focused on the bias in the Marshallian demand schedule in respect of consumer's surplus. The resultant measure of the reduction in consumer's surplus is indeed biased as far as it diverges from the GCV. But the corresponding increase in producer's surplus as calculated in the Marshallian way is also in error if it is viewed as an observation on MIA. Moreover the two sorts of error curiously tend to cancel: while the GCV is understated, so too is MIA. Recall that the latter is deducted from GCV to obtain NCV.[5]

In calculating consumer's surplus, Hicks (1956, p. 169) has held that there must always be "a sufficient background of fixed-price commodities, to serve as 'money'." In relating NSV to NCV I have not only taken x_2 as numeraire but have assumed that it is produced competitively under conditions of constant cost. Hick's requirement, therefore, has been fully met. Note, however, that there was no need to assume constant costs in defining NCV to begin with. Also in relating NSV to NCV, that assumption can be dispensed with again, but there are then two further, in some degree offsetting, sources of error in NSV viewed as an observation on NCV. Thus suppose that there are diminishing returns to labor in the competitive as well as in the monopolistic industry. Then $(R - V)$ evidently fails to allow for the additional producer's surplus generated by increased production of the numeraire good. Or rather that is so if $(R - V)$ is calculated by reference to a marginal cost schedule reflecting the wage rate prevailing when the monopolist charges a competitive price. But with the shift to a monopoly price and the transfer of labor to the competitive industry, the wage rate itself falls. Hence $(R - V)$ as so calculated also fails to allow for that reduction. For my purposes here, I continue to suppose that the monopolist acts as a competitor in hiring labor even though the wage rate ultimately varies in dependence on his price policy.

I assumed that labor is the only variable factor of production. Where there are two or more such factors, their relative prices are apt to vary as they are reallocated between monopolistic and competitive industries. Here too, therefore, the observation on MIA that is obtained from pre-Hicksian surplus analysis is affected.

In reformulating the Hicksian analysis in a general equilibrium context and in relating the result to pre-Hicksian analysis, I have considered only one monopolized product. Suppose there are many? In my previous essay I considered the question thus posed as to the welfare loss when there is monopolistic pricing for many products. While reference was to a linear production possibilities schedule, it should not be too difficult to extend the analysis to the curvilinear schedule. I will accordingly leave that to the reader.

Attention has been focused on producer's surplus accruing to an enterprise. A producer's surplus has traditionally been envisaged as possibly accruing also to suppliers of factors, but what might be said on that score too is sufficiently evident not to need laboring. A principal case in point, of course, is the surplus accruing to labor when hours vary, but as long understood that seems more properly viewed as a form of consumer's than of producer's surplus.

Although I have focused on the welfare loss due to monopoly pricing, the analysis can be extended to appraisal of welfare variations originating on other accounts.

While it has seemed of interest, at least doctrinally, to view the pre-Hicksian computation of the welfare loss due to monopoly pricing in a fresh perspective, the computation, as so viewed, is subject to error, partly of a familiar and partly of a novel sort. Moreover welfare variations often may be calculated without the kind of error that the pre-Hicksian computation provides.(Bergson 1975). In the cited article, I referred only to the error in the use of the Marshallian demand schedule to gauge one or another of the Hicksian representations of benefit. But that argument applies at once to the GCV considered here, and one surmises that the pre-

Hicksian computation may also be improved insofar as it relates to the MIA, the other element figuring in a welfare variation as I have represented it.

My theme is an appropriate one for an essay in a volume honoring Abba P. Lerner. Lerner himself, in a now famous essay (1934), found it in order to apply what I have discussed as the pre-Hicksian analysis (though one somewhat different from that here) to the measurement of the welfare loss due to monopoly pricing.[6] From one standpoint, my concern here has been in part simply to update that analysis.

Notes

1. The concern here is only conceptual. Extension of the calculations of my previous paper to the case of curvilinear production possibilities is left for separate inquiry. But on that, see S. Togan, "On the Welfare Costs of Monopolistic and Average Cost Pricing," *European Economic Review* (forthcoming).

2. For simplicity, I pass by fixed coefficient production functions that might associate unemployment with realization of production possibilities.

3. May we also conclude that the loss due to the misallocation is thus overstated by Hicks's measure? One surmises that it ordinarily is, but conceivably a measure of the loss due to that misallocation alone could be even greater than Hicks's compensating variation. That would occur if, in figure 2.1, x''' were to the left of DE. On x''', see below.

4. On the concept of producer's surplus, see Currie, Murphy, and Schmitz (1971, pp. 753ff).

5. The cancellation is not complete, but in trial calculations made in connection with my previous essay, the error in the observation on MIA actually turned out to be larger than that on the GCV, so NCV on balance was understated. The calculations assume linear production possibilities, and it remains in question how the results might be affected if reference is instead to a curvilinear schedule. But these results, relating also to a linear Marshallian demand schedule for the monopolistic product (demand varies linearly with price and income), may be of interest (see table).

	Unadjusted for Income Effects			Adjusted for Income Effects		
	GCV	MIA	NCV	GCV	MIA	NCV
$N_{xp} = 1.5$; $N_{xI} = 1.0$	8.69	7.65	1.04	9.10	8.33	.77
$N_{xp} = 3.0$; $N_{xI} = 1.5$	9.38	7.29	2.09	10.11	8.33	1.78
$N_{xp} = 6.0$; $N_{xI} = 3.0$	10.42	6.25	4.17	12.21	8.33	3.88

On the left are the observations on GCV, MIA, and NCV indicated by variations in consumer's and producer's surplus, as determined by reference to the Marshallian demand schedule, and on the right the corresponding figures, after correction for income effects. I consider alternative cases in respect of the price (N_{xp}) and income (N_{xI}) elasticities of demand for the monopolist's product. Data on GCV, MIA, and NCV are expressed as percentages of the household's full-employment income under monopoly pricing for x_1. I assume throughout that the monopolist's price-cost ratio is 1.2, and that with x_1 so priced that good accounts for one-half of the indicated income.

6. The treatment of the welfare loss due to monopoly pricing in Lerner's 1934 essay is properly still singled out for replication in the survey on consumer's surplus of Currie, Murphy, and Schmitz (1971).

References

BERGSON, ABRAM. "On Monopoly Welfare Losses." *American Economic Review* 63 (December 1973): 853–870.

———. "A Note on Consumer's Surplus." *Journal of Economic Literature* 13 (March 1975): 38–44.

CURRIE, J. A., MURPHY, J. M., and SCHMITZ A. "The Concept of Consumer's Surplus and Its Use in Economic Analysis." *Economic Journal* 81: (December 1971): 741–799.

HICKS, J. R. *A Revision of Demand Theory.* New York: Oxford University Press, 1956.

LERNER, A. P. "The Concept of Monopoly and the Measurement of Monopoly Power." *Review of Economic Studies* 1 (June 1934): 157–175.

Chapter 3

William Fellner

Neo-Keynesianism, Monetarism and the Short and the Long Run

Much of the history of economic thought has been written in terms of rival schools, and the temptation is great to continue this habit in the interpretation of contemporary Western controversies. The distinction between economists representing merely different views on various professional problems and economists belonging to different schools of thought has never been very sharp but, despite the absence of truly articulate criteria, in many instances it would be possible to reach a fair degree of agreement on whether differences of opinion reflect characteristics of different schools. I shall return to this question later in the specific context of the problems to be discussed.

My concern here will be some aspects of recent controversies to which monetarist and neo-Keynesian writings have given rise and in which authors not identifiable by these labels have also participated. As I go along, I shall express my own position on matters involved in these debates. But I shall start with an attempt to describe differences of opinion at two distinct levels of discourse because I believe that failure to separate these two levels has led to confusion in the appraisal of opposing professional views. At the first of these levels the controversial problem relates to the main objective of demand-management policies, that is, of policy measures bearing on the effective (current-dollar or nominal) demand for goods and services. At this level, the question is this: What considerations should guide the authorities in deciding how much demand to create? At the second of the two levels, the controversies center on views concerning the role of specific policy variables—particularly of monetary and of fiscal ones—in the determination of the quantity of aggregate effective demand that will be forthcoming.

Economists have taken several specific positions at these two levels of discourse. There seems to exist a correlation between favoring, at the first of the two levels, one of two specific positions to be described in that context, and favoring at the second level the corresponding specific position to be described in the other context. But the correlation is imperfect, and since I belong among those whose views illustrate the imperfection of this correlation or overlap, I will try to explain not only the reasons why the correlation exists but also why it is not perfect.

Controversies on Objectives of Demand Management

According to one view the authorities of demand-management policy should take for granted the money-wage and the price trends they will face at alternative rates of resource utilization: different trends for different rates of resource utilization and possibly different trends for different types of direct wage-price interference administered by other branches of the government. Given these trends, the authorities should aim for the effective demand in current dollars—say, for the money GNP—that will establish unemployment rates falling within a narrow acceptable range. It is implied that for given levels of resource utilization, demand management as such—monetary and fiscal policy—cannot alter the money-wage or the price trend, though policies involving administrative wage-price interferences may be able to achieve this.

The other view maintains that, by its effect on price expectations, a consistent demand-management policy can exert a significant influence on the money-wage trend and on the price trend for given levels of resource utilization within a wide range of these levels. According to this view, utilization rates are not sustainable over a reasonable time horizon if they are so high that at any of those rates demand-management policies cannot significantly influence the behavior of the cost and price trend; thus one would get into an impasse by postulating that only those rates are acceptable. It is further maintained that supplementing monetary and fiscal policy by administrative wage and price regulations does not describe a way out of such an impasse because these measures are unsuitable for suppressing inflationary tendencies in the Western institutional setting. Hence, according to this view, the demand-management authorities should aim for the effective demand (money GNP) that will lead to the highest levels of resource utilization consistent with the requirement that price expectations and the cost and price trend should fall in line with known policy objectives concerning the behavior of the price level.

According to both views demand-management policies must be concerned with generating effective nominal demand—demand in current dollars—on specific assumptions concerning the variables that determine the total demand as it expresses itself, say, in the money GNP. But according to the first of these two views, the money GNP to be generated should be such that given the money cost and the price trend developing at an acceptable level of the real GNP—trends that according to this view are given to the demand-management authorities—the level of the real GNP should in fact be acceptable, in the sense of corresponding to an acceptable unemployment-rate target. According to the second view, the money GNP to be generated should be such as to leave no more room than is needed for the specified price-behavior target of the demand-management authorities plus the growth of real GNP compatible with this price target. According to this second view the money cost and the price trend developing in the markets will adjust to a consistent policy at the best levels of resource utilization that can be sustained over a reasonable time horizon by any demand-management policy operating in a market economy.

There is a considerable difference between these two ways of viewing the take of demand-management. The difference is brought out clearly when the adherents of these two views become faced with an uncomfortable question, a different question in the two cases, respectively, but in each case with one that cannot be neglected.

I start with the first of the two views. Do its adherents believe that the money-wage and cost trends, which they suggest should be taken for granted in the pursuit of specified low unemployment targets, are likely at all to be those developing in the markets without substantial and effective interferences? Or, if not, just what type of wage-price regulations do they visualize? After all, given numerically specified targets for the measured unemployment rate, a combination of expectational factors and market power may generate steepening money-wage and price trends, and this kind of destabilizing process cannot be allowed to last very long. What then? The answer that has been suggested by the adherents of the first view has been changing to some extent over the years.

For some time the emphasis was usually placed on the suggestion that the inflation rate will settle down at some level—that is, it will not in fact be steepening but will become a stable rate to which the economy can adjust—unless the unemployment target is set too ambitiously; and that within a specified range of acceptably low unemployment rates, there is a choice as to whether a country should opt for a higher steady rate of price increase and a correspondingly lower unemployment target or the other way around. The number of economists proposing this answer and the degree of confidence with which the answer is given has been declining significantly over the past years. The answer involves a belief in the existence of a long-run Phillips trade-off, and that hypothesis has become increasingly suspect even to those who had considered it convincing for several years.

Another answer to the same question, which has been gaining ground, involves administrative interferences with the wage and price structure. Economists who continue to argue for demand-management policies accommodating the cost trends for the sake of low unemployment-rate targets now usually are making allowances for the fact that such a policy involves unreasonable inflationary dangers unless government exerts a direct influence on money-wage and price trends. Indeed, belief in the hypothesis of the long-run Phillips trade-off characterized influential thinking during a period that was both preceded and succeeded by the advocacy of supplementing a full-employment policy with controls administered by other branches of the government.

In the *General Theory* Keynes himself had not anticipated the need for such controls in an economy in which the full-employment threshhold (as he had defined it) was not quite reached or was not overstepped, but before World War II was over, Sir William Beveridge did advocate a policy of full employment with reliance on direct controls.[1] Shortly thereafter Abba Lerner expressed himself in favor not of price regulations as conventionally interpreted but of a governmental commitment to the purchase and sale of commodities at prices that would describe a noninflationary trend and would, on the microlevel, satisfy the requirements of a competitive price structure; wages would then also have to be made to satisfy a competitive condition, that of equality with the value of labor's marginal product.[2] Phillips's article was published more than a decade later.[3] Under its influence the view was spreading for a while (without Phillips's endorsement) that when a demand-policy choice is made between alternative constant levels of labor market tightness, it is appropriate to assume that these levels can be made to correspond to alternative rates of inflation that would become stabilized after an adjustment period. Inflation would become stabilized, and an inflationary equilibrium could become established without direct controls—at a higher rate for tighter than for less tight labor markets. In view of the accumulating evidence, models incorporating this hypothesis have become increasingly suspect, and by now it has become more usual to recognize that a policy directed at specified low unemployment-rate targets must be supplemented by administrative wage-price interferences to prevent major instability resulting from accelerating inflation.

The meaning of these interferences is generally left vague. In the United States and in some other countries, a program of comprehensive wage and price controls would be rejected by a high proportion of the population. It is very likely that only in a political environment having many characteristics regarded as highly undesirable in the Western world could such a policy of controls achieve even its proximate objectives. This is true particularly of large countries in which no substantial part of the observed relations between economic variables is determined by processes developing abroad and in which the political authorities have a great deal of leeway for being guided by vote-getting considerations. Consequently the use of colorful and evasive terminology—ranging from the advocacy of "jawboning" to that of bringing about a "social compact"—has been spreading to express the belief that democratic governments can beneficially influence the money-wage and price trend without imposing on workers and on the sellers of goods politically inspired decisions that need to be enforced with reliance on substantial police power. Having exerted this beneficial influence, democratic governments can then let those in charge of demand-management policy validate the resulting wage and price trends to create what is referred to as "practical full employment."

I shall call this view of the central task of demand management policy the cost-accommodating view, remembering that its adherents are placing increasing emphasis on the need to use other policies for shaping the cost trend that demand management should validate or accommodate.

The second of the two views describes the cost-conditioning position. It basically suggests that the authorities should aim for the money GNP that is compatible with the highest utilization rates (say, the lowest measured unemployment rates) that develop in the markets when the market participants have become conditioned to expecting a price-level behavior the policy makers consider sustainable. Those subscribing to this view consider wage and price controls harmful and, in many Western countries, not even workable over a reasonable time horizon. Also they are skeptical about evasive terminology that suggests major wage-price interferences falling in an area between controls and no controls. Most economists arguing for this cost-trend conditioning (rather than "accommodating" or "validating") position consider practical stability of the price level the objective that can and should be achieved by the policy they have in mind. This has to do with the fact that the success of a cost-trend conditioning policy depends greatly on its consistency and credibility. A policy starting out with the promise to accommodate, say, an "underlying" inflation rate of 4 percent and to become restrictive if the "underlying" rate rises next year to 5 percent or higher is very unlikely to acquire the needed credibility and, judging by experience, rightly so. Hence cost trends will steepen under such a policy. A high degree of uncertainty will develop, because at each stage there will be substantial variance about the mean value of expectations concerning the further rise of the inflation rate.

But while moving consistently toward noninflationary conditions is typically advocated by those representing the conditioning approach, few have suggested an attempt to move in the United States from the recent double-digit inflation rate promptly to the close neighborhood of the zero rate. A comparison of the risks of gradualism with those of abruptness poses problems of considerable interest to economic analysis. Yet when making this comparison, most advocates of the cost-conditioning idea have been mindful primarily of the shock that abruptness would cause in view of the inflationary expectations already built into wage contracts and into other elements of the cost structure.

Earlier we faced the adherents of the cost-trend accommodating view with an uncomfortable question, and we should repeat this exercise in relation to those advocating the cost-trend conditioning position. What if, the conditioning effort should fail, and if such a policy should get the economy into a state of long-lasting stagnation at low levels of activity, or even into a state of long-lasting "stagflation" (low activity levels associated with continuing significant price inflation)?

If these difficulties became pronounced and extended enough, our economic and political system would become unworkable. This possibility cannot be excluded, nor can the outlook be improved by introducing into a market economy wage and price regulations that greatly increase the uncertainty facing the investors and soon start becoming increasingly ineffective even by their own standards. But before accepting prophesies of doom in this regard, we should remind ourselves that a credible policy preventing the creation of excessive nominal demand did prove successful in putting an end to many past inflationary outbreaks. Even in the rather recent past the cost-trend conditioning effort was quite successful in the United States.

From 1951 to 1965, the United States had practical stability of the price level; the consumer price index (CPI) and the implicit deflator rose at an average compound rate of less than 2 percent with a smaller than 1 percent annual price increase as measured by the material-goods component of the CPI (that is, disregarding the service component). There were three recessions during that period, but there is reason to believe that in a future period of price-level stability, the improved predictive ability of economists concerning the money GNP during spans of reasonable duration could keep the economy on a somewhat steadier path.[4] Moreover even in the 1951–1965 period, there was 3.4 percent average yearly increase in real GNP and a 1.9 percent average yearly rise of per-capita real disposable income. The average unemployment rate of the period as a whole was 4.9 percent, and in 1965, the unemployment rate was at 4.5 percent. Yet for successive subperiods, unemployment had a rising trend; the average rate for 1957–1965 was 5.5 percent. Although this resulted from cyclical instability, it also (and importantly) was connected with facts for which allowance needs to be made in the interpretation of unemployment statistics. There occurred during the period a significant growth of the proportionate representation in the labor force of groups with a high ratio of new entrants and reentrants and thus with high specific unemployment rates. The shifts in the labor-force composition have continued since 1965, and there has also taken place a significant extension of our unemployment compensation system and of our system of transfer payments in general.

The 1951–1965 record should not be ruled out as irrelevant; into the early 1960s there was an awareness by the American public of a focusing of American demand-management policy on the objective of price stability. Price-level expectations were presumably so conditioned. Although more than a decade has elapsed since the end of that span, I see no reason for fearing that in the United States a consistent effort to return to a cost-coditioning demand policy would fail. In some other countries the odds are worse, but even there the possibility remains that the political pressures to change highly damaging wage-setting practices will grow. The more responsive these practices become to competitive forces, the more the outlook will improve for cost-conditioning demand policies also in those countries.

The Controversy on Objectives: Opposing Views on a Timely American Problem

It is an essential characteristic of the cost trend conditioning position properly interpreted that no promise must be made to achieve a numerically specified low measured unemployment rate. Instead such a policy aims for moving an economy that is unconstrained by wage and price controls into the neighborhood of the highest sustainable growth path—thus of the lowest sustainable unemployment rate—recognizing that a state of the economy brought about by the stimulus of unanticipated inflation is not sustainable. Most economists supporting this policy share the view that trying to condition cost behavior to a significant and yet steady inflation rate is unlikely to succeed because of the lack of credibility of the authorities' persistence in such an effort.

If in this spirit a decision were reached to abstain from policies that backfire with a brief delay, only vague guesses can be made about the measured unemployment rate sustainable in the United States after an adjustment period that has followed years of steep inflation. If approached gradually, that rate is very likely to be lower than the 7 percent prevailing at this writing. Yet because of large changes in the composition of the labor force and because of the rapid spread of what may be described as subsistence guarantees, the achievable rate is very likely to be significantly higher than 4 percent which was said to correspond to the conditions prevailing in the mid 1950s. Even the close to 8 percent unemployment rate of 1976 was compatible with a rise of real as well as of money wage rates; while this rise was in turn compatible with a deceleration of inflation during the year, it nevertheless follows that even at a close to 8 percent rate of unemployment the unemployed did not underbid a rising real wage trend. In general those favoring a cost trend conditioning policy realize that one can not guarantee subsistence and promise also the achievement of specified low unemployment rates as we measure them in this country. Adherents of the cost conditioning line in demand policy have the conviction that it would be a mistake not to adopt it because the alternative—the cost-accommodating policy line—would bring back the economic disturbances of the past decade with an increasing deterioration of the state of the economy.

All advocates of the cost conditioning policy line recognize, and some strongly stress, that the outlook for the success of the policy would greatly deteriorate if the forces limiting competition on the supply side of the labor and commodity markets were not kept within reasonable bounds. Such forces obviously reduce the sustainable rate of resource utilization quite aside from causing malallocation of resources.[5]

An analysis of the distorting effects of competition limiting forces belongs among Abba Lerner's major contributions of which we need to take account in the discussion of any kind of demand management policy, including a non-Lernerian cost-conditioning policy. Like most other economists who have shown much more understanding for Keynesian than for monetarist views, Lerner has favored demand-management policies that would accommodate rather than condition cost and price trends; in his conception, these trends would have to be strongly influenced by specific kinds of government intervention. Yet much of what he has contributed to the understanding of the problem of competition-limiting forces has remained of importance to economists in general. Since the time of Lerner's early work on this subject, the possibility of intensifying competition by removing barriers to free international trade has improved substantially, though the world so far has made only limited use of this opportunity.

In contrast to the cost-conditioning position, the cost-accommodating line in demand-management policy regards a slow reduction of the American measured unemployment rates of the recent past to an unspecified level as too high a price for avoiding the risk of a renewed steepening of inflation and of whatever administrative wage-price interferences would have to be tried out again in the event of such steepening. There probably also is disagreement about how grave the risk is of a renewed inflationary outbreak if cost trends should become accommodated by a policy aiming for unemployment-rate targets specified in terms of narrow ranges.

The foregoing remarks relate to the general characteristics of conflicting views on demand-management, in the present-day American setting. In 1973, however, and since then, the difference between the conflicting views on demand management came to the fore also in relation to a specific problem that cropped up suddenly. As a result of exogenous changes, the prices of specific raw materials—first of farm products and thereafter mainly of energy materials—rose significantly and unexpectedly; the prices of these products enter into the costs of other products. Economists who favor accommodation argued that the creation of nominal demand should be stepped up by more expansionary monetary and fiscal policies, because it is inevitable that such cost increases should raise the general price level through pricing practices by which the costs are passed through. The other components of the price level (say, of the GNP deflator) would not become adjusted downward to offset the cost increases.

The argument on the other side has been that although expectational factors and imperfections of competition may indeed make a temporary rise in the general price level inevitable, it would nevertheless be wrong to generate more nominal demand in order to make room for the price increases. In the first place, the pass through is likely to be less complete even initially if demand-management policies are known to adhere firmly to a line of nonaccommodation. Second, and more important, in this situation the acceptance of real burden by the population is an inescapable necessity, and thus it is desirable to make it clear to the sellers of goods whose costs have risen that an effort to get rid of the cost burden by price pass-throughs is costly in terms of the sales volume they can achieve. If the sellers of goods or services will not learn this lesson without going through the experience, then not only will there occur a temporary increase in the general price level but, under a nonaccommodating policy, output trends will weaken promptly, and the possibility of a recession cannot be excluded. Yet even this is distinctly less undesirable than stepping up the creation of nominal demand and thereby leading the public to proceed as if they could avoid the burden by passing it back and forth among themselves, noticing after each round that the higher prices they were charging as sellers have now acquired a counterpart in higher prices they need to pay as buyers. This latter sequence, describing the consequences of accommodation, is the scenario of an accelerating inflationary process, and such a process must be stopped before long at a substantial cost. This is likely to be far in excess of the cost of a typical cyclical setback.

The Role of Variables in Demand Determination

Neo-Keynesians tend to subscribe to the demand-policy position favoring the accommodation of cost trends, while monetarists tend to adhere to the cost-conditioning policy conception. However, the overlap is not complete—the correlation is imperfect. The problem is whether there is a convincing explanation of a significant but incomplete overlap of neo-Keynesian thinking with the cost-accommodating position on the one hand and of monetarist thinking with cost-conditioning on the other.

In posing the problem I am implying that cost accommodation and cost conditioning are not definitional characteristics of neo-Keynesianism and monetarism. Trying to define the difference between neo-Keynesianism and monetarism is a worthwhile effort in spite of the fact that in the background of these approaches one may detect the same common model of noncommittal generality. What matters is that the two groups are placing the emphasis on different relations among the variables when using constructs that are sufficiently specific or simplified to lead to substantive conclusions.

The definitional characteristic of monetarism is its emphasis on the crucial role of the size of money aggregates in the determination of nominal demand, this being a role that over a reasonably chosen time horizon dwarfs that of pure fiscal policy in the process of demand determination and dwarfs also the role of interest-rate effects (particularly of those brought about by changes in the money aggregates). The definitional characteristic of neo-Keynesianism is the advocacy of the view that money aggregates influence effective demand mostly by effects on interest rates and that fiscal policy, which too has an effect on interest rates, should also be regarded as a significant determinant of nominal demand.[6]

There is no purely logical reason for the major overlap between monetarism so defined and the cost-conditioning position or for the major overlap between neo-Keynesianism so defined and the cost-accommodating position. There are no purely logical grounds for concluding that the efforts of a cost-conditioning demand management must be based exclusively or even mainly on the regulation of money aggregates; or for concluding that authorities aiming for cost accommodation should judge monetary policy not by its effects on money aggregates but by its effects on interest rates and that they should attribute great importance to fiscal policy. Indeed the overlaps are incomplete, even if substantial. Yet I believe that there does exist a reasonable explanation of the overlaps and that it is understandable also why the overlaps should be imperfect.

The monetarist emphasis on the demand-determining role of money aggregates, with little or no regard to interest-rate effects and with no importance attributed to the role of pure fiscal policy, discloses a 'long-run' orientation. It is based on the conviction that realistic insights can be obtained into the process by which effective demand (say, money GNP) is determined over the longer run, provided policies are credibly directed to longer-run objectives. Further, it is implied that in this case the short-run behavior of market participants will also be strongly influenced by the expected long-run results, provided the public is not prevented from responding to market forces. These convictions underlie the monetarist position on the central role of money aggregates in the determination of nominal demand and also the cost-conditioning position in the area of demand-management policy. The latter implies the same kind of orientation toward long-run objectives, with the same presumption concerning influences exerted on short-run market behavior as well.

On the other hand, in a sense to be explained, a 'short-run' orientation is reflected in the neo-Keynesian view of demand determination, with its emphasis on fiscal policy in general and on the interest effects of monetary and of fiscal variables. We shall soon see that the same statement applies also to the cost-accommodating demand-policy position.

To begin with, a major part of the effects of demand-management policies on real rates of interest develops merely temporarily, during a period in which the interest rates on specific types of securities have been lowered or raised by the monetary or the fiscal authority's purchases or sales of these securities but in which the supply of other types of securities and of claims to goods in general has not yet adjusted in an offsetting fashion. Even if all interest-rate effects of monetary and fiscal policy were merely temporary, it could still be maintained that the effect of demand-management policy on current-dollar demand goes through the interest-rate mechanism, but since in the longer run there would be no interest effects, the long-run effectiveness of demand-management policy could not be gauged by the size of its effect on interest rates.

This is another way of saying that if the Hicksian IS curve always tended to become infinitely interest elastic, the fact that an increase in the money supply temporarily reduces interest rates before the infinite elasticity actually manifests itself would not justify appraising the long-run effectiveness of the money supply on investment by a relationship between the size of the effect of money on interest and by the effect of the change in interest rates on investment. Furthermore in these circumstances fiscal deficits and surpluses would have no long-run effect whatever on effective current-dollar demand because deficit spending would merely displace the equivalent amount of private investment at unchanging interest rates (and a fiscal surplus would merely have the contrary effect).

Short-run effects *would* be produced on effective current-dollar demand. This follows not only from what was said above but also from the fact that expansionary policies may increase or turn on productive investment as a result of their short-run effect on capacity utilization rates. This short-run effect may supplement the positive effect on total demand and on investment of the temporary reduction of interest rates caused by expansionary monetary policy, and the same short-run capacity-utilization effect may outweigh the negative effect of the temporary rise in interest rates on investment caused by a deficit. The negative effect of a deficit-induced rise in interest rates on aggregate current-dollar demand will in any event be outweighed if velocity is higher at higher interest, but the negative effect of higher interest rates on investment could be outweighed only as a consequence of the short-run effect of higher capacity utilization rates.

This relates to the case in which all interest effects of demand-management policies are merely temporary. If that is not so, lasting effects may indeed develop on aggregate current-dollar demand, but, as concerns fiscal policy, the real effects for which the authorities are aiming will still be merely of a short-run character. Even if deficits should raise the current-dollar demand in the long run, this will be associated with a long-run reduction of the real supply of the goods on which the additional money incomes are spent because (outside the liquidity trap) interest rates will rise and have an adverse effect on investment.

Yet this line of reasoning leaves the important question open whether a long-run oriented theory of demand determination should imply that realistic long-run conclusions can be established without paying attention to the effect of fiscal policy on the successive short-period events that lead up to the long run.

According to neo-Keynesian views the temporary (short-run) stimulus provided by a fiscal deficit can serve long-run objectives as well. Indeed the stimulus carries over into the long run, this being a conclusion reached by turning around the monetarist chain of reasoning considered above— a chain linking short-run market behavior to reasonably predictable longer-run trends. Neo-Keynesian views disclose the belief that in order to understand the long run, we must first acquire an understanding of a system of relations among variables, including policy variables, determining the short-period results. A theory incapable of explaining how policy variables, including the fiscal ones, can be used for shaping the successive short-period developments overlooks the tendency of short-run difficulties to perpetuate themselves and to prevent the system from arriving at a differently described long run. The same conception underlies also the cost-accommodating position in the area of demand-management policy since this too is based on skepticism about the view that a long-run oriented policy effort would condition cost trends by exerting the proper influence on market behavior during the successive periods of which the long run is made up.

This concept explains the overlaps I have described. The reason why these overlaps are not complete is that both these ways of constructing a link between the short and the long run involve oversimplification. One may want to construct the link one way for most purposes and yet remain aware of the fact that in some situations it is advisable to construct it in the other direction; and one may be much more inclined to be selective in this regard in one's concern with one type of problem than in one's concern with another.

I belong among the firm believers in the need to shift consistently from a demand policy of inflationary cost accommodation to one of cost conditioning, and I feel opposed to making concessions to the short-run position favoring cost accommodation, except that I would make the transition to noninflationary conditions gradual. On the other hand, I find the proposition unconvincing that the short-run character of fiscal influences on demand would justify attributing little importance to fiscal-policy variables for demand determination over an extended period of time. The position so described illustrates the incompleteness of the overlap discussed in this paper. My view that fiscal variables may in some phases play a significant role in the determination of demand is not based simply on the observation that central banks are often pressured to gear the policies to the size of fiscal deficits. That in itself does not bear on the question of whether demand theory should attribute importance to pure fiscal policy, that is, to fiscal policy given the rate of increase of the money supply. Here I am concerned with pure fiscal policy in this latter sense. In view of the very limited knowledge available on the process by which economies are moved along their paths, I suggest that the long-run orientation of monetarists to demand determination does provide a useful point of departure for analysis; yet even in a long-run oriented approach, it is necessary to remain aware of the short-run effects of fiscal-policy variables to avoid falling into the trap of describing a long run different from that which is evolving from the sequence of short runs.

Regularities Suggesting Significance of a Money Aggregate in the Determination of Money GNP

Of the money aggregates computed by the Federal Reserve, the M_2 stock is that which through 1975 showed a noteworthy regularity in its relation to the money GNP (the latter to be expressed here at an annual rate). M_2 consists of currency and checking deposits owned by the public, and of savings accounts and time deposits (other than large-denomination negotiable certificates of deposit) held in the commercial banks. The relation of M_2 and of other M aggregates to money GNP has been explored by several authors.[7]

The Cambridge k type ratio defined as the ratio of M_2 to simultaneous money GNP, had been trendless since 1962 (or even since 1960, though I consider it somewhat preferable to regard 1962 as the year that separates a preceding period of downward trend from the following period of trend horizontality). The Cambridge k so defined (M_2/GNP, which is the reciprocal of the GNP velocity of M_2) had a mean value of 0.421 since 1962, with an average deviation of about 0.7 percent and a standard deviation of about 1 percent when these dispersion measures are related to the whole period's mean. This applies to the annual series; the standard deviation rises to about 1.2 percent of the mean in the quarterly series. The maximum deviation was, through 1975, less than 2 percent in the annual and about 3 percent in the quarterly data. Measures of dispersion would come out higher if each year's M_2/GNP ratio were compared with the ratio observed for the preceding year. If each post-1962 year's ratio is compared with the known mean value of the ratio from 1962 to 1975 preceding that for which we are estimating the ratio in retrospect, then the average deviation is somewhat higher than the average deviation of all yearly ratios from the mean of the entire period from 1962 to the present, but these two measures of deviation are close to each other. A moderate reduction of the measures of dispersion can be obtained by introducing brief lags between M_2 and the corresponding money GNP, but the improvement is attributable to subperiods in which money creation either accelerated or decelerated significantly (and, we may conjecture, unexpectedly). In most other periods the simultaneous relation wins over lagged ones.

Efforts to interpret the trendlessness of the M_2/GNP ratio as a consequence of offsetting movements of explanatory variables have not been entirely unsuccessful, and I would not place much confidence in the numerical results of the underlying pieces of regression analysis; the adjustment coefficients tend to be unconvincingly low and the parameter values are not sufficiently stable over time. Nevertheless the interest-elasticity of the M_2/GNP ratio appears to be very small in regressions postulating a rise of the ratio with rising real income on the one hand, and a decline of the ratio with rising money-market rates on the other, thus in constructs explaining the trendlessness of M_2/GNP by the roughly zero net effect of these two opposing forces.[8] At least as far as these analytical models are concerned, the potentially significant role of fiscal policy does not express itself to any large extent in interest-rate effects that would develop in a continuous fashion when interest rates vary over the ranges over which we have observed their movements.

Such results are derived from very simple analytical constructs but, given the significant uncertainties attaching to the results obtained from large models aiming at comprehensiveness, I regard the neo-Keynesian tendency to neglect the simple regularities as unconvincing. On the other hand, these regularities, or even somewhat more complex ones, should not be projected mechanically into the future. This is not only because of the uncomfortably aggregative character of most of the approaches from which such regularities are derived or only because such regularities are apt to be significantly affected by institutional changes. Quite aside from these considerations, the type of approach discussed here raises the question of what variables have kept the system within a region in which the observed monetary regularities came through. Because of its complexities, this question is more elusive than are those to which the usual kinds of quantitative analysis can be applied with convincing results. Elusive though the question is, it is very likely that the so-called fiscal stabilizers belong among those that have kept the economy within the ranges in which it has in fact been fluctuating. Recently the protracted inflationary experience seems to have reduced the M_2/GNP ratio to a somewhat lower level.

Importance of Fiscal Variables for Demand Determination

During recessions built-in fiscal flexibility results from the automatic reduction of fiscal revenues relative to expenditures, given the tax rates and the government's spending commitments; in expansion phases built-in flexibility results from the automatic reversal of this relationship. Aside from lags that could occasionally become disturbing, this flexibility works in the direction of stabilization during the short-run sequence of events. To my knowledge, no major contributor has contradicted the claim that the fiscal variables on which these built-in stabilizing features of the system impinge do exert a short-run influence on aggregate demand. It would, of course, be wrong to conclude that we are better off the more we have of the fiscal instruments that incorporate such flexibility in both directions, since the types and the levels of taxation as well as of fiscal spending during the various phases of the cycle can have serious adverse effects on the average level of activity. But it would be equally unconvincing to argue that the short-run character of the effect of built-in flexibility greatly reduces its importance for demand creation or to argue that it would be impossible to make good use of this short-run influence in the framework of a basically long-run oriented policy. The proposition that, given a consistent long-run policy, the short-period behavior in unimpeded markets will adjust properly and will not normally vitiate the expected long-run outcome can serve as a general guiding principle, but it cannot have the validity of a rigorous theorem. It is useful, and it may even be necessary, to have supplementary arrangements to help the system in overcoming short-run impediments without large or even indefinite delays. This is essentially another way of saying that variables other than the monetary ones, including the fiscal variables, in all probability have played an essential role in shaping the environment in such a way that, within the resulting range of movements of the economy, the observed monetary regularities could establish themselves. Theories of the determination of current-dollar effective demand should not overlook this, even if, at the present stage of knowledge, approaches stressing the role of money aggregates lend themselves well to being used as a point of departure.

Built-in fiscal flexibility may play the essential role of a safeguard in the framework of a policy steering a long-run course, and discretionary flexibility—adjustment of tax rates and of fiscal spending commitments in the various phases of the cycle—may also be a safeguard. Yet in practice there exist substantial differences in this regard between automatic and discretionary flexibility. The differences stem from the unanticipated character of ad hoc fiscal-policy adjustments, from the lags in reaching fiscal-policy decisions, and from the risk of making too large discretionary moves in circumstances in which the basic fiscal variables had been set in a manner compatible with good performance. These risks need to be remembered, but specific situations may develop in which they become small as compared to the risk of an undue prolongation of short runs with highly undesirable properties. Nor can it be taken for granted that monetary policy can always achieve the short-run effect at which fiscal-policy measures can be aimed, since in its depressed phases an economy may find itself in the close neighborhood of a liquidity trap.

The Incompleteness of the Overlap

A basically long-run oriented monetary theory of demand determination (money-GNP determination) should not overlook the short-run fiscal influences. A theory that has no room for these would move us onto a long-run plane of discourse from which it is impossible to see that short-term effects, including those of the fiscal variables, are supporting the plane itself. Does it follow that a basically long-run oriented cost-conditioning demand policy can make good use of short-run cost-accommodating measures as supports or safeguards? The answer to this question, I suggest, is no. At this point the analogy ceases to be valid. This is why the overlap is incomplete between adherence to a uniquely money-minded position in the theory of money-GNP determination on the one hand and adherence to the cost-conditioning policy view on the other. Both are long-run oriented, and this is why they overlap. Nevertheless in addition to stressing the significance of money in the determination of demand, one may want to insist on recognizing also the importance of the short-run effect of fiscal variables for demand determination, and yet one may be unwilling to make room for cost-accommodating qualifications in a cost-conditioning policy approach (except to the extent that it is possible to regard conditioning to a gradually declining rate of inflation as representing at the same time temporary cost accommodation at a consistently diminishing rate).

The reason for this negative conclusion is that if, in order to spur the economy inflationary money cost trends are accommodated, then keeping the stimulus alive would require stepping up the inflation rate. This is so because a stabilized and foreseen rate will not continue to provide stimulus. On the other hand, withdrawal of the stimulus is apt to cause a recession, which is almost certain to be more severe the longer the stimulus had been administered before its withdrawal. Consequently while a short-run oriented concern with the effects of fiscal policy can *supplement* a long-run oriented monetary policy, cost accommodation *contradicts* cost conditioning. As I see it, the sustainability of anything that can reasonably be described as a market economy operating in a political system of the contemporary Western type depends in large part on our willingness to use the cost conditioning approach consistently and on our determination not to allow market power to grow to a size at which even a consistent cost-conditioning policy becomes helpless.

Schools of Thought

In my appraisal one would be focusing on an unduly narrow range of problems if one decided to define monetarism and neo-Keynesianism as distinct schools of thought. Neo-Keynesians recognize the importance of money-demand functions, and monetarists do not generally deny the existence of a relationship between the demand for money and interest rates.[9] In terms of these fundamentals, there exists no cleavage.

As for existing differences, Milton Friedman is correct in suggesting that neo-Keynesians are more inclined to a "Walrasian" approach in the sense of using comprehensive models, and that monetarists on the other hand have a "Marshallian" tendency to keep in the background the role of variables they consider to be of lesser significance for the analysis in which they engage.[10] But in this regard methodological preferences shade over into one another. There is, to be sure, a further difference in judgment between the two groups as to which of many variables is performing merely a minor role in various analytical contexts. This is a difference bearing particularly on the role of changes in real rates of interest in response to changes in the money supply and on the role of fiscal variables in the determination of demand (money GNP). These explanatory variables weigh much more heavily in neo-Keynesian than in monetarist analysis. Yet this difference is a reflection of the neo-Keynesian inclination to build up the long run analytically from successive short runs and of the monetarist inclination to visualize short-run behavior in unimpeded markets as falling in line with expected long-run results.[11]

This same difference expresses itself more importantly in disagreement on whether demand policies should accommodate money-cost trends (such as may have to be regulated by other types of policy measures) or whether they should be used for conditioning the trends in money costs and the price level. From the purely logical point of view, this latter disagreement—essentially a disagreement on how much demand is to be generated—must be carefully distinguished from the disagreement between neo-Keynesians and monetarists on the role of sets of variables in the determination of demand. The second of these two disagreements goes less deep than the first, and it justifies a much higher degree of compromise-mindedness.

I suggest that the nearest we can come to distinguishing among currently influential schools of thought in the United States and in several other Western countries is to draw a distinction between (1) approaches suggesting a need to explore short-run relations among a substantial number of variables in order to understand how long-run sequences evolve under alternative policies bearing on the short run and (2) approaches stressing longer-run relations and suggesting that these will become established under a long-run oriented policy consistent and credible enough to exert a strong influence on the short-run behavior of the market participants as well. Approaches of the former type imply much greater optimism concerning our short-term forecasting methods than do the latter, and they lead to a more ambitious interventionistic outlook. Approaches of the second variety are based on the conviction that long-run trends in market economies describe in many significant respects a success story that could unfold only under a steady policy directed at long-run objectives. These latter approaches imply at the same time that market imperfections must remain within reasonable limits for short-run market behavior to become consistent with an expected long-run course of events—an expected course that in this case is not much affected by short-run disturbances encountered as the economy moves along.

Any useful approach must leave quite a bit of room for the pursuit of policy objectives that the market mechanism does not achieve automatically even under the most efficient demand management. But while it is possible to formulate political judgments the acceptance of which would make market economies unworkable, the United States belongs among those major countries of the industrialized world in which these judgments are held by only a small minority. I limited my discussion to controversies belonging in the mainstream of economic thought in the United States and in a number of other Western countries.

Inclinations remain strong to link the short to the long run in one of the two ways I have discussed. However over the years there has occurred a shift away from a short-run oriented outlook that had been inspired by the 1930s. At that time the risks were high of getting stuck in a very dismal kind of short turn while keeping one's eye on an ever-receding long run. The safeguards suitable for supplementing a long-run oriented policy were far too weak. In those circumstances it made sense to sound an emergency signal by turning an uncontested biological fact into a proposition in social-science methodology: "in the long run we all are dead." Yet remembering that emergency signals had to be sounded on specific occasions justifies no more than a concern with what I here called safeguards. There is nothing in our past experience to suggest that we should construct our theories and our policy line as if we were chronically stuck in a phase reminiscent of the 1930s or as if we were particularly prone to fall into that hole.

We have created for ourselves a far greater risk of falling into a hole through being guided by short-run oriented cost-accommodating policies that have gradually become counterproductive in almost any time frame. Also in some countries more than in others, developments during the era of cost accommodation have reduced the sensitivity of wage-setting practices to competitive forces to such an extent that overcoming the political difficulties involved in a return to cost-conditioning demand management may require going through a phase with very unusual characteristics. In those circumstances gradualism would not turn out to be the answer, and the shock involved in an abrupt readjustment may be unavoidable.

The long run has had a belated comeback in the outlook of many economists. To some extent recently it has had a real comeback, not merely the earlier apparent comeback that suggested that normal long-run relations need to be studied carefully but that these tendencies will come through only if we keep shaping each successive short run by new policy efforts. If his life span had not been so brief, Keynes might well have shown a good deal of understanding for this comeback. At any rate, neither side in the contemporary debates has good reason for claiming his authority.

Notes

1. Sir William Beveridge, *Full Employment in a Free Society* (London: Allen and Unwin, 1944).

2. Abba P. Lerner, *The Economics of Control* (New York: Macmillan, 1946).

3. A. W. Phillips, "The Relation Between Unemployment and the Rate of Change of Money Wages," *Economica* (November 1958).

4. On the improvement of the forecasting record of official agencies, see William Fellner, *Towards a Reconstruction of Macroeconomics* (Washington, D.C.: American Enterprise Institute, 1976), pp. 118–124.

5. See Gottfried Haberler, "Stagflation: An Analysis of Its Causes and Cures." In Bela Balassa and Richard Nelson, eds., *Economic Progress, Private Values and Public Policy* (Amsterdam: North-Holland Publishing Co., 1977).

6. This statement about the interest-rate effects of fiscal policy loses its validity in Keynes's "liquidity trap" such as could develop in a depression. In the liquidity trap neither monetary nor fiscal policy would have an effect on interest rates. While monetary policy would be completely ineffective, expansionary fiscal policy would possess effectiveness by leading at constant interest rates to a substitution of government securities for money holdings of the public and by leading to the spending by the government of the money balances previously held idle by the public. Outside the liquidity trap—in the circumstances mainly visualized by neo-Keynesians—the effectiveness of monetary policy is viewed as depending on the size of its interest-rate effects. As for the neo-Keynesian view of fiscal policy (say, of the expansionary kind), this raises interest rates, thereby reducing investment, but the adverse effect on investment is outweighed by the increase in government spending because at the higher interest rates total expenditures are higher for any given money supply. To the extent that such increased total expenditures induce more investment (notwithstanding somewhat higher interest rates), even the adverse effect on investment of the higher rates may be wholly suppressed or turned around.

7. For a recent contribution and references to various earlier ones, see William Fellner and Dan Larkins, "Interpretation of a Regularity in the Behavior of M_2," *Brookings Papers on Economic Activity* 3 (1976): 741–761.

8. For instance, a rise in interest rates on money-market instruments by 50 percent of the rates would reduce M_2/GNP by about 3 percent of the ratio itself. See 6 ibid.

9. As Milton Friedman has argued on several occasions, recognition of a potentially significant influence on the demand for money exerted by interest rate changes such as develop due to changes in variables other than the money supply does not contradict the monetarist conception that neglects the effect of changes in the money supply on real interest rates over the time horizon relevant to their analysis. The fact that inflationary policies will raise the money rates of interest, in contrast to the real rates, is not only not denied but is strongly emphasized by monetarists.

10. This, too, has been stressed repeatedly by Friedman, most recently in Jerome L. Stein, ed., *Monetarism* (Amsterdam: North-Holland Publishing Co., 1976), pp. 310–317.

11. While Alan S. Blinder and Robert M. Solow have not formulated this statement in the same fashion, the meaning of the statement in the text is clearly implied in their article, "Does Fiscal Policy Still Matter?" *Journal of Monetary Economics*, Vol. 2 (1976): 501–510.

Chapter 4

R. A. Gordon

A Skeptical Look at the "Natural Rate" Hypothesis

The hypothesis that there is a 'natural rate of unemployment', which is invariant to the rate of change in wages or prices, is only a decade old but has already been widely accepted, particularly by non-Keynesian economists but also by those who continue in the Keynesian tradition. In the long run, however long the 'long run' may be, the Phillips curve is vertical, although it may have a finite negative slope in the short run.

By coincidence, and in the context of somewhat different analytical models, the natural rate hypothesis was put forward at approximately the same time by Milton Friedman and Edmund Phelps—although, as is usually the case in important scientific developments, there had been precursors.[1] In this paper I shall concentrate upon the variant Friedman presented, which is not so deeply imbedded in so-called search theory as is Phelps's version, and I shall also consider the new variant of the natural rate hypothesis (NRH) that Friedman recently put forward in his Nobel lecture.[2]

Friedman's version of the NRH assumes the operation of a national labor market with the following characteristics, among others.

1. In any period short or long, there are demand and supply functions for labor; the quantity of labor demanded and supplied depends upon anticipated real, not money, wages. While Friedman uses the term *real wages* in both his presidential address and his Nobel lecture, he means "product wages" for employers (money wages divided by the prices of the products sold by employers) and "real wages" for workers, (money wages deflated by the prices of the particular bundle of goods and services purchased by workers).[3] The demand for and supply of labor, and therefore

The Institute of Industrial Relations, University of California, Berkeley, kindly provided financial help, which made possible the useful assistance of Thomas O Grady. An earlier version of this paper was presented at the annual meeting of the Midwestern Economic Association, April 1, 1977.

employment and unemployment, do not depend, as the Phillips curve implies, on the behavior of money wages, except insofar as mistaken anticipations lead realized product or real wages to be different from those that were anticipated.

2. The level and shape of these demand and supply functions for labor, in terms of anticipated product and real wages, are those that would result from a Walrasian system of general equilibrium equations, "provided there is imbedded in them the actual structural characteristics of the labor and commodity markets."[4] Much is hidden in this condition.

3. Long-run equilibrium in the national labor market occurs only when realized product and real wages equal those that were anticipated by employers and workers.[5] The level of employment that results from such a long-run equilibrium, given the size of the labor force in such an equilibrium, yields an equilibrium rate of unemployment called the '*natural* rate.'

4. The achievement of such an equilibrium, in which employers' and workers' anticipations as to product and real wages are being fully realized, takes a long time. In his presidential address, Friedman suggested that, for rates of inflation similar to those experienced in the United States until then, a long time was "a couple of decades."[6] In his Nobel lecture, he was more pessimistic. The long run becomes the "long-long run," which "may well extend over decades."[7]

In his Nobel lecture, Friedman introduced an intermediate period between the short and the "long-long run" periods in which anticipations are not realized and a negatively sloping Phillips curve is possible. In this intermediate period, the Phillips curve may be positively sloped—corresponding to recent experience in which accelerating inflation has been associated with rising unemployment.

Friedman does not deny the possible effect of the oil crisis and other independent forces in imparting a common upward trend to both inflation and unemployment in the last few years. But, he believes, something else is also involved:

However, a major factor in some countries and a contributing factor in others may be that they are in a transitional period—this time to be measured by quinquennia or decades not years. The public has not adapted its attitudes or its institutions to a new monetary environment. Inflation tends not only to be higher but also increasingly volatile and to be accompanied by widening government intervention into the setting of prices. The growing volatility of inflation and the growing departure of relative prices from the values that market forces alone would set combine to render the economic system less efficient, to introduce frictions in all markets, and very likely, to raise the recorded rate of unemployment.

On this analysis the present situation cannot last. It will either degenerate into hyperinflation and radical change; or institutions will adjust to a situation of chronic inflation; or governments will adopt policies that will produce a low rate of inflation and less government intervention into the fixing of prices.[8]

Thus after a long enough transition period, measured in quinquennia or decades, the Phillips curve will no longer appear to be positively sloped. A new, long-long run, vertical Phillips curve will emerge at a natural rate of unemployment that will reflect the future institutional environment.

Thus the experience of the last fifty years or so is translated into a forecast that presumably carries into the twenty-first century. But it is a tentative forecast. A "major factor in some countries and a contributing factor in others," Friedman says, "may be that they are in a transitional period."

The question of the amount of calendar time involved in the achievement of the natural rate is bothersome. This is true whether one takes Friedman's, Phelps's, or some other model that purports to explain the underlying forces that determine the level of the natural rate of unemployment.[9]

Friedman's natural rate is presumably the national unemployment rate that would be achieved in equilibrium in the long run (presidential address) or in the "long-long run" (Nobel lecture). It has been said that "in the long run we are all dead." (In the long-long run, I presume, we are not only dead but fossilized.)

The notion of long-run equilibrium has a long and respected tradition in classical and neoclassical economics. It is an integral part of the comparative statics that is still the basis of virtually all microeconomic theory and most of macroeconomic theory. It is, of course, the technique used in *The General Theory*. But it is an approach that creates serious problems in Friedman's development of the natural rate hypothesis.

The NRH explicitly involves a dynamic adjustment process—an adjustment process that, Friedman believes, involves decades. Further, the adjustment is toward an equilibrium that can never be achieved. There are at any point of time, at least conceptually, underlying demand and supply curves for labor, with the quantities of labor demanded and supplied being functions of anticipated product and real wage rates. But these anticipations are always in error. In a continuously changing world in which information is imperfect, particularly about the future, anticipations are always in error to some degree. And the introduction of stochastic notions is of little help. Different groups of employers and workers have different sets of expectations about future wages and prices, which they hold with different degrees of confidence, and, with many workers and small businessmen, expectations are little more than the product of inertia.

In short there is little evidence that in the long run—or even the long-long run—anticipations of future wages and prices approach and eventually reach those that are actually realized. Yet the vertical Phillips curve implied by Friedman's natural rate hypothesis is "for alternative rates of *fully anticipated* inflation."[10]

Let us consider this question of the time periods involved a bit further. In his presidential address, Friedman states that, "At any moment of time, there is some level of unemployment which has the property that it is consistent with equilibrium in the structure of *real* wage rates." He continues: "The 'natural rate of unemployment' . . . is the level that would be ground out by the Walrasian system of general equilibrium equations, provided there is embodied in them the actual structural characteristics of the labor and commodity markets."[11]

There is a problem here that is common to all exercises in comparative statics, and the more so the longer is the amount of calendar time required to reach "long-run equilibrium." Friedman suggests that there is a natural rate of unemployment "at any moment of time" that is consistent with the then existing (but also temporary) level and structure of real and product wage rates. It is impossible, however, to achieve this natural rate except in the long run or the long-long run. But in the long run in a dynamic world, conditions are completely different from what they were several decades earlier. And starting from any particular year, there is no reason to believe that anticipations as to wages and prices a year or two ahead will be much more accurate ten, twenty, or thirty years from now than they are at the beginning of the period. Even professional forecasters have not been notably accurate in their short-term price forecasts, and I am not aware that these forecasts have improved significantly over the last decade or two. Can much better be said of the rank and file of workers and businessmen?

It is not merely that it is so difficult to acquire information about the future, even for a given set of underlying conditions. (And the assumption of a given set of underlying conditions is an integral part of the statement that I have just quoted from Friedman's presidential address.) The really important problem is that these "underlying conditions" are continuously —and sometimes erratically—changing. In time series analysis, we tend to decompose change over time into secular trends, semisecular movements such as the so called Kuznets long swings, cyclical and irregular movements, and seasonal variations. We have trouble in predicting even the presumably most regular of these movements, as evidenced by the problems that are currently being debated as to how to adjust for seasonal variation, notably seasonal variation in the official unemployment series. The problem is much worse, of course, with respect to cyclical-irregular movements. It exists even with respect to long swings where they exist, and even seemingly predictable secular trends can surprise us. (Witness some recent demographic trends, for example, in the birth rate.)

So far as reducing uncertainty merely through the passage of time is concerned, the problem is made worse by the crucial role now played by policy makers in shaping the course of events—and, in democratic societies, by the interaction between policy makers and the political pressures that are brought to bear on them. Indeed in his Nobel lecture Friedman cites such politicoeconomic pressures as the source of the increasing volatility of price changes and of the increasing government intervention that generate a positively sloping Phillips curve in a long run that is not yet a long-long run. But in that long-long run, he suggests, institutional changes will be made, the rate of inflation will become less variable, and we will return to a vertical Phillips curve. All of this hardly seems to describe a world in which, at every moment of time, there is an underlying Walrasian equilibrium, yielding a natural rate of unemployment, which would be achieved in time—if only the world would stop changing.

At this point, in fairness to Friedman, I should retrace my steps. There is a sense in which one might speak of a natural rate of unemployment at every moment of time, given underlying institutional arrangements, even if we can never know or measure what that momentary natural rate is. There might be, at any moment of time, a set of underlying conditions that, if they prevailed long enough, would yield a pattern and average of sectoral unemployment rates and values for other relevant variables that resulted in a steady rate of inflation that neither accelerates nor decelerates. The fact that the current unemployment rate and other relevant variables are different from these momentary equilibrium values—that there is disequilibrium in this sense at that point in time—will generate pressures leading to a different rate of inflation, higher or lower, than the present rate. But that is as far as I am prepared to go. I cannot take the next step and posit a theory of the formation of expectations that leads inevitably to the conclusion that deviations from this momentary equilibrium rate of unemployment lead not only to a change in the rate of change in prices but to an accelerating change.

Even in his recent Nobel lecture, Friedman continues to be completely symmetrical with respect to departures from the natural unemployment rate. Lower unemployment rates, if maintained, lead to steadily accelerating inflation; higher rates lead, in a comparable way, to steadily accelerating deflation. And the accelerating deflation, if the unemployment rate continues above the natural rate, is apparently without limit. Wage rates would not only stop rising; they would eventually fall by ever larger decrements. This is obviously nonsense. At most, in today's institutional setting, the long-run (or long-long-run) Phillips curve can be vertical only at some positive rate of increase in money wages. At some low rate of wage increase, the curve, even in the long-long run, would presumably become horizontal.[12]

But here again it seems futile to engage in hypothetical exercises about what will happen over periods of several decades, particularly when political as well as economic forces are involved. A decade or more of falling or even constant money wages, with the levels of unemployment that are implied, would yield a quite new set of institutional arrangements —and an entirely new long-run Phillips curve.

Advocates of the natural rate hypothesis have been cautious about attempting to provide quantitative estimates of the natural rate, either in particular years or over a succession of years. There is, however, virtually universal agreement that the trade-off between unemployment and inflation has worsened since the mid-1950s. The Phillips curve has certainly shifted to the right by a significant amount during this period. Nonaccelerationists would also now agree that the Phillips curve is significantly steeper in the long run than in the short run. But nonaccelerationists do not accept the argument that below some figure for the national unemployment rate, the rate of inflation not only increases but that acceleration in the rate of inflation goes on without limit.

A number of attempts have been made to estimate how much the inflation-unemployment trade-off has worsened in the United States since the mid-1950s. If unemployment is measured by the official unemployment rate, there is no question that the trade-off has worsened significantly, but this fact alone tells nothing about whether the long-run Phillips curve is vertical, as the natural rate hypothesis implies.

One of the most important reasons for the worsening trade-off has been the changing age-sex composition of the labor force. The significant increase in the share of the labor force accounted for by teenagers and women, with their relatively high unemployment rates, means that a given national unemployment rate today implies a much tighter labor market for adult males than was the case fifteen or twenty years ago. In a pioneering paper in 1970, George Perry constructed a weighted unemployment rate that allowed for the different productivity and number of hours typically worked by different age-sex groups. The use of this weighted unemployment rate (and to a lesser extent of a measure of the widening dispersion of unemployment rates by age and sex) largely explained the apparent upward shift in the Phillips curve in the 1960s but provided no support for the accelerationist argument.[13] The long-run Phillips curve had shifted, but it was not vertical.

As inflation accelerated in the first half of the 1970s, additional data suggested that the natural rate hypothesis could not be so easily dismissed. Econometric studies of the Phillips curve typically regress some measure of the rate of change in wages on some variant of the unemployment rate, on a proxy for the expected rate of change in some price index, and on some combination of other variables, which varied from one investigator to another. The expected rate of inflation is typically based on a weighted average of price changes over some part of the recent past. As such regressions took in more data covering the accelerating rates of price increase in the late 1960s and early 1970s, the coefficient on the proxy for the expected rate of price change increased until some regressions showed it as being not significantly different from one in the usual statistical sense. And a coefficient of one for expected price changes implied accelerating inflation and the natural rate hypothesis.[14]

Although there have been numerous efforts to fit Phillips-curve type regressions and to estimate the coefficient on the proxy for price expectations, advocates of the natural rate hypothesis have been cautious about making direct estimates of the natural rate, either for single years or for any significant part of the postwar period. (And as is so often the case today, experience before World War II is largely ignored.) Robert J. Gordon has offered some alternative estimates of the natural rate and of the extent to which it increased between 1956 and 1974.[15] More frequently estimates are offered as to the size of the "noninflationary rate of unemployment" (or 'NIRU'), to use the term coined by Modigliani and Papademus.[16] This rate, as the term suggests, is the unemployment rate below which the rate of increase in prices will accelerate. In this respect it is like the natural rate. But it is different from the latter in that it does not necessarily imply a vertical long-run Phillips curve and therefore ever-accelerating inflation, when unemployment is below the 'noninflationary rate.'

Whereas it is usual to define the natural rate in terms of what would happen if the actual rate were maintained below that rate, Modigliani and Papademus define their NIRU in terms of what would happen if the actual rate is above it: "a rate such that, as long as unemployment is above it, inflation can be expected to decline—except perhaps from an initially low rate."[17] If the actual rate is below the NIRU, what happens depends on whether one assumes a vertical Phillips curve or one with a finite negative slope. In the latter case, there will be a limit to the extent of wage and price acceleration, and eventually a point will be reached on the negatively sloping Phillips curve.[18]

Current estimates of the noninflationary unemployment rate in the United States, applicable to the period since the severe recession of 1974–1975, tend to fall in the range of 5 to 6 percent, particularly in the upper half of this range. Those who have ventured estimates of the natural rate also tend to place it in this range. This is true, for example, of some recent estimates of the natural rate by Robert J. Gordon, who suggests that it rose from about 4.1 percent in 1956 to about 5.6 percent in 1974.[19] Michael Wachter's estimates of the noninflationary unemployment rate led to similar results.[20] Modigliani and Papademus in 1975 estimated the noninflationary rate of unemployment as "somewhat over $5\frac{1}{2}$ percent."[21] And an official source, the Council of Economic Advisers in the 1977 *Economic Report of the President* put what they called "the full-employment unemployment rate" at close to $5\frac{1}{2}$ percent.[22] While the council speaks of an unemployment rate corresponding to full employment, their estimate, like the others cited, is of an unemployment rate that will not lead to accelerating inflation: "The full-employment unemployment rate is generally understood to mean the lowest rate of unemployment attainable, under the existing institutional structure, that will not result in accelerated inflation."[23]

This represents a definition of full employment quite different from that used in the Kennedy and Johnson administrations (or in the early years of the Nixon administration). Then it was assumed that there was a negatively sloping Phillips curve that permitted a choice among various combinations of unemployment rates and rates of nonaccelerating inflation. The target of 4 percent unemployment reflected the belief that this rate was achievable at a satisfactorily low rate of inflation. While it was assumed that a lower unemployment rate would generate an uncomfortably high rate of inflation, it was assumed that this higher rate would be stable and would not recessarily accelerate. Thus a choice among various combinations of unemployment and stable inflation rates was possible. Now, reflecting the influence of the "accelerationist" literature, the council in the 1977 *Economic Report* suggests that this range of choices is no longer possible. The choice now is between an unemployment rate high enough to lead to a stable or declining rate of inflation or a lower rate that leads to presumably ever-accelerating inflation in the absence of countervailing policy measures.

At an earlier point, I said that I would comment further on Friedman's statement in which he defines the natural rate "as the level that would be ground out by the Walrasian system of general equilibrium equations, provided there is imbedded in them the actual structural characteristics of labor and commodity markets." Among these characteristics he mentions "market imperfections, stochastic variability in demands and supplies, the cost of gathering information about job vacancies and labor availabilities, the costs of mobility, and so on."[24]

I shall pass over briefly the statement that the natural rate is that which "would be ground out by the Walrasian system of general equilibrium equations." The world Friedman is talking about is not a Walrasian world.[25] Above all, as I have already suggested, it is a dynamic, not a static, world. The complex of relationships that determines the behavior of the economy is subject to a wide range of lags, which are not constant. Further the structure of the economy is subject to continuous as well as sporadic change. Not only do shifts occur in the behavioral equations that can be identified but the variables that must be taken as exogenous are subject to a variety of changes that go considerably beyond what he refers to as "stochastic variability." In short we live in a world in which expectations, of quantities as well as prices and wages, never catch up with realized values, even in the long-long run.

The "structural characteristics"of labor and commodity markets to which Friedman refers do not result in a homogeneous labor force of interchangeable workers. The single figure for the national unemployment rate that is so widely cited is, in a significant sense, an artificial construct. It is a weighted average of many different unemployment rates, which can be constructed by averaging along different dimensions of the labor force—age, sex, occupation, industry, and so on. Along any dimension of the labor force—age, for example—the inflationary implications of relatively low or high unemployment rates for particular groups vary widely. Is there at any time a natural unemployment rate for teenagers and young women as well as for prime-age males, for nonwhites and whites separately, for workers in each major occupation and industry? Friedman has said that "emphasis on the single unemployment percentage, as if it were meaningful and homogeneous, gives a misleading impression of both the nature of the problem and its magnitude."[26] Here he was speaking of the degree of hardship implied by the official unemployment statistics, particularly in view of the availability and liberalization of unemployment compensation. But the same issues arise in discussing the natural rate for a heterogeneous labor force.[27]

With Friedman the nature of the institutional environment determines the level of the natural unemployment rate, and in the postwar world changes in this environment (including broadening the coverage of the minimum wage and more generous unemployment compensation) have increased the natural rate and thus have shifted the vertical Phillips curve to the right. In addition, at least until the last few years, changes in the institutional environment have led to increasing pressures on governments to keep the actual unemployment rate below the natural rate. (These pressures have certainly been relaxed in the last few years.) And, he further argues in his Nobel lecture, a high rate of inflation tends to be volatile. It is the increasing volatility of inflation together with the increasing government intervention in the price system that yields the seemingly upward sloping Phillips curve of the last fifteen years or so.

This is a great deal to infer from the experience of the last decade and a half—indeed less than a decade in the case of the United States. It is true that changes in the institutional environment have been making for a more rapid and, until the 1974–1975 world recession, a seemingly accelerating rate of inflation.[28] Among these institutional changes have been the postwar commitment in all advanced countries to a high level of employment (stronger in Europe than in the United States), the reluctance to cover increasing public expenditures fully by taxation, the growing tendency to link wage and other payments to the consumer price index, the increasing aggressiveness of trade unions and other organized groups of income receivers, an apparent weakening of the willingness of employers to resist wage demands (which is closely related to the government's commitment to high employment), and the intensification of inflationary expectations engendered by past inflation.

Some of these changes have moved us higher on a given Phillips curve, some have shifted the curve, and some also have made the curve steeper. Together they have significantly worsened the trade-off between inflation and unemployment. But these changes do not necessarily imply some magical unemployment rate below which the rate of inflation will accelerate without limit.

Indeed there is one essential aspect of the institutional environment that ensures that, at least north of the tropics, inflation will not accelerate without limit: the existence of government. While it is fair to say that pressure on government generates rapid and sometimes accelerating inflation, it is also the resistance of government that leads eventually to the deceleration of inflation. "Stop-go" policies are a fact of life in all of the advanced economies of the postwar world. Although progress toward decelerating inflation may seem painfully slow, the stop signs are up even in the United Kingdom and Italy. Economists all too often forget, in viewing the real world, that they need to be not merely economists but political economists. High rates of inflation, like high levels of unemployment, can and do generate strong pressures on government to take countervailing action. These pressures vary among countries and over time in the same country, and limits of tolerance may be lower with respect to unemployment than to inflation (although tolerance of unemployment seems to have increased significantly in most advanced economies in the last few years). But high and accelerating rates of inflation lead to countervailing government action in the same cause-and-effect way as lower levels of unemployment may lead to higher rates of inflation.

There was a time when the almost exclusive emphasis in macroeconomic theory was on expectations with respect to real variables. Given a presumed stable consumption function (in real terms), the problem of the business cycle, and of short-run economic instability generally, was analyzed in terms of the determinants of the marginal efficiency schedule for investment—and, of course, the role played by government expenditures, other exogenous variables, and tax rates. Changing expectations played a major role in short-run shifts in the investment function and therefore in the unstable behavior of private investment. And these unstable expectations, however they were formed, were concerned with the probable future behavior of aggregate demand and its components expressed in real terms. All this reflected the emphasis on unemployment and on growth, although increasing attention came to be paid to the problem of inflation through the 1950s and into the 1960s.

In the first three decades or so after *The General Theory*, theoretical and econometric macromodels explicitly or implicitly utilized employment functions that tied employment directly to the level of output; and it was the behavior of output, in either the short run or the longer run, that was the chief concern of the analysis. It was the expected behavior of output that was important, and a variety of lagged relationships were developed, for consumer and investment expenditures and for other variables, that made future values of the variables depend in various ways on the present and the past. To this extent, the notion of adaptive expectations was implicit in these relationships (of which, I suppose, the acceleration principle is the simplest and the oldest).

In these neo-Keynesian models employment varied primarily because of expected or actual changes in the level of real output. Changes in expected real or product wages played a minor role or none at all. Indeed changes in real or product wages were considered to be more the result than the cause of changes in the level of employment.

While these neo-Keynesian macromodels continue to be widely used in forecasting and in many types of analytical research, the new concern with inflation, which is closely related to the rapidly increasing influence of the monetarists, has led to a new and different treatment of the role of expectations in macroeconomic analysis. What has become important is not expectations as to the future behavior of aggregate demand in real terms but expectations as to the future behavior of prices and wages. And this new emphasis on price and wage expectations has led to increasing attention being paid as to how these expectations are formed—and to how soon realizations catch up with expectations. At the very heart of the natural rate hypothesis is the process by which expectations of future inflation eventually catch up with realized inflation—if they ever do.

We need to pay renewed attention to the problem of changing expectations with respect to the real macrovariables. Friedman and other advocates of the natural rate hypothesis emphasize that, even in the relatively short run, increases in employment are associated with declines in product wages as perceived by employers.[29] The possibility of an upward shift in the demand curve for labor, reflecting more optimistic expectations of employers, seems to be ignored. Similarly the supply of labor as a function of the real wage is assumed, even in the short run, to have a positive slope. Whatever the level of unemployment, some rise in the expected real wage is required to induce those unemployed at any time to accept jobs. I have always assumed and still assume that, at even lower unemployment rates than those now prevailing in the United States and most of Western Europe, no increase in prevailing wage rates would be needed to induce a substantial fraction of the unemployed to accept jobs.[30]

This discussion of expectations brings me finally to the subject of "rational expectations," to use the term John Muth made popular.[31] Muth was not concerned directly with the level of aggregate output and employment. His analysis was entirely at the micro level, in terms of a single commodity market under the most simplified conditions, and applying only to the very short run. Neither Friedman nor Phelps made use of the notion of rational expectations in their formulations of the natural rate hypothesis, and Friedman has expressed some skepticism as to the validity and usefulness of the concept. But since the beginning of the 1970s, the concept of rational expectations has been seized eagerly by a number of economists, and some—for example, Lucas and Sargent—have argued that the validity of the natural rate hypothesis is strengthened by the assumption of the "rational" formation of expectations.[32] Or in Lucas's words, "The hypothesis of rational expectations *does* lead to the natural rate theory."[33] The hypothesis does more than this; it makes the natural rate hypothesis apply even in the short run, and not merely in the long run or Friedman's long-long run.

When are expectations "rational"? For Muth rational expectations, "since they are informed predictions of future events, are essentially the same as the predictions of the relevant economic theory."[34] Or as Sargent puts it, citing Muth, "Expectations of inflation are assumed to be endogenous to the system in a very particular way: they are assumed to be 'rational' in Muth's sense—which is to say that the public's expectations are not systematically worse than the predictions of economic models. This amounts to supposing that the public's expectations depend, in the proper way, on the things that economic theory says they ought to."[35]

Let us pause over the last part of Sargent's definition: "the public's expectations depend, in the proper way, on the things economic theory says they ought to." The public's expectations depend "in the proper way." What does this mean? And the public's expectations depend "on the things that economic theory says they ought to." What aspects of economic theory? What and whose theory of inflation? Does "the public" refer to everyone from the most sophisticated businessmen, union negotiators, and economists to the rank and file of small businessmen, workers, and consumers? I confess that I can make no sense out of the notion of rational expectations as it has been applied in recent macroeconomic theory.

The macro and monetary theorists who cite Muth's original article in their use of the notion of rational expectations need to take a closer look at the original than they have apparently done. Muth's analysis is entirely at the micro level and is confined to the presumed operation of an organized market for a single homogeneous product, the production and consumption of which depend only on actual and expected price and a catch-all error term. Further, and Muth emphasizes this: *"All the variables used are deviations from equilibrium values."*[36] Apparently, with Muth, rational expectations are "informed predictions" of the equilibrium values from which "informed predictions" about deviations from these equilibrium values can also be made.[37]

If, as Lucas and Sargent contend, the validity of the natural rate hypothesis depends on the validity of the assumption that the public's expectations are "rational" as they define that term, then clearly the natural rate hypothesis cannot be taken seriously. But the natural rate hypothesis, whatever problems there are with it, does not have to depend on the assumption of rational expectations.

Notes

1. Friedman's contribution is generally associated with his presidential address, "The Role of Monetary Policy," *American Economic Review* 58 (March 1968): 1–17. The same idea was put forward in his "Comment" in George P. Shultz and Robert Z. Aliber, eds., *Guidelines, Informal Controls, and the Market Place* (Chicago: University of Chicago Press, 1966), esp. p. 60. For Phelps's contribution, see his "Money Wage Dynamics and Labor Market Equilibrium," in E. S. Phelps et al., *Microeconomic Foundations of Employment and Inflation Theory* (New York: Norton, 1970), pp. 124–166, "Phillips Curves, Expectations of Inflation, and Optimal Unemployment Over Time," *Economica* 34 (August 1967): 254–281, and *Inflation Policy and Unemployment Theory* (New York: Norton, 1972). Phelps mentions as precursors Fellner, Wallich, Lerner, and von Mises.

While in the article by Lerner that Phelps cites, the former does talk about the role of expectations in the inflationary process, he says nothing to suggest that there exists a natural rate of unemployment that is impervious to government policy. See Abba P. Lerner, "The Inflationary Process. I. Some Theoretical Aspects," *Review of Economics and Statistics* 31 (August 1949): 193–200. Indeed, as one of the leading disciples of Keynes, Lerner believed precisely the opposite.

2. "Inflation and Unemployment," Nobel Lecture, November 29, 1976. Published as "Nobel Lecture: Inflation and Unemployment," *Journal of Political Economy* 85 (June 1977): 451–472.

3. In the Nobel lecture, Friedman states that what matters to workers is the purchasing power of wages "over all goods in general" (p. 457). Surely the prices that concern workers are limited almost entirely to retail prices of goods and services that enter into their cost of living.

4. Friedman, "Role of Monetary Policy," p. 8.

5. Edmund Phelps offers essentially the same equilibrium concept when he says that the "essential hallmark of macroequilibrium is that the actual inflation rate is turning out equal to the (average) expected inflation rate." *Inflation Policy*, p. xxi.

6. Friedman, "Role of Monetary Policy," p. 11. His presidential address was written in 1967.

7. "Nobel Lecture," p. 465.

8. Ibid., p. 470.

9. Phelps is much less explicit about the amount of calendar time involved than is Friedman.

10. Friedman, "Nobel Lecture," p. 464.

11. Friedman, "Role of Monetary Policy," p. 8.

12. See James Tobin, "Inflation and Unemployment," *American Economic Review* 62 (March 1972): 11. This suggestion has also been made by Robert J. Gordon and, I presume, by others. See R. J. Gordon, "Recent Developments in the Theory of Inflation and Unemployment," *Journal of Monetary Economics* 2 (April 1976): 193–194.

13. See George L. Perry, "Changing Labor Markets and Inflation," *Brookings Papers on Economic Activity* 3 (1970): 411–441.

14. For a useful summary of some of these studies, redone to apply to data through 1970, see Robert J. Gordon, "Wage-Price Controls and the Shifting Phililps Curve," *Brookings Papers on Economic Activity* 2 (1972): 385–421. For a more recent study, which, among other things, presents a number of Phillips-type regressions fitted to data through mid-1975, see Michael L. Wachter, "The Changing Cyclical Responsiveness of Wage Inflation," *Brookings Papers on Economic Activity* (1976): 115–159.

15. Robert J. Gordon, "Structural Unemployment and the Productivity of Women," in K. Brunner and A. Meltzer, eds. *Stabilization of the Domestic and International Economy* (Amsterdam: North-Holland, 1977), pp. 181–229. Interestingly, several years earlier, Gordon had remarked that "even if the natural rate hypothesis is valid, the exact value of the natural rate will always be uncertain." "The Welfare Cost of Higher Unemployment," *Brookings Papers on Economic Activity* 1 (1973): 135. Phelps has suggested that the value of the natural rate should be thought of as falling in a band rather than being a precise figure. *Inflation Policy*, p. 57.

16. Franco Modigliani and Lucas Papademus, "Targets for Monetary Policy in the Coming Years," *Brookings Papers on Economic Activity* 1 (1975): 141–165.

17. Ibid., p. 142.

18. Ibid., pp. 145–149.

19. Gordon, "Structural Unemployment."

20. Wachter, "Changing Cyclical Responsiveness."

21. Modigliani and Papademus, "Targets," p. 142.

22. *Economic Report of the President* (January 1977), p. 51.

23. Ibid., p. 48.

24. Friedman, "Role of Monetary Policy," p. 8.

25. Cf. Tobin, "Inflation," pp. 5–6, 11.

26. *Newsweek*, February 7, 1977, p. 63.

27. Robert J. Gordon has offered some alternative estimates of the natural unemployment rate for the total labor force that vary depending on which age-sex group is considered the key group in determining the relation between unemployment and wage changes. See his "Structural Unemployment."

28. This paragraph borrows heavily from my "Rigor and Relevance in a Changing Institutional Setting," *American Economic Review* 66 (March 1976): 9.

29. Cf. Friedman, "Role of Monetary Policy," p. 10.

30. Cf. Arthur Okun, "Inflation: Its Mechanics and Welfare Costs," *Brookings Papers on Economic Activity* 2 (1975): 356.

31. John F. Muth, "Rational Expectations and the Theory of Price Movements," *Econometrica* 29 (July 1961): 315–335.

32. See, for example, Robert E. Lucas, Jr., "Econometric Testing of the Natural Rate Hypothesis," in Otto Eckstein, ed., *The Econometrics of Price Determination: Conference* (Washington: Board of Governors of the Federal Reserve System and Social Science Research Council, 1972), pp. 50–59, and Thomas J. Sargent, "Rational Expectations: The Real Rate of Interest and the Natural Rate of Unemployment," *Brookings Papers on Economic Activity* 2 (1973): 429–472.

33. Lucas, "Econometric Testing," p. 58.

34. Muth, "Rational Expectations," p. 316.

35. Sargent, "Rational Expectations," p. 431.

36. Muth, "Rational Expectations," p. 317.

37. *Business Week*, April 11, 1977, p. 24, referred to "rational expectations" as a concept that "used to be called market psychology." This is certainly a more useful concept that that developed by Lucas and Sargent.

Chapter 5

Charles P. Kindleberger

Is Symmetry Possible in International Money?

The topic of this paper is only loosely tied to the impressive achievements of Abba Lerner in economics. The slight connection runs to his classic article on the symmetry between import and export taxes, which showed that an export tax was identical to an import tax in its effects on trade, the terms of trade, revenue, and the like—but not in its determination of the rate of exchange.[1] My contention is that symmetry may be possible in all else but that it is difficult to achieve, perhaps impossible, in the realm of money. This topic is important because of the interest of the world in modifying the asymmetrical system of the dollar-exchange standard, an interest shared by the United States as well as by the rest of the world. An asymmetrical distribution of costs and benefits, or rights and duties, is politically unacceptable in a world of sovereign states. If it is inescapable, we have one more in the dilemmas posed by the conflict between a politically acceptable and an economically efficient world.

The asymmetry between commodities and money is well known. Take a list of commodities $A, B, C, D, \ldots, N$, and choose one commodity, say N, as numeraire. We now have an asymmetrical system. The numeraire, or money, is needed for efficiency to reduce the number of prices from $N(N - 1)/2$, which obtains in barter, to $N - 1$. All commodities have prices; money does not. Or the price of money can be considered to be the reciprocal of the prices of all other commodities than N, somehow (properly) weighted.

The same is true with $A, B, C, D, \ldots, N$ national currencies, and one currency, call it N, which becomes international money. If the dollar becomes the unit of account in international measurements and transactions, the price of each currency is expressed in terms of dollars, but the price of the dollar is the reciprocal of all other national currencies on a weighted basis.

Asymmetry in pricing is related to asymmetry in how balance-of-payments equilibrium should be determined in the two cases. For A, B, C, D, . . . , $N - 1$ countries, basic balance is a serviceable criterion for most purposes and may be expressed in this way,

$$X - M - LTC = 0 = STC + G \tag{5.1}$$

where X stands for exports of goods and services on current account, M for imports of goods and services, LTC for long-term capital exports (and has an implicit negative sign when long-term capital is being imported), STC for short-term capital outflows (and has an implicit negative sign when short-term capital takes the form of inflow), and G for gold imports (with an implicit negative sign for gold exports). On this definition, in equilibrium an export surplus is matched by an export of long-term capital, or an import surplus on current account is matched by a long-term capital inflow, and the sum of short-term capital outflows (inflows) is matched by a gold outflow (inflow). The matter may be put that the autonomous elements in the balance of payments on the left-hand side of the equation (or above the line) sum algebraically to zero, so that there need not and cannot be any net compensating movements on the right-hand side of the equation, or below the line. If basic balance does not hold, the left-hand side of the equation equals the right-hand side, but both depart from zero. When both sides are positive, there is a basic-balance surplus; when negative, a deficit.

For the Nth country, the currency of which serves as international money, this criterion of equilibrium will not serve. Such a country balances its accounts not through its assets but through liabilities. This is the element of truth in the U.S. Department of Commerce's (Walther Lederer's) insistence in the late 1950s that the United States shift from presenting its balance of payments in terms of the "basic balance" definition of equilibrium to a "liquidity-balance" measure. Under this definition

$$X - M - LTC - STC_a = 0 = STC_1 + G \tag{5.2}$$

where STC_a is short-term capital flows representing increases or decreases in U.S. assets, or claims on foreigners, and STC_1 is such flows through changes in foreign short-term claims on the United States (U.S. liabilities to foreigners). On the right-hand side of this equation, equilibrium is achieved if the sum of gold outflow (inflow) plus the decrease (increase) in U.S. liabilities to foreigners is zero. If the right-hand side of the equation is positive (a short-term capital outflow plus a gold inflow, or larger than a gold outflow, or a gold inflow larger than a short-term capital inflow), the liquidity balance of payments is in surplus; if the right-hand side is negative—and I refrain from spelling out the various combinations to produce this result—the accounts are in deficit. Implicit in the asymmetry between (5.1) and (5.2) is that ordinary countries balance their accounts through changes in assets, accumulating or reducing their holdings of, say, dollars, while the United States, as the issuer of dollars in this case, balances its accounts through increases or decreases in liabilities. If symmetry is to be achieved, the United States should balance its accounts through assets, like other countries in the system.

The weakness with liquidity balance is that it made no allowance for the possibility of increasing the supply of international money through borrowing. In an ordinary banking system, money is created by banks making loans and investments, which they pay for through the issuance of deposits. As financial intermediaries, banks lend long and borrow short, the latter representing increases in deposits or money. If the money supply is fixed, liabilities of banks are transferred by various depositors from one account to another. New loans and investments cannot be made net. But if the money supply is expanding, banks must be lending and investing long, and borrowing short, on a net basis. In the process they experience an increase in liabilities, which results not from a disequilibrium excess of absorption over production but merely from the need for increased money supplies in the system. If international financial intermediation is allowed to increase the supply of international money, the criteria for balance-of-payments equilibrium must be changed both for the $A, B, C, D, \ldots,$ $N - 1$ and for the Nth country.[2] For the former, equilibrium is achieved when

$$X - M - LTC - STC_{FI} = 0 = STC_o + G \qquad (5.3)$$

where STC_{FI} is the increase in money sought through long-term borrowing, or financial intermediation, and STC_o is all other short-term capital outflows (inflows). For the reserve-currency country, increases in liabilities sought by the rest of the world for expansion of the world's money supply can be offset against long-term lending as part of normal and necessary financial intermediation. The equilibrium criterion for a reserve center thus becomes

$$X - M - LTC - STC_a - STC_{1_{FI}} = 0 = STC_{1_o} + G \qquad (5.4)$$

where $STC_{1_{FI}}$ is money issued in regular financial intermediation and STC_{1_o} is all other outflows of short-term capital through liabilities (or inflows). It must regretfully be noted that equilibrium definitions (5.3) and (5.4) are nonoperational because it is impossible to determine from objective statistical evidence the appropriate size of normal and necessary financial intermediation. One can have an idea of such appropriate size, however. On earlier occasions, I have suggested that a liquidity-definition deficit—(5.2)—of about $3 billion a year for the United States in the late 1950s and early 1960s was consistent with equilibrium on the basis of definition (5.4). This seemed to be about the amount of liquidity the world wanted and was prepared to achieve through borrowing over and above the proportion of gold production entering the central-bank circulation. The number fit neatly with the results obtained by Fritz Machlup, although he did not accept my analysis. He found that the United States succeeded in transferring abroad each year in real terms, through an export surplus, all but about $3 billion of its long-term lending, and he referred to this as the transfer "gap."[3] Our differences in interpretation arise from differing criteria for measuring balance-of-payments equilibrium.

If one accepts the view that international financial intermediation is a legitimate activity—and many do not—that fact disposes of the possibility of an additional asymmetry under the exchange standard in the form of seignorage, seignorage being available to the country the currency of which is used as international money but to none other. The position taken here is that there is no seignorage, that interest paid to holders of the short-term claims on the United States, plus the value of the liquidity acquired by countries borrowing long and lending short, is equal to the earnings on long-term loans and investments acquired by the banking country—in this case the United States. This attitude is debatable and debated.[4] The reader is cautioned against accepting it without scrutiny.

There are a number of asymmetries under a dollar standard other than those found in exchange rates and balance-of-payments definitions. One is the possible range of fluctuation of exchange rates under a fixed-rate system. If the dollar is the reserve currency, the range or band of fluctuations of the dollar is half that of any other two currencies. With a 1 percent range on either side of parity, the vehicle currency can never be more than 1 percent above or below any other currency, whereas any pair of other currencies can vary between them by 2 percent—one country at the top of its range against the dollar, the other at the bottom. This asymmetry runs not between the United States and all other countries but between pairs of countries, one pair involving the United States, others not involving it.

Under a dollar standard with gold as a reserve asset, moreover, power with respect to the price of gold is asymmetric. Foreign countries under the dollar-exchange system could change the value of their currency against the dollar; the price of the dollar could not be changed by the United States, as it was the reciprocal of the value of all other currencies in terms of dollars. But the United States could change the price of gold, and other countries could not. If France had tried to change the price of gold, as she would have liked to do, she would have succeeded only in depreciating the franc.[5]

Consider further the asymmetry implicit in the so-called assignment problem posed by Robert Mundell.[6] This is closely related to the $N - 1$ discussion earlier. Take two countries, the United States and the rest of the world (ROW), closely joined through capital movements, with the financial markets of the United States larger, more efficient, and therefore dominant. The United States can fix the world rate of interest under these circumstances, but not its balance of payments. Other countries can use small differences between their domestic rates of interest and that set by the United States to determine their balances of payments. Outside of these narrow limits, however, they cannot set domestic rates of interest. If the United States and ROW both seek to determine the levels of their balances of payments, the system is overdetermined, since just as the exchange rate of the United States is the reciprocal of that of ROW, so is its balance of payments. Mundell has proposed that the United States set world monetary policy in the interest of price stabilization, and neglect its balance of payments, while ROW neglects or ignores domestic monetary policy apart from the small differences needed to balance its international payments, and incidentally those of the United States.

If the United States and ROW are of approximately equal size, and ROW has unified decision-making comparable to that of a nation, this system is not so much asymmetric as overdetermined, which almost certainly calls for an asymmetric solution. The US and ROW may agree upon their objectives for monetary policy and for the balance of payments between them, and further agree on a division of the policy instruments between them. Since targets are interrelated, instrumental variables must be harmonized or related. Symmetric solutions are possible, but in a world of sovereign states, equilibrium appears unstable.

A number of suggestions have been made that foreign-exchange could be retained in international reserves, but asymmetry eliminated, by shifting from a single to a multiple-reserve standard, and adopting—to avoid the uncertainty just referred to in the previous paragraph—a rule for uniform settlement. Such a rule might require intervention by the deficit countries, which would sell off reserves to support their currencies at lower limits or floors; or intervention by surplus countries, which would buy the currencies of deficit countries to hold their own currencies down when they reached the upper limits of possible fluctuation, or the ceiling. The crippling asymmetry in these suggestions was quickly detected. Deficit settlement means that world reserves are continuously declining; surplus settlement that they grow without limit. If reserves are to stay steady around a given level or trend, a country must accumulate reserves when it has surpluses and sell them off when it experiences deficits; thus it must intervene both at the floor and the ceiling rather than follow a world rule that permits only one.

Apart from seignorage, there are thus asymmetries in the exchange standard—relating to the setting of exchange rates, band width, the price of gold, balance-of-payments definitions to establish equilibrium—and they are likely to occur in the assignment problem. Let us now assume that the dollar exchange standard is abandoned in favor of either the gold standard, the special drawing right (SDR) standard, or fluctuating exchange rates. First, however, we must determine that such a transformation is possible.

Gresham's law—bad money drives out good—is matched by another empirically observed phenomenon: markets prefer an efficient to an inefficient money. Gold as international money has the drawback of being expensive to use in payment settlements, except notionally through earmarks, since it must be transported and assayed. It serves well enough when its price is fixed, for long-term reserves, but it is expensive to use for transactions. The gold standard has a clearly discernible tendency on this score to convert itself into a gold-exchange standard, using gold as reserves perhaps, but currencies convertible into gold as the vehicle for payments, for inventories that turn over, rather than ace-in-the-hole, rock-bottom reserves against catastrophe. Gold may serve as time deposits but never as demand deposits or useful money. Triffin believes that the gold-exchange standard is inherently unstable.[7] The gold standard would seem to be equally unstable as markets choose an efficient money for transactions to use alongside the designated official reserve, if there by only one.

Little experience with the SDR has accumulated as yet, and there is doubt as to how the system will develop if it continues to grow. Whitman forecasts the necessity to retain the dollar standard, despite the SDR as international reserves, and fluctuating exchange rates.[8] Much turns on the rules that ultimately evolve for the use of SDRs. If the SDR is not allowed to be privately held and traded, it seems inevitable that a currency standard would grow up in parallel to it if the dollar standard were effectively suppressed. Trading firms, corporations, and banks would be unwilling to go without working balances and even inventories of final means or payment, or foreign exchange. Economy dictates that such inventories be held in a single currency—perhaps one in each of the major regions of the world—and the SDR system would develop into the SDR-exchange standard. Even if SDRs can be held by private institutions, it is by no means certain that such institutions would not want to hold foreign exchange that can be spent without conversion involving transaction cost, at least for the major foreign currencies in which such institutions deal. Only if the SDR were to become a world currency, spendable in transactions in major countries, as well as holdable as reserves, would the incentive to convert an SDR standard into an SDR-exchange standard be seriously weakened. Such a development seems remote.

Finally many economists have predicted that adoption of fluctuating exchange rates will not eliminate private holdings of foreign exchange but may even increase them. If the public good of foreign-exchange reserves for stabilizing foreign expenditure intertemporally is not provided publicly, pressures will be felt to provide it less efficiently privately. Reserves would be held in the currencies most used, and in a hierarchy, with major amounts, on the insurance principle, held in the strongest currency. There is even the possibility that if central banks are unwilling to stabilize foreign-exchange rates, that public good—the provision of international money—will be provided privately by stabilizing speculation, as the proponents of fluctuating exchange rates think.

On all three scores, there is the possibility that the currency-exchange standard may not be easily eliminated but that any other standard will evolve, or degenerate, into an exchange standard. Is every exchange standard asymmetric? The answer is probably yes. Leaving the instability of Gresham's law aside, let us take a look at the gold-exchange standard.

Settlement through gold is settlement through assets. Settlement through exchange is settlement through an asset on the part of one participant, and settlement through a liability for another. There is a strong tendency on the part of countries settling through foreign exchange to pick a single one, the dollar in the post–World War II world and sterling for the most part, but also the French franc and the German mark, in the period from 1870 to 1914.[9] It is not necessary to agree with Triffin that the gold-exchange standard is an absurdity to recognize that, for the exchange pàrt, there will be at least some asymmetry. Triffin and others exaggerate when they claim that reserve centers pay no attention to changes in liabilities. Presidents Eisenhower, Kennedy, and Johnson agonized at length (and in my judgement excessively since they did not recognize the role of international financial intermediation, though perhaps they failed to do much about it). In my thesis forty years ago, I sought to demonstrate that an increase in liabilities to foreigners could have the same effects on the internal banking system as a decrease in assets (gold and/or claims on foreigners).[10] This assumed, however, that there was no incentive on the part of central authorities in the reserve center to sterilize short-term capital movements and that foreign holders of claims on the reserve center would be more interested in risk than in the (then) low returns on market assets, and would hold their claims either at the central bank or in the commercial banks, as demand deposits. If, as today, foreign holders of claims on the reserve center hold market assets, they themselves act to sterilize the effects of capital inflow on commercial-bank reserves. The gold-exchange standard need not be completely asymmetrical if foreign-exchange reserves are accumulated at the central bank. It cannot claim to be completely symmetrical, however.

Adoption and maintenance of the pure gold standard, if it were possible, would not eliminate all asymmetry in the international monetary system. With a fixed amount of gold, it is possible for all countries to abide by rules of settlement through assets, with no country settling through liabilities, but asset settlement itself is asymmetrical between creditors and debtors. There is no limit to accumulations from surpluses; a limit is reached on deficits when a country runs out of gross assets and credit. Interest is not involved in gold reserves, to be sure, but interest is charged on gold loans contracted by persistent-debtor countries and earned on such loans by persistent creditors. At the Bretton Woods negotiations, Keynes objected to this asymmetry, maintaining that persistent creditors were as likely to be responsible for disequilibria as persistent debtors. At that time the position received no sympathy from the United States. Since 1968, however, this country has changed its view. In one of his many provocative dicta on international money (but one unhappily that I cannot place) Mundell has suggested that in a world of inflation, deficit countries should bear the responsibility for disequilibrium; in a world of deflation, the creditor countries. The insight is acute, but the institutional framework for putting the policies that derive from it is hopelessly out of reach. In a world where capital is productive, interest is earned on lending and paid on borrowing.

Assume, however, a pure gold-exchange standard, with domestic policies that operate to forestall persistent creditors and persistent debtors.[11] Is such a system symmetrical? Starting from a given distribution of gold, and assuming no need for monetary growth, with a two-tier system for gold such as that adopted in March 1968, one price for gold in the central-bank circuit and another for new production, industrial use and private hoarding outside, the system may be said to be symmetrical. The two-price system for gold sets up tensions, to be sure. Central banks, especially those of smaller countries that have no sense of responsibility for the world monetary mechanism, will be tempted to buy gold for sale to other central banks if the outside price is below the central-bank price; or to buy central-bank gold to sell outside if the outside price is above the central-bank price. If all arbitrage between the central-bank stock and the outside market can be prevented, however, the only asymmetry in the system is that between central-bank gold (money) and noncentral bank gold (a commodity).

But assume that there is a unified private and central-bank market as on the ordinary gold standard, which has the expectation that the money stock should grow from year to year and that the common price is high enough and low enough to provide the central-bank circuit with exactly the amount of gold needed each year to meet world liquidity needs—a price difficult to calculate with accuracy and confidence. There now arises an asymmetry between gold producers and purchasers of newly mined gold, the former treating it as a commodity export, in X, the latter as monetary gold, which appears in the balance of payments as G. Such symmetry has no political drawbacks to be sure and perhaps can be overlooked as trivial. It does underline, however, that there may be asymmetries arising from the need to introduce new money into the system.

All this, however, assumes that the gold stock of each country is increased or decreased through changes in the current account that give rise to gains or losses in reserves, and there is no market for lending and borrowing gold reserves through international financial intermediation. If countries borrow for the sake of adding to international reserves, and other countries serving as financial centers lend, asymmetries are back. Basic balance of international payments becomes

$$X - M - LTC - G_{FI} = 0 = STC + G_o \qquad (5.5)$$

where G_{FI} is gold acquired by borrowing from a financial center, and G_o is other gold flows. Gold acquired through long-term borrowing is not an indication of surplus in the balance of payments. And the converse is true in the lending country, which can use the same definition of equilibrium: a loss of gold, blanced by long-term lending as part of the financial-intermediation process, is not a sign of deficit. The balance-of-payments criteria for balance, surplus, and deficit may be the same, but the banking country is in equilibrium when it lends for gold outflows; the borrowing country when it borrows for gold inflows.

Nineteenth-century economic history is replete with gold flows that were borrowed to increase reserves. The Bank of England borrowed from the Bank of Amsterdam in 1696, from the Bank of France in 1832, 1839, and 1890, from Hamburg in 1839, and from Russia in 1890.[12] Williamson has made clear that gold flows to and from the United States in the nineteenth century were not always compensating but were frequently autonomous. The United States borrowed in booms to acquire gold to expand the money supply in the upswing and paid it back in subsequent contraction when the need for money was reduced.[13] Even with the gold standard then, and with no foreign-exchange reserves in the system, financial intermediation involving bullion enabled some countries to settle balances with assets and others to do so through liabilities. Again the criterion of balance-of-payments equilibrium is nonoperational, since in practice it is impossible to distinguish G_{FI} from G_o by any objective test. Again, moreover, the fact of asymmetry takes on a less awkward political coloration since the borrowers that settle payments through increasing their liabilities are the many trading countries rather than the few financial centers.

We arrive at the SDR standard. Assume some initial appropriate distribution, no need for increased stocks in the system, no financial intermediation, and universal agreement, which is credible, that the system will never be dissolved; there is no asymmetry. But asymmetry creeps in if any of these rigorous conditions is not met.

Let us deal first with the question of ultimate dissolution as against permanent existence. Domestic bank reserves in a national banking system are "outside" money because they represent a liability of government, which will never be paid off and which need not be paid off. The basic asymmetry involved in fiat money—that it is an asset for a holder but not necessarily a real liability of some debtor—is matched by a contrary and offsetting asymmetry—that debts of governments within their own borders differ from debts of all others and from foreign debts in that they will never be requited. Like gold, government money, issued directly or through a central bank that holds claims on the government, can last forever. The debt that is its counterpart is equally immortal.

With the SDR, however, one cannot be sure. The SDR is an asset of all countries in the system, but it is also a liability of the same countries. The possibility, or prospect, that some countries in the system would act as persistent debtors, and others as persistent creditors, led the originators of the scheme to put maximum limits on the amounts of SDRs an individual country would be obliged to hold—three times its quota—and minimum holding ratios—40 percent of its quota—that it would be required to reconstitute from time to time, if it did not already hold the minimum, as proof of its readiness to accumulate as well as to spend this sort of international money. With each country holding at least 40 percent of its cumulative allotment, the dissolution of the system and cancellation of existing holdings against initial quotas, and the funding of excess and deficiencies, would not be an insuperable undertaking. Limits and holding ratios thus imply that there is a liability potentially outstanding against the asset of the SDR. They also imply that a country might on some remote occasion have to settle its cumulative accounts with liabilities while others acquired claims, a source of asymmetry.

Whether there will be financial intermediation in SDRs is unclear. It is possible to contemplate an international market in SDRs like the national federal funds market in the United States that makes it possible for some banks to pay by running down assets while others do so through increasing liabilities. To the extent this occurs, the system will be asymmetric. If SDRs are traded only among central banks, the SDR system may evolve into an SDR-exchange standard in which private traders and financial institutions hold a national currency as an international liquid asset. This again would make the system asymmetric. If private firms are allowed to deal in and hold SDRs, one would expect a rise of international financial intermediation of SDRs against debt in SDRs. Again the system would be asymmetric, insofar as it was possible for some countries to settle balance-of-payments liabilities by going into debt.

Consider increases in SDR allotments. I choose not to address the well-worn question of whether SDRs produce seignorage that is available for distribution to the less developed countries. To the extent that the SDR is outside money, it is available for distribution as seignorage, but the more it is so distributed, the less the SDR retains the attribute of outside money. Of more interest for present purposes is the possibility of finding asymmetry in the distribution of increased allotments.

Under the gold standard, additional international reserves are distributed to countries that earn them through an export surplus, or acquire them by borrowing, which entails a matching increase in liabilities. SDRs, on the other hand, were initially to be distributed on the basis of financial capacity and responsibility in the world, as measured by quotas negotiated under the General Arrangement to Borrow (GAB), a basis that was later modified by shifting to the quotas arrived at for the International Monetary Fund (IMF). These quotas have an odd history; they were decided on the basis of a compromise between Keynes, who sought IMF quotas based on national shares in world trade, and White, who favored a criterion related to shares in gross world product. The GAB came into being because quotas based on a compromise between trade and gross output failed to allow, except very indirectly, for reserves needed by the financial centers of the world.

In a world of persistent debtors and persistent creditors, new issues of international money to increase world liquidity, distributed in a fixed and arbitrary way decided ab initio, would be too great for the creditors if they were adequate for the debtors and too small for the debtors if they were adequate for the creditors. What might be called poker-chip or helicopter money, distributed in predetermined quantities to individual countries without any net saving or any incurred liability by the units acquiring the money, is necessarily distributed in a skewed fashion. Only if all countries maintain their balances of payments in continuous equilibrium on some consistent basis would the fixed regular distribution of more money to all countries meet the requirements of the system. And in this case the asymmetry between the distribution of domestic and international money would be complete: the former distributed to savers and borrowers, the latter from on high by helicopter.

If there were a world central bank, new supplies of SDRs could be put into circulation in ways which closely resembled the issue of domestic money. For the bank to operate effectively, there would need to be an international financial asset, held by all countries in financial portfolios and traded internationally, much like government bills, notes, and bonds in a domestic banking system. In the absence of world government issuing its own debt, the closest we have come to this is the U.S. government debt, which was held widely under the dollar-exchange standard, the system we are trying to escape. If the bank were allowed to hold and trade in the government obligations of separate countries, the amount of liquidity could be restricted to the amount needed, but the bank would quickly find its assets consisting of the debts of deficit countries, raising once more in acute form the question of possible dissolution of the SDR system. Although there is merit in a system where balance-of-payments surpluses and deficits are settled in long-term securities, as Ingram has made clear, the balance-of-payments criteria for equilibrium are rendered more complex.[14] (Readers can work out their own algebraic definition like (5.6) and decide its operationality.)

A system of discounting shifts the initiative, to some degree at least, from the world central bank to the deficit countries. The differences between open-market operations and discounting should not be exaggerated. With open-market operations, the bank has to obtain consent from national monetary authorities before conducting operations in a particular market; with discounting, in the absence of an established international financial asset, the bank will have to establish criteria for the sorts of assets it is prepared to rediscount and to make explicit decisions to discount (or not) in particular cases. The distinction between them may be too small to be worth making. But a discounting system presumably creates money on demand; under an open-market system the initiative rests with the supply. Both differ in efficiency from SDRs created on trend, like helicopter money, distributed to creditors and debtors alike on the basis of politically negotiated criteria in which output and trade, rather than the health of financial markets, play the leading roles.

It thus may be possible to build a symmetric world monetary system based on the SDR, distributed on trend in arbitrary fixed amounts. The system would be inefficient. Whether symmetry for political purposes is desirable at the expense of economic efficiency is something the economist is not competent alone to judge.

Notes

1. See Abba P. Lerner, "The Symmetry Between Import and Export Taxes," *Economica*, n.s. 3 (August 1936): 306–313. As further evidence of Lerner's fascination with the question of symmetry at that time, see his "Further Notes on the Elasticity of Substitution, III, The Question of Symmetry," *Review of Economic Studies* 3 (February 1936): 150–151.

2. See my "Measuring Equilibrium in the Balance of Payments," *Journal of Political Economy* 77 (November–December 1969): 873–891.

3. Fritz Machlup, "The Transfer Gap of the United States," *Banca Nazionale del Lavoro Quarterly Review* 21 (1969): 195–238.

4. See, for example, George N. Halm, "International Financial Intermediation: Deficits, Benign and Malignant," *Princeton Essays in International Finance*, no. 68 (1968).

5. See my "The Price of Gold and the N-1 Problem," *Economie Appliquée*, t. xxiii, n° 1 (1970): 149–162 (Archives de l'ISEA).

6. Robert A. Mundell, "The Appropriateness of Monetary and Fiscal Policy for Internal and External Stability," *International Monetary Fund Staff Papers* 9 (March 1962): 70–77.

7. Robert Triffin, *Gold and the Dollar Crises: The Future of Convertibility* (New Haven: Yale University Press, 1960).

8. Marina V. N. Whitman, "The Current and Future Role of the Dollar: How Much Symmetry?" *Brookings Papers on Economic Activity* 3 (1974): 539–591.

9. Peter Lindert, "Key Currencies and Gold, 1900–1913," *Princeton Studies in International Finance*, no. 24 (1969).

10. Charles P. Kindleberger, *International Short-Term Capital Movements* (New York: Columbia University Press, 1937).

11. An assumption of no persistent creditors or debtors may well be utopian. I am confirmed in this thought by the recollection of the experience of a wartime carpool in Washington in 1944 and 1945 that consisted of four economists: Philip S. Brown, Emile Despres, George A. Eddy, and Walter A. Salant. From the beginning, it was understood that various circumstances affecting the particular circumstances of automobiles and families made it impossible to balance ride accounts each week or month, and it was recognized further that intertemporal balancing was in any event more efficient. The carpool then bought a set of poker chips, divided it evenly among the participants, and paid the driver on the occasion of each ride one white chip. Very quickly the group divided into persistent debtors and persistent creditors. Long-term loans were provided to the former by the latter, outside of current accounts. The debtors sought an infusion of new liquidity into the system; another set of chips was bought and distributed. I have mercifully forgotten the identities of the Populists, on the one hand, and the Wall Street hard-money types, on the other, nor do I recall the ultimate dissolution. That there is a tendency toward persistent surpluses and deficits, however, cannot be doubted, even in a microcosmic experiment operated by sophisticated economists.

12. Jacob Viner, *Studies in the Theory of International Trade* (New York: Harpers, 1937), p. 274.

13. Jeffry G. Williamson, *American Growth and the Balance of Payments, 1820–1913: A Study of the Long Swing* (Chapel Hill: University of North Carolina Press, 1964).

14. James C. Ingram, "State and Regional Payments Mechanisms," *Quarterly Journal of Economics* 73 (November 1959): 619–632.

Chapter 6   **Political Aspects of Economic Control**

L. R. Klein

Control as a Branch of Economic Policy Analysis

The concept of economic control is not new in analytical economics. but control theory in one form or another is one of the most promising frontier subjects in econometrics, and it is my intent to put the subject into place, both theoretically and applied, from the point of view of political economy. What are the possibilities of introducing more automaticity into economic policy, achieving stability, and achieving optimality? Eventually I hope to be as realistic as possible, but first I want to form some historical perspective and formulation of concepts.

The idea of economic control is certainly not new. In 1944, Abba Lerner, in *The Economics of Control*, took up control in both microeconomic and macroeconomic terms. His approach was a precomputer, prelarge-scale modeling approach to comprehensive economic control, using the market system to the fullest extent. I do not intend to take up control from the viewpoint of complete socialist planning with replacement or supplementation of the market mechanism. I want to confine my attention to macroeconomics and overall guidance of the economy. Lerner stated the problem succinctly: "The uncontrolled economy may be likened to an automboile without a driver but in which many passengers keep reaching over to the steering wheel to give it a twist while complicated regulations prescribe the order and degree to which they may turn the wheel so as to prevent them from fighting each other about it. The controlled economy has a driver, so these regulations are unnecessary." [8] This analogy is actually taken from an article of the suggested name "The Economic Steering Wheel," published as early as 1941 [7]. A more recent analogy is "fine tuning." It conveys essentially the same idea of overall

This paper was originally presented to the IFAC/IFORS Conference on Dynamic Modelling and Control of National Economies, Vienna, January 24–27, 1977.

guidance as does the "steering wheel." Generally the Lerner and later positions would be to use overall fiscal and monetary policies to stabilize the macroeconomy at a high level of aggregate activity. Fiscal policies would concentrate on public spending and taxing changes, while monetary policies would deal with interest rate and money supply policies. To a large extent, these ideas were nonquantitative and nonformal. They were put forward not on the basis of a numerical model but on the basis of highly aggregative versions of the Keynesian theory of effective demand.

At a more formal, mathematical level, J. Tinbergen proposed a theory of economic policy designed for use with macroeconometric models [14]. He classified variables into instruments and targets, the former being changed by policy makers in order to attain the goals set for the latter. In the particular case of equality between numbers of instruments and targets, this problem may be interpreted as an arithmetic or algorithmic procedure involving the reclassification of variables from the "given" to the "determined" categories. That is to say, we are ordinarily given instrument variables and asked to solve for target variables. Tinbergen posed the problem in the opposite way and asked for determination of the instrument variables, by endogenizing them, for given values of the target variables, by exogenizing them. If a meaningful solution exists, this is a straightforward problem. If no solution that makes political or economic sense exists or if the number of instruments is less than the number of targets, an economic choice mechanism must be introduced. This was done by Theil and others who constructed loss or gain functions to be optimized, subject to the constraints set by the model of the economic system [13]. This really is the foundation for most recent investigations by econometricians into the methods of optimal control.

There is another aspect to the control concept besides optimization. That is stabilization, usually thought of as the formation of economic policy designed to reduce the amplitude of economic fluctuations. Stabilization methods date back to the steering wheel concept and earlier, but the significant new dimension to be investigated is automaticity, introduced in a formal way by A. W. Phillips [9]. He proposed the use of engineering concepts of level, derivative, and integral correction factors, automatically triggering fiscal and monetary policies. He too introduced targets. Deviations from targets of economic variables—present level, present change, and historical cumulated level—with given weights for each type of factor, automatically determine instrument settings in order to stabilize the path of the economy.

The development of control ideas in economics proceeded from general reasoning with small informal models to formal mathematics with large or small nonnumerical models and finally to concrete applications in the context of estimated statistical models.

Let me first review some of the literature on applications in order to show how the subject now stands, on the threshhold of new developments. The Phillips-type stabilization schemes were worked out some years ago for the Brookings model in the United States. V. G. Duggal formed the following criterion functions and policy rules [2]:

1. Lagged discrepancy between real GNP and target GNP

$$\xi \quad = 0.965 L_{-1} \left[\frac{\text{GNP}^{58}}{E} \right]_{-1} - \text{GNP}^{58}_{-1}$$

where

L	= labor force	3.5%	= target level of unemployment
E	= employment	GNP^{58}	= real GNP (1958 dollars);

2. Tax policy rule

$$\Delta TP = 2.4\xi + 0.4375 \sum_{i=1}^{7} \xi_{-1} - 0.1875 \, [\text{GNP}^{58}_{-1} - \text{GNP}^{58}_{-2}]$$

TP = personal income taxes;

3. Public expenditure rule

$$\Delta G^{58} = 1.4\xi + 0.4375 \sum_{i=1}^{7} \xi_{-i} - 0.1875 \, [\text{GNP}^{58}_{-1} - \text{GNP}^{58}_{-2}]$$

G^{58} = real government expenditures.

These are alternative rules. Each is a weighted combination of a level (ξ), integral ($\Sigma\xi_{-i}$), and derivative [$\text{GNP}^{58}_{-1} - \text{GNP}^{58}_{-2}$] correction factor. The weights were eventually selected on a search basis and appear to stabilize the economy. In retrospective simulations with the Brookings model, Duggal found that these policies stabilized fluctuations in the rate of unemployment between 3.5 percent and 4.6 percent, while actual values ranged from 3.9 percent to 7.4 percent. It does so, however, at the expense of adding about 10 percent to the general price index over the course of nine years, although there were real income gains.

This early experiment with automatic control showed what was possible and gave exposure to some well-known problems. It showed how the vast powers of the electronic computer could be harnessed for these advanced applications in macroeconometrics of control, and it also showed the need for reconciling trade-offs not only with respect to other target variables but also with respect to instruments.

As we move from the concept of automatic stabilization to optimal control (also automatic), we have a technique for dealing with the trade-off and side-effect problems: by adopting a criterion function for losses or gains, we can seek an "optimum" policy. Such procedures have been long known and in use in engineering systems but often for smaller and more tractable systems than those used in macroeconometrics. The Brookings model Duggal used for the Phillips-type stabilization policies was considered large in its day—some three hundred equations—but now a system with a thousand equations is fairly commonplace in econometric practice. The solution and dynamic simulation of such systems is at the heart of control theory applications, and the problem is made somewhat more difficult by the superimposition of the controllers' optimizing conditions. (That control theory calculations can in practice be superimposed on such large systems is shown by the applications reported by R. S. Preston et al. [10].) In the early 1960s, the computer was first used on a broad scale in econometrics and routinely adapted to large model solution in connection with research on the Brookings model [3]. In the last few years, it has been used to deal with the optimal control calculation for large-scale systems. An interesting array of such applications was presented to meetings of the American Economic Association (Dallas, Texas, December 28, 1975) [4, 11, 12]. These were summaries of studies done for the Model Comparisons Seminar of the Conference on Econometrics and Mathematical Economics. This seminar meets semiannually to examine joint standardized applications of the leading American models, and control theory has been on the agenda for the past two years. The original presentations have recently been revived and brought together in a single paper to be published soon.

Control theory has much to offer econometrics by way of enhancing understanding of model properties, establishing a theory of economic policy, and making concrete contributions to actual policy formation. Its use thus far has been mainly in the first two of these offerings. Now that the computational problem has proved to be manageable, one of the main barriers to application has been removed. New methodological and theoretical advances on the frontiers of econometrics will continue to be made regardless of numerical applications, but these nonnumerical results will have only limited impact or applicability without the full implementation for realistic policy formation.

Statement of the Control Problem for Macroeconometric Models

A model of a national economy may be represented in general terms as

$$F(y'_{t}, y'_{t-1}, \ldots, y'_{t-p}, x'_{t}, \theta') = e_{t}.$$

The vector of functions is understood to be represented as

$$F = \begin{pmatrix} f_1 \\ f_2 \\ \vdots \\ f_n \end{pmatrix},$$

with arguments,

$$y_t = \begin{pmatrix} y_{1t} \\ y_{2t} \\ \vdots \\ y_{nt} \end{pmatrix} \quad n \text{ dependent variables (endogenous)}$$

$$x_t = \begin{pmatrix} x_{1t} \\ x_{2t} \\ \vdots \\ x_{mt} \end{pmatrix} \quad m \text{ independent (exogenous)}$$

$$e_t = \begin{pmatrix} e_{1t} \\ e_{2t} \\ \vdots \\ e_{nt} \end{pmatrix} \quad n \text{ random errors}$$

$$\theta = \begin{pmatrix} \theta_1 \\ \theta_2 \\ \vdots \\ \theta_r \end{pmatrix} \quad r \text{ parameters (unknown).}$$

The independent variables may also be lagged, but we could adopt the convention of renaming such lag values as different independent variables; therefore we simply include them among the m. This is written as a finite lag system, but we could equally well handle many classes of infinite lag processes. The errors are assumed to be drawn from a fixed probability distribution with unknown parameters. The parameters θ are response characteristics of the system, and individual components need not be present in more than one equation.

The models of Project LINK are among the better known ones throughout the world that have the representation F [15]. Also the various American models in the CEME group are typical of those that I have in mind for this representation [6].

The variables in y_t are prices, wage rates, interest rates, production volumes, hours of work, expenditures, depreciation, work force, and so forth. They are the economic variables that the model is trying to explain. The variables in x_t are not generated by the system. They are the givens. The initial conditions for a dynamic solution (simulation) include both lag values of y_t and values of x_t. In dynamic solutions, y_t are subsequently generated, but values of x_t must be given assigned magnitudes.

Random variables must be generated by some probability process for a solution or assigned mean (zero) values. The parameters in θ are not known, but solutions can be obtained for estimated values $\hat{\theta}$.

Choose a subset of y_t, say $y_{1t}, y_{2t}, \ldots, y_{n_1 t}$ and a subset of x_t, say x_{1t}, $x_{2t}, \ldots, x_{m_1 t} (n_1 \leq n; m_1 \leq m)$. The designated subset of y_t are to be target variables, and the designated subset of x_t are to be instrument variables. Over a simulation horizon $t = T + 1, T + 2, T + 3, \ldots, T + H$, preassigned target values are decided upon for $y_{1t}^*, \ldots, y_{n_1 t}^*$. The problem is defined to be to calculate estimates of $x_{1t}, \ldots, x_{m_1 t}$ that optimize the distance between y_t and y_t^*. This will generally be taken to mean minimizing the distance such as the weighted sum of squared or absolute value deviations. Let us construct a loss function as follows:

$$L = L(y_{1,T+1} - y_{1,T+1}^*, \ldots, y_{n_1, T+H} - y_{n_1, T+H}^*, x_{1, T+1}, \ldots, x_{m_1, T+H}),$$

which depends on all the deviations from target for the subset of y_t over the horizon and on the instrument settings for the subset of x_t over the horizon. The reason for putting the values of x_t in the loss function is to avoid side effects from instrument instability. It may be that instrument values exist that bring y_t close to y_t^* but such instrument values may be wholly unreasonable; therefore we allow the central decision makers to take account of their instrument preferences (or dislikes) in the formulation of optimal policy in the first place. In general, many policy makers prefer not to intervene in the economy; hence I introduce a cost of instrumentation.

The problem can now be stated as

$$L = \min \text{ w.r.t. } x_{1, t+1}, \ldots, x_{m_1, T+H}$$

s.t.

$$\hat{F} = 0.$$

The notation $\hat{F}$ signifies that $\theta = \hat{\theta}$, and the zero values on the r.h.s. imply that $e_t = 0$ (its expected value).

The computation problem originally bothered econometricians, but that does not appear to be an issue at this time, apart from its cost. It is a manageable problem that can be handled by a variety of algorithms. The analysis, the formation of rules, and the computations are especially easy if F is linear and L is quadratic. These are simplifying but by no means essential conditions.

A solution to the problem may be said to be an optimum, but this description needs qualification. It is an optimum only with respect to the estimated constraint system. The estimate $\hat{F}$ may be inaccurate or even incorrect. It is also capable of change. Some of the most interesting economic policies are those that alter F, either by completely changing some of the components of f_i or by imposing restrictions on their performance. Price controls or guideline rules, for example, suspend operations of those elements in F that govern price formation.

Other reasons why the control theory solution may not be optimal are that the underlying data are inexact and subject to revision, as often occurs. Moreover even if observation is accurate, we may not know future values x_{T+j} with any certainty.

Finally the specification of L is arbitrary. We do not know the policy makers' preferences, and they may not be able to formulate them in our terms. If there are many persons involved, it may not be possible to obtain agreement about the form of L. Results can depend significantly on the assumed specification of L, and we may not be using a good approximation.

The lack of certainty about $\hat{F}$ and the setting of $e_t = 0$ imply that we should be extending our analysis from the subject of deterministic to stochastic control theory. In the linear case, Johansen has introduced sampling error into the estimates of θ and derived formulas that allow for parameter uncertainty [5]. We must go further, however, and treat the dynamic, nonlinear case, as well as allowing for variability of e_t over the control horizon. Uncertainty can be attacked through the medium of stochastic simulation of models, with optimal decision rules. It is unlikely that satisfactory rules in simple formulas can be worked out for the nonlinear case. Stochastic simulation, with replication, seems to be the most feasible method apart from linear approximation. The latter have been developed by Chow [1]. The work to date with large-scale systems has been done mainly by deterministic simulation, meaning that uncertainty problems have been avoided or ignored, but one of the next steps is surely to allow for uncertainty in the whole calculation, allowing it to enter wherever it is relevant.

Given that there is much uncertainty, there are two or more research strategies possible. One is to make the best possible optimal control calculations and try to use them in the context of model advice on contemporary economic problems. Another approach, however, is to eschew optimal control calculations and concentrate on research to improve the constraint system $\hat{F}$. We can look for better coefficient estimates; we can urge reconsideration of the specification of the constraint system; we can look for more detail in the constraint system and hope, thereby, to improve model performance, especially in certain subsectors where performance is relatively poor.

A control theory view may be that it is not of prime importance to improve the constraint system because a powerful control system can possibly overcome constraint system deficiencies. I am reluctant to move in this direction, however, because I see little definitive evidence that control methodologies are powerful enough to outweigh the faulty estimation of the functioning of the economy.

Political Implementation of Economic Control

In spite of deficiencies (inaccuracies, misspecifications, and lack of knowledge), are we on the verge of large-scale applications of optimal control theory (optimal economic policy) in attacking contemporary economic ills? I want to caution against movement toward practical policy use of optimal control at this stage of knowledge. I want to encourage work on these problems and see fascinating potential, but I think that real-life economic policy should be implemented differently.

What are the desiderata of economic policy for statesmen? They need accuracy and credibility, speedy manipulation and an ability to introduce change, a flexible system, and, particularly, a planning system that can cope with legislative delays, gestation periods for policy implementation, and legal technicalities.

In the United States during the past decade or so, economic policy makers have tended to discredit the economics profession by making careless forecasts or claims so inaccurate that credibility was lost. This loss of economic policy credibility came at a time when the whole American political fabric was torn with lack of credibility, and economists were held in the same contempt as general politicians. Some economists have tried to minimize the role of forecast accuracy, claiming that they can "play by ear" and make corrections repeatedly to put the system back on track. It is much like the control theorists claims that a poor constraint system (the model of the economy) can be compensated by a good control system, but unless we have the confidence of the public at large, it will not be possible to carry out policy. Widespread cooperation is needed in order to render policy successful, and this will not come about if there are serious forecast errors. It is especially dangerous to cite goals as though they are forecasts, when the hope or expectation of achieving those goals is remote.

A major characteristic of economic, in contrast with many physical or engineering systems is the presence of an unusually large noise component—a low signal-to-noise ratio. Generally economic relationships that make up the equations of an econometric model are loose, both in data base and underlying parametric specifications. We do better with such noisy relationships than without them, but we should not treat them as being more precise than they actually are. Not only are they noisy but they are subject to "outlying" shocks that arise on short notice. Weather shocks have hit agricultural production in recent years and had enormous repercussions. Politico-military shocks associated with embargoes and cartel pricing have been equally large and far-reaching. We do not know where the next shock is coming from, but we can be fairly sure that it will come in the next few years; therefore we need control systems that permit quick adaptation to greatly changed situations. It is possible to program a smooth model result that looks good on paper from the point of view of economic performance, but if it is based on a benign mother nature working in a serene, peaceful world, it is almost sure to be wrong and misleading.

Through appropriate stochastic treatment of statistical models of the economy, we can allow for disturbances with average variance, but we could not have and cannot predict on any scientific basis such events as the Korean war, the Suez Canal closing, Sputnik, the Cuban missile crisis, the Bay of Pigs, the Vietnam War, Sino-Soviet harvest failures, or the oil embargo. The list can be lengthened with events of lesser magnitude that have occurred during the past three decades. The principal point is that such events are always occurring, that they have highly specific impact, and that they cannot be foreseen but that models can indicate how to react once their occurrence has been discerned. That means that economic policy formation must be quickly changeable to take into account events of large magnitude and consequence. Models must be readily manipulated to factor in the latest information. They should not be too complicated, but they must be detailed enough so that the affected parts of the economy have good exposure in highlighted equations. The software for programming must be highly understandable and worked up into fast algorithms.

None of these aspects would have been possible before the days of the computer but are all feasible to some degree at the present time.

These considerations mean that systems cannot be very small or too large. Let me exclude some polar cases: small systems of ten or fewer equations are not reliable and are bound to break down at crucial moments. They are good pedagogical devices for demonstrating principles but not for use as working systems. At the other extreme, systems of tens of thousands of equations are probably too complicated for easy manipulation and comprehension. I doubt that the human mind can do a very good job in gaining full understanding of the workings of such large systems. That leaves us in the region of one hundred-equation systems that are fairly commonplace in most major countries today, or even a few hundred equations, up to large-scale systems that are in use in a few places consisting of one or a few thousand equations, say up to five thousand. In terms of the previous discussion, the equation system $F = e_t$ might have upwards of a hundred equations, to a ceiling of perhaps five thousand.

To the extent that the structure of F is decomposable, either recursively or otherwise, it may be possible to deal effectively with large systems, even by extending the elastic upper limit on size. Many of the so-called equations of a system may be very simple ratios or large number of input-output coefficients (also defined as ratios), thus permitting large numbers of very simple equations. Decomposability into hierarchical systems permits different decision makers to participate at each of several layers in a causal structure, thus taking the burden off any single operator.

Finally a system may be enlarged in a horizontal way by using the device of satellite systems. Attached to one master model of the economy as a whole, we can have various sector models. Two variants of this design are in use now in the Wharton group. One is a local area or regional model. It is used for metropolitan areas, states, or broader geographical groupings. The area satellite usually runs off output values from the master model without feedback, but, in principle, feedback could be introduced. National wage rates, prices, interest rates, or production definitely affect local area economic performance. If the local area is large enough or strategic enough, it can have an observable feedback effect on the nation.

A second case concerns energy modeling. Satellite models for large energy-using (steel, cement, exports, transportation) or energy-producing sectors (mining, extracting, fuel transport, refining, imports, power generation) are attached to a master model in a full feedback relationship. The advantage of satellite models for policy planning is that technical advances can be directly entered through the medium of parametric changes. Many satellites, each of one-hundred-plus equation size, can be hung on a single macromodel so that there are few limitations other than manageability and storage, to the indefinite elaboration of system size. As long as the satellite design fits with the flow of policy choices (as long as the available energy options are included explicitly in the range of energy satellite models), we are in a good position to formulate energy policy. If options not covered in model design are to be considered, say by the need for parametric change in a sector that possesses no satellite model, it is all right to say, in principle, that the appropriate satellite may be built and then used for policy formation, but that is a time-consuming procedure and will do little to help the politician who must respond quickly. If we date the energy crisis from 1973, we can say that in the three to four years that have elapsed, we have not been able yet to build the kind of energy sector models that are needed for wise policy formation, and we have not yet had satisfactory energy policies. This is definitely the case in the United States where researchers are building energy models. They may come up with good models, but it is a time-consuming process and cold comfort to the two previous American administrations whose energy policies did them or the country little good. If we are searching for an optimal policy, it must be understood that any solution that professes to be optimal must be so named relative only to the constraints imposed on the policy evaluation algorithms; I feel safe in claiming that the appropriate restraints have not yet been found. Any policy formed now will not be likely to be deemed optimal, retrospectively, in a few years when we have a better model view of the energy sectors. Models that had some limited energy content, explicitly displayed, should have performed, and probably did perform, better in recognizing appropriate policy, but they did not have enough content to guide policy makers toward an optimum set of choices.

These thoughts lead me to an alternative strategy for the making of socioeconomic policy in the political environment. Models are built so as to be capable of comparatively easy simulation. Models are invariably dynamic, so a simulation is essentially the integral of a finite difference equation from fixed initial conditions. The standard way of formulating policy is to search among alternative input values for exogenous variables, parameter readings, and imposition of constraints until an improved integral is obtained. Improvement would be judged by inspection of turning points, amplitude of fluctuation, frequency of turning points, and overall distance from target. These are less formal criteria than those used in the statement of the optimal control problem but are probably closer to what policy makers actually use than any scalar measure of welfare gain or loss. Attention would be focused on improving the existing situation and being ready to move at the next opportunity toward another improvement step rather than attempt to reach a stated optimum position directly. Some analysts feel that they know their models sufficiently well that by alternative simulation search they can, in fact, come very close, quickly and inexpensively, to the implied optimal position.

Let us now turn to a living situation in model-based economic policy formation to see how political practice fits with standard applications of optimal control. The problem was to work out a hypothetical four-year policy program for the challenger for the presidency of the United States in Campaign '76. This was something less than realistic because it was developed only for a political campaign, but some of it appears to have survived during the actual running of the economy.

The Preference Function

In lieu of a formal mathematical function with weights, I interpreted the following leading characteristics of the policy maker's criterion function:

1. Preference for use of the private sector to achieve goals.

2. Desire for more monetary policy stimuli.

3. Desire for more fiscal policy stimuli.

4. Gradual attainment of stated goals by 1980.

5. Standby authority for wage and price controls (later rescinded).

Within the framework of these general preferences, the following targets were chosen by the policy maker:

1. Full emplyment (4.5 percent unemployment) by 1980.

2. Inflation rate of 4 percent by 1980.

3. Balanced federal budget by 1980.

4. Federal outlays held to 21 percent of GNP by 1980 (1976, 23 percent).

An even lower inflation rate and a very low interest rate would have been in the target listing had the candidate not been willing to listen to technical advice that ruled them out as infeasible for the next few years. Instruments, targets, and general preferences are thus set out. Rather than try to build a formal function to describe the candidate's preferences, and follow the control theory calculus, guesses were made about how the Wharton model would respond to various fiscal and monetary changes. Through mixtures of fiscal (tax reduction/spending increase) and monetary (easier credit with lower interest rates) stimuli, it was found that the unemployment rate could be lowered to about 5.5 percent and also that policies designed to push it lower would trade off some gain in the labor market against a loss with regard to the inflation rate. The campaign economic task force therefore devised a job-training program that would try to attack structural unemployment on a cooperative basis with the private sector and bring down the unemployment rate, eventually, in simulations to 4.5 percent (finding one million jobs through training programs) and stay within budget target figures (balance and 21 percent rule). The budget targets were met because the scheme was shared between the public and private sectors and because the extra overall stimulus created by this program provided a better public revenue base, together with a decline in federal transfer payments. Finally the Wharton model found a simulated solution that met all the targets simultaneously and agreed with the general preferences of the policy maker. This set of policies had to be searched for and discovered; it would not generally fall from an optimal control calculation. Had the policy analysis been confined entirely to more or less taxes, public spending, and monetary reserves, an optimal solution could have been computed, but it would not have been as desirable for the policy maker as the solution that was finally adopted. A mixture between a structural policy and a purely macroeconomic quantitative policy is difficult to obtain from a formal control theory approach; however, given the structural policy, once it has been decided upon, we might ask for the calculation of the optimal macropolicy, but it is my opinion that an answer that is quite close can be obtained readily by experimental simulation. Given appropriate margins of error surrounding all estimates, whether from alternative simulations or optimal control calculations, we shall probably conclude that there are no differences between the two methodologies.

While these considerations and associated calculations looked all right for several months, in summer and autumn 1976 economic performance was turning out to be poorer than estimated, suggesting an extra stimulative policy early in 1977. This was unplanned and not due to a particular disturbance but nevertheless the kind of miscalculation that will always be happening and causing a revision of policies. The problem that is caused by the application of extra stimulus in early 1977 is that the attainment of 1980 targets is made that much more difficult and set back at least one year. Also the path to one of the targets is fundamentally altered. To get to a federal budget balance by 1980 (or later), it was formerly calculated that the budgetary path would be steady and monotonic. In the new situation, it appeared to be necessary to incur some added deficit in the immediate period in order to achieve a smaller deficit later. To put over this kind of policy path requires great credibility. Both the legislature and the voting public at large have to be educated in the belief that some aspects of economic performance, or indeed the economy as a whole, will eventually be better if it is first a bit worse. In addition there is a normal cyclical pattern in the solution for output and employment. It is the usual four-year business cycle that has been functioning in the United States since the end of World War II. It does not show up in the policy-supported simulation as an actual cycle but as a distinct growth slowdown in 1978–1979. This means that higher deficits in 1977 will be followed by fairly poor growth in 1978–1979 before a strong revival sets in. To tell the lay public that the growth slowdown would be much worse without the policy will be of little help in trying to explain a deficit of $40–50 billion followed one year later by a 2–3 percent rate of real economic growth. This is the point at which political acceptance of a scientifically devised economic policy becomes critical.

The contemporary debate over a fiscal-monetary stimulus was conducted along the following lines:

fiscal options
   lower taxes
      permanent or temporary?
      personal or business?
   increase expenditures
      transfers from the federal to the state/local sector?
      public works projects?
      public service employment?
monetary policy
   accommodation.

These were the considerations and options for the policy maker. What could he learn through alternative simulations and through optimal control? His preferences would be for programs that show up as quickly as possible in the more favorable unemployment programs, that retain the business confidence that was recently built up, and that interfere as little as possible with the 1980 targets.

In principle the policy solution ought to be balanced. Some of various kinds should be used to satisfy different groups and regions of the country—the public at large, the business community, and large urban centers with economic hardship. Also the solution should be balanced because of uncertainty. We did not know which policies would perform up to standard and which below standard; therefore we recommended diversification.

The total also had to be determined. Alternative simulations that add up to $10 billion or $20 billion in public sector costs were calculated. Although larger totals would be needed in order to make significant and highly visible decreases in the unemployment rate, a smaller figure may have been desired in order to keep the deficit within bounds. This kind of trade-off could be handled with the proper construction of a loss function with a high penalty applied to large deficits, but other constraints are not so easily treated. The number of months to validate and approve public works projects is an uncertainty but probably determines a maximum amount through this policy medium. Whether local officials would spend federal transfers wisely is hard to know in advance. Public service jobs may be effective, but they do not use the private sector as much as the policy maker might like. Temporary tax cuts or rebates leave more flexibility for medium-term policy choices than do permanent cuts. These considerations have to be taken into account.

It probably would be possible to construct a complicated loss function that would bring out all these ideas in proper perspective, but it was found to be more direct and quicker to make alternative simulations with public works up to a maximum of $3 billion phased in gradually, grants-in-aid (federal transfers) of $2 billion, personal tax rebates of $8 billion, and investment tax credit of $2 billion. In this way, a package of $15 billion was constructed that could be simulated with longer term programs aiming at 1980 targets.

Monetary policy was not particularly changed because it was assumed that the authorities were already on a course of accommodation. As to the personal tax cut, the model defied the pessimistic conclusions of the permanent income hypothesis and programmed a temporary rebate on the grounds that this kind of distribution was successful in 1975 and that when the tax program is put in the context of a total four-year program, it is no longer purely temporary. As events turned out, the temporary tax rebate was first decided upon and then dropped, three months later.

These are the practical political considerations that must enter model-based implementation of economic policy. At one remove, they look very practical and even realistic. But to the layman, they probably seem to be very much "ivory tower" calculations. They are, however, more realistic from a political point of view than policies that could be derived from formal applications of optimal control theory.

References

1. CHOW, G. "An Approach to the Feedback Control of Non-linear Econometric Systems," memo # 180, Econometric Research Program, Princeton University.

2. DUGGAL, V. G. "Fiscal Policy and Economic Stabilization." In *the Brookings Model: Perspectives and Recent Developments*, edited by G. Fromm and L. R. Klein, pp. 221–252. (Amsterdam: North-Holland, 1975).

3. FROMM, G., and KLEIN, L. R. "Solutions of the Complete System." In *The Brookings Model: Some Further Results*, edited by J. Duesenberry et al., pp. 363–421. (Amsterdam: North-Holland, 1969).

4. HIRSCH, A. "Econometric Review of Alternative Fiscal and Monetary Policies, 1965–75: I." Paper presented to American Economic Association, Dallas, December 28, 1975.

5. JOHANSEN, L. "Targets and Instruments under Uncertainty," University of Oslo.

6. KLEIN, L. R., and BURMEISTER, E., eds. *Econometric Model Performance*. Philadelphia: University of Pennsylvania Press, 1976.

7. LERNER, A. P. "The Economic Steering Wheel." *The University Review* (June 1941).

8. ———. *The Economics of Control*. New York, Macmillan, 1944.

9. PHILLIPS, A. W. "Stabilization Policy in a Closed Economy." *Economic Journal* (June 1954): pp. 290–323

10. PRESTON, R. S., KLEIN, L. R., O'BRIEN, J., and BROWN, B. W. "Control Theory Simulations Using the Wharton Annual and Industry Forecasting Model." Paper presented at the April 1976 meeting of the Eastern Economic Association, Bloomsburg, Pa.

11. SHAPIRO, H. "Econometric Review of Alternative Fiscal and Monetary Policies, 1965–75: II." Paper presented to American Economic Association, Dallas, December 28, 1975.

12. ———. "Optimal Control and Macroeconometric Models." NSF-CNRS Conference on Macroeconometric Models and Economic Forecasting, Gif-sur-Yvette, France, November 22–26, 1976.

13. THEIL, H. *Economic Forecasts and Policy*. Amsterdam: North-Holland, 1958.

14. TINBERGEN, J. *On the Theory of Economic Policy*. Amsterdam: North-Holland, 1952.

15. WAELBROECK, J. *The Models of Project LINK*. Amsterdam: North-Holland, 1976.

Chapter 7

Fritz Machlup

The Effects of Fiscal Policy and the Choice of Definitions

The spectacle of contradictory advice by renowned economists on current policy regarding price inflation, unemployment, fiscal expansion or restraint, and related matters, is a disgrace. Are we not getting tired of the continuous arguing over the supposedly optimal combination of budget deficit, money supply, and interest rates? Are we not fed up with advisers who seem cocksure about the effectiveness of their prescriptions and contemptuous about the abominal unwisdom of their fellow advisers?

To be sure, we cannot expect agreement among people with beliefs in and loyalties to different social and economic systems. (One cannot reasonably expect that those who wish to strengthen the system of free enterprise and free access to free markets will prescribe the same policies as those who prefer a system of direct controls by government, fixing and policing thousands or millions of prices of products and wages of labor; not to speak of those who want to replace the decentralized enterprise-and-market system with one of central, comprehensive planning of production, investment, and consumption.) There is not much point in trying for a consensus on policy among adherents of totally different ideologies. But it should be possible—and it is urgent—to seek a consensus and understanding among economists who share a preference for a competitive market economy free from direct controls.

Some of the continuous controversies between fiscalists and monetarists can be traced to differences in terminology, but a much larger part to incomplete specifications of assumptions essential to the argument. Perhaps we can come to understand how it is possible that eminently brilliant, well-read, and reasonable economists persist in employing fundamental terms in meanings different from those intended by their friends and colleagues and different also from the meanings intended in their own earlier writings. Among the economists selected for this review will be my admired friend Abba Lerner, in whose honor I am writing this essay. The review of

alternative meanings of the terms will enable me to arrive at the least misleading sense of fiscal policy and to proceed to presenting a simple model
of the process of fiscal expansion with a fixed stock of money.

Fiscal and Monetary Policy

A sharp definition of fiscal policy presupposes an agreement on the definition of monetary policy because, under the institutions prevailing in
almost all developed countries, fiscal and monetary policies, as usually
defined, are interdependent.

The Interdependence of Fiscal and Monetary Changes

It is possible and, from an institutional point of view, perfectly adequate
to distinguish fiscal policy and monetary policy by the prerogatives and
actions of the authorities concerned. Thus fiscal policy would be defined as
the policy pursued by the fiscal authorities regarding taxing, subsidizing,
borrowing, lending, repaying (of previous debts), buying (spending for
goods and services), and selling (goods and services). The biggest three of
these fiscal functions are spending, taxing, and borrowing. Monetary
policy would be defined as the policy pursued by the monetary authorities
determining the magnitudes of some monetary quantity or aggregate,
such as central-bank money, currency and bank deposit-liabilities of various types or, alternatively, targets for interest rates and foreign-exchange
rates, or some different kinds of targets for economic quantities which the
monetary authorities can influence only indirectly but which guide the
authorities' actions concerning the variables they can control directly.

Alas, such institutional definitions are inadequate for an economic
analysis of the effects, intended, expected, or actual, of the policies in question. For it is not possible to say anything about the effects of "fiscal"
policy without making precise stipulations regarding associated (reinforc-
ing or compensatory) changes in monetary variables; and it is similarly
impossible to say anything about the effects of "monetary policy" without making precise stipulations about associated changes in the fiscal
variables.

Fiscal measures have monetary repercussions, and one must ask how
the monetary authorities will respond. Will they allow such repercussions
to take place, will they perhaps reinforce them, will they resist them, neu-
tralize them, or offset them? Similarly, monetary measures have fiscal
repercussions; how will the fiscal authorities respond to them? The effects
of any particular fiscal policy will significantly depend on the reactions of

the monetary authorities, and the effects of any particular monetary policy will depend to some extent on the reactions of the fiscal authorities. Thus failure to specify the mutual reactions renders any definite statements regarding the effects of the policies rather vacuous. One should not be surprised if economists differing in their "tacit specifications" come up with different and even contradictory conclusions.

Beginning with the less crucial but by no means negligible *fiscal repercussions to monetary policy*, it is easy to understand that induced increases in business spending and consumer spending financed by monetary expansion may increase the revenues from various taxes at unchanged tax rates. It will surely make a difference for prices, production, and employment if the fiscal authorities react by lowering the rates of all kinds of taxes to keep their revenues at the previous levels. They might reduce the sales taxes and value-added taxes to keep total tax revenues unchanged; they might accept the increase in tax revenues and use it for repaying short-term debts or long-term debts of the government; they might use the additional funds collected for holding larger cash balances either with the central bank or with commercial banks; or they might also use them for increasing public expenditures, perhaps transfer payments to the poor, subsidies to agriculture or industrial producers, construction of highways or river dams, increased outlays for higher education, or increased salaries of civil servants. These are only some examples; the actual number of alternatives is impressive, and certain kinds of them may influence the total effects of measures taken by the monetary authorities. This is obvious since some of the reactions of the fiscal authorities would reduce prices charged to consumers, some would increase salaries of public employees, some would release loanable or investable funds to consumers and investors, and some would result in larger holdings of idle cash balances.

The *monetary repercussions to fiscal measures* may be even more varied, so we are even less capable of predicting the effects of any fiscal policy as long as the reactions of the monetary authorities are uncertain or unknown. Assume that the fiscal authorities decide to increase expenditures for highway construction and finance one half through tax increases and the other half through a bond issue. There will probably be an increased demand for bank credit, both on the part of taxpayers unwilling to cut their expenditures by the full amount of their increased tax liabilities, and on the part of bond purchasers unwilling to pay for the bonds entirely with their own funds either out of current receipts (including incomes) or out of their surplus cash balances. The supply of loans by commercial banks is usually elastic; the banks may have unused lending capacity and may try to obtain even more lending capacity by borrowing reserves or selling securities. The central bank may (1) react by buying some of the securities sold by commercial banks and/or by granting additional loans to commercial banks; on the other hand, it may (2) refuse to acquire additional securities and to increase its loans; or it may (3) become even tighter and counteract the credit expansion of the commercial banks by reducing its loans outstanding and selling securities in the open market. These three different kinds of reactions would surely cause the effects of the fiscal measure to be entirely different. The first reaction would add monetary expansion to fiscal expansion not only by allowing commercial banks to use existing excess reserves to increase their deposit liabilities but also by creating additional central-bank money and, thereby, additional lending capacity. The second reaction would merely permit the banks to meet the increased demand for loans by using the lending capacity they happen to have at the time. The third reaction would restrict the money supply to the former level by reducing the reserves of the commercial banks.

Alternative Conceptions of Monetary Policy

There have been attempts to find simple formulas that might avoid the need of choosing among so many possibilities. For example, James Meade proposed to single out a particular stance of the monetary authorities and to call it "neutral." He defined monetary policy as "constant" in a "neutral economy" if it was designed to keep "the" interest rate—the "representative" interest rate—unchanged.[1]

In the case of an expansionary fiscal policy, which would almost certainly increase the demand for credit and most likely also the demand for money, the monetary authorities could succeed only in keeping interest rates from rising if they made sure that the increased demand for credit (as a flow) and money (as a stock) were fully met by a perfectly elastic supply on the part of the commercial banks. This would require positive actions by the central bank to increase the capacity and the willingness of the banking system to expand its lending operations.

What by Meade's definition is seen as neutral monetary policy is, in my terminology and in that of many others, a highly active and definitely expansionary monetary policy. Yet, the outcome of this combination of fiscal and monetary measures would be regarded, according to Meade, as the effects of fiscal policy with neutral monetary policy. With all due respect for freedom of definition, I must suggest that the language is highly confusing to the uninitiated. (I submit that, in the long run, after expansionary fiscal and monetary policies have resulted in expectations of continuing or even accelerating price inflation, the monetary authorities will be *incapable* of keeping interest rates from rising; hence it is impossible to pursue this supposedly neutral monetary policy in the long run.)

It has frequently been suggested that monetary policy be defined in terms of foreign-exchange rates. To say that the monetary authorities pursue a policy of keeping the exchange rate of a selected key currency or reserve currency fixed and are determined to subordinate all other possible objectives or targets of monetary management to the sole or primary aim of maintaining exchange-rate stability (without exchange controls), does make sense, but does not allow prediction of the effects of fiscal policy. The same fiscal measures—say, the ones used in the earlier illustration of a government project financed half by tax increases and half by bond issues —may have different monetary repercussions in different circumstances. The increase in the demand for credit may result in higher rates of interest, which may sometimes attract capital funds from abroad and, therefore, produce an increase in the supply of foreign exchange (at fixed exchange rates) with the consequent increase in the reserves of the central bank as well as of commercial banks. At the same time the increase in the effective demand for goods, services, and labor may result in higher prices and higher wages, but also in an increase of imports, with an increase in the demand for foreign exchange and (at fixed exchange rates) a consequent decline in the reserves of the central bank as well as of commercial banks. Which of the two possibilities will outweigh the other depends on too many circumstances to enumerate, let alone evaluate. If the positive change in the balance of capital movements surpasses the negative change in the balance of trade, the banking system acquires in the process both foreign and domestic assets (claims against foreign borrowers and claims against domestic borrowers).[2] If the negative change in the trade balance predominates, the banking system will find its portfolio of domestic assets increased but its holdings of foreign assets reduced. It is also possible that the fiscal expansion results in a decline of confidence in the country's ability to maintain fixed exchange rates; in this case both capital balance and trade balance may change in the negative direction. It is not possible to predict the effects of fiscal policy just on the assumption that the monetary authorities pursue a policy of maintaining fixed exchange rates.

To define monetary policy in terms of a double target of interest rates and exchange rates makes even less sense in that it would, even in the medium-long run, be impossible to achieve the double target. For example, to hold interest rates constant implies an infinitely elastic supply of credit and domestic money; to maintain fixed exchange rates implies an infinitely elastic supply of foreign money. The monetary authorities can perhaps create as much domestic money as they wish, but they cannot create infinite amounts of generally accepted foreign money.

A Full-Employment Standard of Monetary Policy

Some students of Keynes have thought that monetary policy can be defined in terms of a full-employment target. This illusion seems to have been destroyed. Virtually all economists now realize—after an incredibly long learning period—that the value of money in purchasing labor is apt to decline as the nominal quantity of money is increased. If wage rates increase faster than the quantity of money and/or the rate of spending, employment must fall.[3] Whether we like it or not, a full-employment standard of monetary policy is unworkable, and there is no point in analyzing the effects of fiscal policy on the assumption of a monetary policy aiming at an illusive full-employment goal. Keynes himself had noted that an increase in effective demand (in terms of nominal money) could not lead to an increase in employment and production if "the elasticity of money wages with respect to effective demand" were equal to unity. In this case "output will be unaltered and prices will rise in the same proportion as effective demand in terms of money."[4] Keynes did not consider the possibility of the elasticity of money wages being *greater* than unity —as, in fact, it sometimes is. Yet even if it is below unity, but the supply of labor increases with the growth of population of working age, the rate of unemployment may increase—not despite but as a result of the full-employment policy pursued by fiscal and monetary authorities and reflected in the wage contracts demanded by labor unions and accepted by employers.

Lerner's Conceptual Schemes

Abba Lerner seems to have accepted a full-employment standard of fiscal policy (aided by money creation) without serious reservations. In 1944, he wrote: "The wise course for the government is the brave one of going all out and bringing about full employment no matter how much it has to resort to deficit spending."[5] In 1949, he conceded that "under full employment strong trade unions can continually raise wages more rapidly than productivity increases. This results in higher prices, further wage increases, . . . the expectations lag, and the spiral of open inflation."[6] He proposed to break this "vicious circle" by a system of regulation of wage rates in accordance with scarcities and abundances of labor, a scheme he called "an artificial free market," which he had developed in 1947 and later elaborated in greater detail.[7] However he also seemed to suggest another way out of the frustrations of a full-employment policy that has always led to wage-and-price inflation and never to full employment: one could redefine "full" employment as "that level of employment at which inflation begins."[8] This redefinition, I must admit, is quoted here out of context and should not be taken seriously; but it points to the fact that much of the controversy about fiscal and monetary policies designed to secure full employment is a matter of mere definition.

Definitional entanglements are especially troublesome in the controversy about monetary policy and the degree to which money "matters." Keynes has frequently been accused of having neglected or underrated the role of money in the determination of economic activity. Some have defended him against this accusation, citing chapter and verse to show that money was a strategic factor in the Keynesian system.[9] Others, however (but also some of the same writers), have attempted to show why it was in fact fiscal policy that alone determined expansion and contraction of economic activity, and why the creation of money was therefore an irrelevant part of the story. The chief exponent of this point of view was Abba Lerner. In his "Functional Finance" the "printing of money" was regarded as subsidiary to the instruments of fiscal policy.[10] The six functions of fiscal policy—taxing and spending, borrowing and lending, buying and selling—were the "effective instruments in the hands of the government for maintaining full employment and preventing inflation."[11] Money creation, by contrast, was not an instrument of policy "but" merely a servant of these policies, just like printing the stationery used in the various government departments.[12] Still, if the government wanted neither to tax more nor to borrow more (because this would raise the rate of interest), "It should provide itself with all the money it wishes to spend by printing it."[13]

Lerner reaffirmed in later publications the low respect in which he held monetary policy and monetary aggregates: "the creation of money does not figure at all in the six [fiscal] instruments. This is because the creation of money has no effects on the economy as long as the printed money stays in the print shop. It is only when the money gets out into the economy that any effects come about."[14] Lerner seems to overlook that virtually all monetary theorists and monetary statisticians speak of money creation only if the money "gets out into the economy." The stock of money (or supply of money) does not include any currency or bank deposit balance unless it is already in the hands of the public, that is, at the disposal of possible spenders, or respenders, be they business firms or consumers. If government was the first spender of newly created money, it evidently had decided against taking existing money away from people ("non-banks") by taxing them or by borrowing from them. This decision is ordinarily regarded as monetary policy. It is perfectly understandable, however, if Lerner prefers to think of a unified government in which the fiscal authorities make all the decisions and the central bank has nothing to say in the matter but must furnish all the money that the treasury wishes to spend without taking it from the people. On the other hand, one may prefer to think of a central bank that is really a monetary *authority* with prerogatives regarding the quantities of the money which it creates and the money which it permits commercial banks to create.[15] It happens that the latter scheme of thinking has advantages in economic analysis, no matter whether the central bank is in fact autonomous or subject to the decisions of the fiscal authorities. That the banks can make loans to others than the government and thus enable businesses and households to be the first spenders of new money is only one reason for preferring this conceptual framework. Several other strong reasons counsel for its adoption.

Friedman's Monetarism

The position that the stock of money, or rather its rate of change, is determined by the monetary authorities, and that monetary policy is what they do to change it or keep it constant, is most strongly argued by Milton Friedman.[16] His terms of reference were the monetary aggregates, that is, the quantity of money in one of its operational definitions. The line separating an expansionary from a contractionary monetary policy was either at the point of zero growth or at a point of "normal" growth (fixed at, say, 3 percent per year). The effects of fiscal policy could then be determined as those that would result from the particular fiscal measures if the quantity of money were not allowed to deviate from that of the fixed (or zero) rate of increase. Any induced deviation from this money stock would be regarded as a definite change in monetary policy, and any effects (on money GNP) of the fiscal measures associated with these deviations of the quantity of money would be attributed partly or chiefly to monetary policy.

Friedman's definitional separation of fiscal and monetary policy has been criticized on several grounds. Least serious is the objection that one has to choose, more or less arbitrarily, which of the various monetary aggregates (M_1, M_2, M_3, and so on) to use for reference. Friedman admits that the rates of increase of these aggregates differ from one another, especially over short periods, but he finds this problem of relatively little significance. More serious is the objection that fiscal policy may have substantial effects on aggregate money income through induced changes in the velocity of circulation of whatever monetary aggregate is taken as *the* quantity of money. Strangely enough, the facts (or rather the interpretations of the statistical records) are controversial. Some observers find the variations in velocity highly significant, both in the short run and in the long, others find them too small to call for a revision or rejection of this approach.

The most serious of the objections to the Friedman standard is the contention that the monetary authorities cannot exercise effective control over the quantity of the assets regarded as money in a sense relevant to the volume of aggregate spending. If changes in the quantity of money relevant for the outcome occurred as a result of fiscal policy but without any possibility of control by the monetary authorities, then it would indeed make little sense to attribute these changes or their effects to monetary policy. Monetary policy, to be meaningful, must be assumed to be practicable in the sense that it can achieve or prevent certain changes in the domain of monetary variables. The possibility of controlling particular monetary aggregates may, of course, depend on the existence of certain institutions, and these institutions may exist in some countries and not in others. Where the monetary authorities can effectively control certain monetary aggregates, one may agree to define monetary policy in terms of the changes that they effect in these aggregates. In more concrete terms, where a central bank can control the amounts of its assets and liabilities, and where changes in the liabilities of commercial banks can be controlled either directly or indirectly through the central bank's changes of its own liabilities and, finally, where the bulk of all payments is transacted through transferring the liabilities of commercial banks, we may judge the control of the monetary authorities to be sufficient for the purpose—for monetary policy to make sense in macroeconomic analysis.

Having worked my way toward what I believe to be a meaningful concept of monetary policy that is independent of any measures that can be designated as fiscal policy, I shall adopt this conception for further analysis of the effects of fiscal policy.

The Effects of Pure Fiscal Policy

I shall once more state the assumptions that allow us to isolate the effects of fiscal policy from any side effects, repercussions and reactions that can be attributed to certain, uncertain, or unknown attitudes of the monetary authorities. These assumptions are designed to define a monetary policy that is independent of the measures of the fiscal authorities and can be defined without reference to intended or expected effects or goals.

1. Virtually all spending, public or private, is done either with central-bank money or with commercial-bank money.

2. The monetary authorities are able to control not only the supply of central-bank money ("high-powered money") but also (through their lending policies, open-market operations, and reserve requirements) the supply of commercial-bank money (deposit liabilities).

3. The monetary authorities exercise their control to keep the rate of increase of the stock of moneys constant; this rate of increase may be (a) zero or (b) equal to the rate at which the active labor force or, alternatively, the real GNP is expected to increase on the average over the next several years.

Assumption 3(a) excludes any increase in the stock of money. Assumption 3(b) allows a small annual increase in the stock of money and, therefore, an elasticity of supply of additional bank credit a little larger than zero. Reasoning and comprehension will be facilitated by adhering initially to assumption 3(a).

Sources and Uses of Funds
A simple model can help us trace the sources of funds needed for an expansionary fiscal policy, chart the flows of these funds, and judge the effects of spending them. Let it be assumed that a fiscal policy of increased public spending is initiated; its sole objective is to increase the employment of labor. The government will raise the funds needed for its increased expenditures partly through increased taxes and partly through bond issues, but other possible sources of funds will also be considered. Four groups of operators are in the model: the government (G), the taxpayers (T), the nonbanks lending and buying assets (N), and the commercial banks (B). The funds that any of these operators use for their spending, lending, or buying come from their idle money balances (m), from their diverting money from alternative expenditures (d), from the proceeds of selling assets or their own promises to pay (p), and, as far as the government is concerned, from tax revenues (t).

The *government* has the following sources of funds available for its new expenditures: any surplus cash balances it has been holding (Gm); funds diverted from other expenditures (Gd); revenues from increased taxes (Gt); proceeds from borrowing from, or selling securities to, non-banks (GpN); and proceeds from borrowing from, or selling securities to, commercial banks (GpB).

Gm is quite limited since the total cash balances of the government are ordinarily only a small percentage of the annual budget, and the part of its cash balances that can be regarded as excessive or surplus is quite small. Gd may be ruled out as inconsistent with the fiscal-policy objective assumed; the new spending is supposed to be additional to the previous level of spending, not a substitute for expenditures omitted. Thus the remaining sources, Gr and Gp have to finance the new spending, and we have to ask how the taxpayers, the nonbanks, and the banks can have or get the money they furnish to the treasury.

The *taxpayers* may draw on the following sources of funds to pay the increased taxes: any surplus cash balances they have been holding (Tm); funds diverted from other expenditures (Td); proceeds from borrowing from, or selling their own security issues to, nonbanks (TpN); proceeds from selling portfolio securities and other assets (inventories) to nonbanks (also TpN); and proceeds from borrowing or from selling securities to banks (TpB).

Tm is, in general, rather limited; some corporations may carry cash balances large enough to be drawn down, but the balances of other corporations and of many individuals may not be larger than needed. As a group, taxpayers may have enough extra cash to pay the increased taxes for a few months, but it is unlikely that their idle balances will be so plentiful that the tax increase can be financed through their activation for long. The diversion of funds from other expenditures, Td, would constitute a case of government spending crowding out investment or consumption expenditures by individuals and corporations, and thus frustrating the government's objective. The remaining sources of funds, borrowing from or selling to nonbanks (TpN) and banks (TpB), leave us with the question what funds these lenders and buyers have available to finance the taxpayers.

The *nonbanks*, lending to or buying assets from the taxpayers, or lending directly to the government or buying its securities, have the same sources of funds for their lending and buying as the taxpayers have for meeting their tax obligations: any surplus cash balances they have been holding (Nm); funds diverted from other expenditures (Nd); proceeds from borrowing from, or selling their own security issues to, other nonbanks (NpN); proceeds from selling portfolio securities and other assets (inventories) to other nonbanks (also *NpN*); and proceeds from borrowing from, or selling securities to, banks (*NpB*).

The limitations regarding the first source of funds, excess cash balances, (*Nm*), are for nonbank lenders and asset purchasers even more stringent than for the treasury and the taxpayers. After all, the treasury has decided, or has been ordered by the legislature, to spend more, and it will have few inhibitions in drawing down its own cash balance. Similarly, the taxpayers are compelled to pay higher taxes and will surely for this purpose use their own surplus cash balances to the extent that they deem it safe to do so. This is different in the case of nonbanks considering lending to, or buying securities from, the treasury or the taxpayers; these nonbanks have to be induced to enter into such transactions, induced by terms of lending made more attractive than they have been. This means that rates of interest have to go up and prices of securities and other assets have to go down if the nonbank holders of surplus cash balances are to be persuaded to part with their funds. Thus not only is the magnitude of idle funds on the accounts of nonbanks limited, but so is also the willingness to run them down in exchange for less liquid assets.[17]

There is a close connection between this source of funds and the second source, the diversion of funds from other expenditures. The increase in the rate of interest that effects the surrender of surplus cash balances to borrowers (treasury and taxpayers) and to sellers of securities and other assets will also induce some investors to give up or postpone their investment plans. Thus the likelihood of funds being diverted from other expenditures is greatly increased. Not only the nonbank lenders and buyers of securities themselves may decide to forego purchases that they would otherwise make, but the reduction in securities prices and the increase in interest rates may induce others to abstain from investment and consumption expenditures that they have been planning. This involves again the probability of private spending being crowded out by the increase in public spending (*Nd*). Where taxpayers try to raise funds through selling inventories of finished products or goods in process, these sales may encroach on the saleability of newly produced goods—another crowding-out effect of the increase in government expenditures, though perhaps a less significant one than that associated with the sales of securities.

The next two sources of funds available to nonbank lenders and asset buyers are other nonbank lenders and asset buyers. This is a case of "infinite regress" and requires no new detective effort. Idle cash balances and switching of funds from other expenditures are the only two possibilities of finding finance for the lenders to the treasury and to the taxpayers. The only source not yet examined is the banking system.

Bank Loans
Banks may lend to, or purchase securities from, the government, the taxpayers, or the nonbanks that lend to the government, to taxpayers, or to nonbanks financing the taxpayers or the nonbanks that finance the nonbanks that lend to the government or to the taxpayers or to the buyers of assets sold by the taxpayers. In any of these cases of banks expanding their portfolio of loans or securities, we must ask what enables the banks to do so.

Were it not for the constraint imposed by Assumption 3(a), we would have no trouble answering: banks may be liquid enough to expand their loans and investments and would be glad to meet the increased demand for credit and to take up some of the increased supply of securities. This, indeed, is the normal way in which fiscal policy affects the activities of the banking system. Alas, this way is blocked by Assumption 3(a) (based on Assumption 1).

Any expansion of loans and investments by the banking system would increase the banks' liquid liabilities to nonbanks and, hence, the stock of money. If the stock of money is kept unchanged (which requires a toughness on the part of central-bank management that many political economists, and especially the central bankers themselves, cannot imagine to exist), the banks cannot make any funds available except those they can obtain through collecting previous loans or selling securities to nonbanks. However, repayments of bank loans and sales from bank portfolios will be associated with activities that, directly or indirectly, involve reductions in private spending—apart from the instances in which the nonbanks concerned use surplus cash balances for the purpose. Thus we have again the same story: there have to be enough surplus cash balances available to enable debtors to repay their bank loans and investors to acquire securities previously held by banks, so that the banks' new loans and new purchases of securities will be fully offset; otherwise we are confronted with the crowding out of private by public spending.

Surplus Cash Balances
Our survey of sources of finance for the government's planned increase in expenditures has with monotonous regularity drawn attention to surplus cash balances held by government, by taxpayers, by nonbank lenders (to government, taxpayers, other nonbank lenders), and by securities pur-

chasers. Activation of surplus cash balances for financing, directly or indirectly, increased disbursements by the government becomes statistically visible in an increased turnover of existing bank deposits, that is, an increase in the velocity of circulation of money. But how much of an increase in public spending can be financed out of excess liquidity of the treasury, the taxpayers, nonbank lenders and nonbank securities purchasers? The answer will depend on the magnitude of excess liquidity at the beginning of the process and the magnitude of the incremental public spending. Even a relatively large stock of idle money will be depleted after some time. When much of it is absorbed into the active circuit flow, even a drastic increase in interest rates will have a relatively small effect on drawing additional funds from what Keynes called speculative and precautionary balances into transactions balances.

The surplus cash balances of the fiscal authorities themselves will be exhausted first, and they are available to them without pushing up interest rates; the taxpayers' surplus balances will be next in reaching a state of depletion; the surplus balances of nonbank lenders and potential purchasers of assets are the ones that have to be attracted by higher interest rates. These interest rates, however, will affect not only some of the remaining potential dishoarders (if we may call them so by this un-Keynesian term) but also real investors. The latter may find that their investment opportunities are not promising a rate of return sufficiently high to warrant sinking money into newly constructed facilities. Their decisions not to undertake such investments are, of course, feeding the source Nd; they constitute crowding out private investment by government expenditures.

Increasing the Moneyness of Other Assets

The assumptions which I have stipulated for my argument do not rule out the possibility of an increase in the liquidity of nonmoney assets feeding the active money stream through the release of money stocks from the use as liquidity reserves to the use as transactions currency. The reasoning in the preceding section presupposed an invariant stock of money, a "monetary aggregate" kept at a constant level under the strict control of the monetary authorities. If the authorities stick to a designation of specified assets (bank liabilities) as money, and if they succeed in holding the total quantity of these assets absolutely fixed, it may be possible that other assets acquire a degree of moneyness in the sense that they can satisfy the demand for liquidity. As increasing numbers of individuals and firms come to regard these previous nonmoney assets as sufficiently liquid to be used for liquidity reserves, increasing amounts of assets with officially recognized moneyness will be released from use as inactive reserve money to the use as active transactions money. Thus the velocity of circulation of the fixed quantity of the specified money assets can increase more than would be possible without the increase in moneyness of assets not included in the money stock controlled by the authorities.

If new assets with increasing moneyness were emerging promptly whenever the demand for credit was rising and interest rates were stiffening, one would indeed have to question the validity of all arguments based on a strict control of the money supply. This condition, however, is purely hypothetical and clearly contrary to fact. It is true and well known that time deposits in commercial banks and even savings deposits in savings banks and loan associations have become endowed with a high degree of moneyness and are now widely used as liquid reserves. It would be absurd, however, to hold that expansionary fiscal policy in general, or an increase in government expenditures in particular, would regularly call forth such an extension of the category of money assets as to defeat a monetary policy of controlling a strictly specified stock of money.

The Limits of Pure Fiscal Expansion

The conclusions from the foregoing inquiry into the sources of funds for fiscal expansion are cogent. If monetary expansion—creation of new money—is excluded, only two sources of funds for net increases in total disbursements are available: surplus cash balances in existence before the fisc embarks on its expansionary policy, and surplus cash balances coming into existence when previous nonmoney assets replace money in its function as the people's liquidity reserves. Both these sources are limited, liable to be exhausted before long. They are not capable of financing for any length of time a net increase in the rate of spending—and hence an increase in government spending (or lending) that is not offset by a decrease in spending by others. In realistic terms, the two sources cannot furnish the funds for net fiscal expansion of a significant magnitude for much more than, say, half a year, if we assume that monetary authorities hold the specified money stock constant or let it increase by only a few percent per year.

The theory of the multiplier was designed to explain how an increase in the rate of aggregate spending could in due time lead to a multiple increase in national income and employment if wage rates and prices remain unchanged and if the primary disbursements (investment or government expenditures) are continued at the higher level. If the primary expenditures, in this case the government expenditures, are not continued in the elevated magnitude period after period, but are reduced, gradually or suddenly, to the level prevailing before the expansionary fiscal policy was launched, the multiplying effect is likewise reduced and, in due course, national income and employment will return to the pre-expansion level. Some fiscal expansionists, confusing multiplier theory with pump-priming theory, contend that the rate of national income and employment will not slump back to the previous low level, because the temporary fiscal stimulus will have "primed the pump" and private business investments will have replaced the loan-and-tax-financed expenditures of the government. Pump-priming theory, however, is based on an elastic supply of bank credit and, hence, monetary expansion. Fiscal expansion can *induce* a demand for bank loans, and monetary expansion can *satisfy* this demand. Monetary expansion, however, was ruled out *ex hypothesi*. Hence, any private demand for loans can be met only by the same surplus cash balances that have already been called upon to finance the public expenditures through loans to government, taxpayers, and buyers of securities. These sources are exhausted by the time they are supposed to be tapped by the "stimulated" investors and other private spenders.

Thus neither the theory of the multiplier nor the theory of pump-priming, let alone the theory of the accelerator, will give fiscal expansion much of a chance to create income and employment if an expansion of the money stock is ruled out. When most of the inactive cash balances are spent, government expenditures at the elevated rate can no longer be continued without encroaching on other kinds of spending. Thus, the demand for labor will not be sustained.

Long-Run Effects on Employment
The temporary effects of fiscal expansion without monetary expansion depended on a strong assumption: that wage rates and prices remained unchanged. If, however, any increase in effective demand leads to greater pressures for higher wages on the part of trade unions and to greater willingness by employers to give in to such pressures, the results may be different:

1. The income-multiplier effect may be different, depending on whether the marginal propensity to save rises or falls as labor incomes are increased.

2. The employment effect in the short period of increased government spending will be smaller if given outlays buy only smaller quantities of labor.

3. A return to the pre-expansion rate of aggregate spending (without a return of wage rates to the pre-expansion level) will mean a reduced level of employment at the increased wage rates.

The first two effects are unimportant in that they make a difference for only a brief transition period; the third effect, however, may be the end-effect of the spell of fiscal expansion. It leaves the economy with higher wage rates and lower employment than prevailed at the outset. A rather sad outcome.

Notes

1. "By 'monetary policy' we mean an alteration in the terms on which capital funds can be lent and borrowed (a change which we shall call, for short, a change in the rate of interest) brought about by the banking system through the creation of additional supplies of money in order to ease the terms on which capital funds can be borrowed or through the restriction of monetary supplies in order to harden the terms on which monetary funds can be borrowed." The "constant monetary policy" of a "neutral economy" would require "that the banking system must be prepared to expand (or contract) the total supply of money to the extent necessary to prevent any scarcity (or plenty) of funds in the capital market which may be induced by any other disturbing factor, from causing a rise (or fall) in interest rates." James E. Meade, *The Balance of Payments* (London and New York: Oxford University Press, 1952), pp. 99 and 48, respectively.

2. The foreign lenders or investors provide foreign exchange, which in the balance sheets of the central or commercial banks that acquire it represents liquid claims against foreigners. This implies logically that the inflow of foreign funds constitutes both borrowing from and lending to foreigners.

3. Back in 1937, Jacob Viner observed that a monetary policy of securing full employment could succeed only if money creation proceeded at a rate faster than wage inflation: "Keynes' reasoning points obviously to the superiority of inflationary remedies for unemployment over money wage reductions. In a world organized in accordance with Keynes' specifications there would be a constant race between the printing press and the business agents of the trade unions, with the problem of unemployment largely solved if the printing press could maintain a constant lead and if only volume of employment, irrespective of quality, is considered important." Jacob Viner, "Mr. Keynes on the Causes of Unemployment," *Quarterly Journal of Economics* 51 (1937): 149. In 1944, I warned that all programs for full employment that "neglect to deal with the problem of wage policy" would be "miserable failures." For "the nearer we get to full employment the faster the wage rates are pushed up—and the objective of full employment moves beyond reach." Fritz Machlup, "Programs to Maintain Employment: The Basis of Social Security," in *Social Security in America* (Washington, D.C.: Chamber of Commerce of the United States, January 1944), p. 22.

4. John Maynard Keynes, *The General Theory of Employment, Interest and Money* (London: Macmillan, 1936), pp. 285–286.

5. Abba P. Lerner, *The Economics of Control* (New York: Macmillan, 1944), p. 320.

6. Abba P. Lerner, "The Inflationary Process: Some Theoretical Aspects," *Review of Economics and Statistics* 31 (1949): 198. Reprinted in Abba P. Lerner, *Essays in Economic Analysis* (London: Macmillan, 1953), p. 341.

7. Abba P. Lerner, "Money as a Creature of the State," *American Economic Review*, 37, Papers and Proceedings (May 1947): pp. 312–317; Abba P. Lerner, *Everybody's Business* (Michigan State University Press, 1961), pp. 88–89.

8. Abba P. Lerner, *Economics of Employment* (New York: McGraw-Hill, 1951), p. 23.

9. See Abba P. Lerner, *Flation: Not Inflation of Prices, Not Deflation of Jobs* (New York: Quadrangle Books, 1972), p. 62.

10. Abba P. Lerner, "Functional Finance and the Federal Debt," *Social Research* 10 (February 1943): 38–51.

11. Lerner, *Economics of Control*, p. 302.

12. Ibid., p. 314.

13. Ibid., p. 309.

14. Lerner, *Economics of Employment*, p. 132.

15. "There is no controversy over government spending financed by printing money. Both sides agree that it will be expansionary; but one group likes to call it fiscal policy, while the other prefers to call it monetary policy. Nothing much hinges on this distinction." Alan S. Blinder and Robert M. Solow, "Does Fiscal Policy Matter?" *Journal of Public Economics* 2 (1973): 323. If one holds that "nothing much hinges on this distinction," one implicitly asserts that it does not matter whether one is understood by discussion partners or by public-policy makers who care to know something about the likely effects of their actions.

16. Milton Friedman, *A Program for Monetary Stability* (New York: Fordham University Press, 1959), and "The Role of Monetary Policy," *American Economic Review*, 58 (March 1968): 1–17.

17. Lerner, *Flation*, p. 63, states that "there are definite limits to the degree to which total spending can be increased if the quantity of money is not increased."

Chapter 8

Jacob Marschak

Efficient Organizational Design

Networks of Tasks

An organization—such as a firm, a hospital, or a government—can be usefully represented by a network of tasks performed by its individual members, or groups of members (agencies, conferences, and so forth). A task consists of processing (transforming) inputs into outputs. The inputs are outside events or messages from other members. The outputs are messages to other members or actions. The actions and the events considered are result relevant; together they determine the gross results, a bundle of criteria, desirable or undesirable. A more extensive bundle is the net result, which comprises, as additional criteria, the organizational costs (both fixed and variable) attached to the tasks (managerial salaries, office personnel, and equipment, for example).

Deterministic and Stochastic Tasks

The input to a member's processing task is a variable or, more generally, a bundle of variables. It may consist of messages received from several fellow members about estimated future demands, or future prices, for several products. It may also include recommendations, or commands, about the set of decisions from which the receiving member should choose: "Increase your stock of brand A to five thousand cans at most" (leaving the exact amount for the member to determine).

The member's output is also a bundle of variables. In neither case need they be numerical. In fact the discussion of networks is both easier and often more realistic if we forego the textbooks' use of continuous ("infinitely divisible") economic variables and define each variable as a discrete set of its values: "estimated price, to the nearest dime per bushel," "weather wet, intermediate, dry," "stop, go," and so forth.

If the processor responds to each input bundle of messages by a unique output bundle, it is usual to say that the latter is a function of the former and also to identify the processor with that particular function. Consider, for example, the rule, "If predicted price high or moderate, stock up; if low, advertise special sales." This is a function, determining for each of the three possible predicted prices (three values of the input variable, in this case three price levels) exactly one of the two possible actions (two values of output).

One processor is more precise than another if its output is specified in more detail. Thus in our example, precision is increased if the responses to high and to moderate price are not the same: for example, "stock up" versus "no stocking up, no special sales." Increased precision may improve (and will never worsen) the organization's gross result, but it also adds to the organizational cost.

So far I have described deterministic tasks: ordinary functions transforming inputs into outputs, with certainty. But such tasks form a special class. The manager who decides on inventories and on special sales may be uncertain about the rule to follow, may be still experimenting, and may exhibit stochastic behavior. When moderate price is predicted, he may hesitate and be inconsistent from one occasion to another. To each of the three possible values of his input, he may assign not a unique, fixed value of output (stocking up versus special sales) but a probability distribution: for example, by stocking up with respective probabilities—0.9, 0.5, 0.1— when the predicted price is high, moderate, or low, respectively. Note that in the previous deterministic case, the probabilities of stocking up were 1, 1, and 0, a special, limiting case.

Now, an experienced manager, rightly sure that his fixed rule of response is a good one, is expensive! The designer of the organizational network has to choose between a good deterministic, a stochastic, and a bad deterministic manager to be placed in this node of the network.

Stochastic processing is natural when the task is to estimate; this is the case with quality control (selecting and classifying materials, products, personnel) and, most important, with the prediction of future events. There are few perfect prophets, but if tomorrow's weather is going to be sunny, today's barometer probably shows high pressure. If next month's price will be moderate, a good market analyst will predict moderate price with high likelihood (the word used by statisticians to mean probability of estimate, given the actual event).[1] An estimate from a sampling survey is better (that is, the errors are less probable) when the sample is larger (and hence costlier).

Just as the increased precision of a deterministic task will typically improve, so will the increased accuracy of a stochastic one typically improve, and never worsen, the organizational result; but it will also increase the organizational cost. (And it can be shown that increased precision is a special case of increased accuracy.)

It will be convenient to tabulate each task as a transition matrix in which, for each value of the input, the probabilities of the several values of output (adding to 1, of course) are aligned. Thus if in our example, the three input values (high, moderate, low price) are denoted by x_1, x_2, x_3, and the output values (stocking up, special sales) by y_1, y_2, the matrix D will represent the deterministic, and the matrix S the stochastic case:

	D				S	
	y_1	y_2			y_1	y_2
x_1	1	0		x_1	0.9	0.1
x_2	1	0		x_2	0.5	0.5
x_3	0	1		x_3	0.1	0.9

Beyond Hierarchic Charts and Oriented Graphs

It is convenient to regard events as "messages from nature" and actions as "messages to nature," where nature includes the physical environment, as well as competitors, customers, suppliers, and so forth.

An oriented graph can describe an organization if it is confined to stating who sends messages to whom. On such a graph, arcs connect some pairs of nodes, and an arrow indicates the direction of the flow along an arc. The speed of the flow and the capacities of the arcs can be used to locate possible bottlenecks and derive the time for the flow to get from the source to the "sink."[2]

For our purposes this is not sufficient. At each node, a particular task must be defined as a processing of possible messages received into messages sent. And our purpose is to evaluate not the minimal time of achieving a fixed result but the nature of the time sequence of results, which varies with the time sequences of events and of actions; the actions themselves are dependent on events and on the network of tasks. (Note that a manufacturing plant, a system of conveyors, would require a similar representation, with physical processors replacing informational ones.)

Even less satisfactory than an oriented graph in general, is for our purposes, its special case, a "tree." Such is the traditional hierarchical chart of an organization, in which every agent except one reports to a unique immediate superior. An organization graph, or a part of it, can look like a spider web or a tree, but it can also resemble an electrical network or a railroad map.

The hierarchic (showing who reports to whom) is replaced by a specification of the individual tasks: Who inquires about what aspects of nature? Who performs which actions, or tells what to whom, in response to what information?

Centralized versus Decentralized Organization: An Example

The two networks in figure 8.1 represents a simplistic illustration about possible operations of an investment fund. They will be called "centralized" and "decentralized", without our claiming any generality for this terminology in any broader context.

The result-relevant action, a is described by the dollar volume of funds to be held, respectively, in stocks a_s and in bonds a_b by performing appropriate transactions. Thus action a equals the pair a_s, a_b. The gross result to the organization depends on a and on the state of nature (relevant events) x. Two members S and B specialize in stocks and bonds, respectively. S receives input from the inquirer, or analyst, of stocks, I_s, who sends as the message p_s information about future prices and yields of individual stocks. These are estimates whose likelihoods depend on the actual future state of nature x. More precisely I_s transforms stochastically the true future prices and yields of stocks—x_s, say—into the message p_s. This transformation is represented by, and I_s can be identified with, a transition matrix relating the probability of each possible message p_s to each possible value of x_s. Extending the usual functional notation to stochastic processing we can write $p_s = I_s(x_s)$, and similarly for the bonds, $p_b = I_b(x_b)$, where p_b is the message about future bond prices sent by inquirer I_b to B, the bond specialist. As both diagrams show, there are two couplings in series: Nature $N \rightarrow I_s \rightarrow S$ and $N \rightarrow I_b \rightarrow B$. These two series are coupled in parallel.

The fifth member, G, has a more general task. G's inputs and outputs,

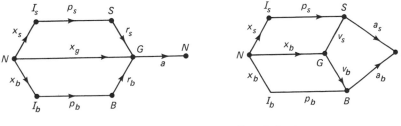

Centralized   Decentralized

Figure 8.1 Two investment funds

and thus also the outputs of S and B, are different in the centralized and the decentralized case. In the centralized case, the output of S is a message r_s that S sends to G, recommending for each individual stock the ratio of its dollar volume to the total dollar volume that might be held in stocks. B sends G similar messages r_b regarding bonds. Thus $r_s = S(p_s)$, $r_b = B(p_b)$. In addition G makes inquiries about some general characteristics x_g of future economy: rate of inflation, interest rates, government policies. (Note that x_s, x_b, x_g may very well be overlapping aspects of the state x of nature: for example, I_b, too, may be concerned with future interest rates.) Thus the input of G is r_s, r_b, x_g. G determines the fund's portfolio, the action a, which is his output: $a = (a_s, a_b) = G(r_s, r_b, x_g)$. Combining this with the previous equations, describing the tasks of the other four members, we can translate our diagram into algebra—$G = (a_s, a_b) = G(S(I_s(x_s)), B(I_b(x_b)), x_g)$, showing how, for any given future state of nature x described by its (possibly overlapping) characteristics x_s, x_b, x_g, the action a depends on the tasks I_s, I_b, S, B, G. This dependence is, in general, a stochastic one, if only because I_s, I_b are stochastic in nature, but also because S, B, and G may exhibit stochastic behavior.

In the decentralized case, the component actions a_s, a_b are decided upon not by G but by the specialists, S and B, respectively. These result-relevant actions are their outputs. Their inputs include the messages (future price, yields) from the inquirers, but, in addition, they receive recommendations from G related to the general aspects of future state x_g. G's recommendations v_s, v_b may be his decision (based on his estimate of future interest rates, inflation rate, and so forth) as to what should be the total value of stocks and bonds, respectively. The algebraic translation of the diagram of the decentralized investment fund would be $a_s = S(I_s(x_s), G(x_g))$ and $a_b = B(I_b(x_b), G(x_g))$, with the processors S, B, and G now defined quite differently from those in the centralized case.

In either case, given the five processors, we can obtain for each future state x the probability distribution of possible portfolios a. That is, we can obtain what may be called the overall transition matrix of the network. This is an essential step for any comparative evaluation of two alternative networks when the set of states x of nature, the set of actions a, and the gross result are the same function of a and x.[3]

Purposive Organizations

In a purposive organization, pecuniary and other compensations to individual members can be regarded as part of the organizational costs, along with the cost of acquiring and maintaining equipment (such as telephones, computers, and offices) and of paying nonmembers. A utility to the organization is associated with each possible bundle of criteria. It is convenient to think of a designer, an organizer who compares alternative networks of tasks to choose an efficient one. That is the designer chooses a network with the highest utility, or rather (because of the uncertainty of events and of the task performances) the highest expected utility.

This problem is complex enough to justify a frequently made simplifying assumption. Assume that the utility to the organization can be represented as the difference between two numbers, the benefit (a function of the gross result) and the organizational cost. Then the expected utility is the difference between expected benefit and expected cost.

Since the benefit is a function of the event (state of nature) and of the members' joint action, the expected benefit is the average of possible benefits weighted by the joint probabilities of all possible event-action pairs. For each such pair, the joint probability is the product of the probability of the even times the conditional probability of action, given the event. That conditional probability depends on the used network of tasks. It is an element of the overall transition matrix, as illustrated earlier by the investment fund networks. Thus for each event-action pair, this conditional probability is to be multiplied by the probabilities of that event and by the benefit yielded by that pair. And summing such products up over all the event-action pairs, the organizer obtains the expected benefit.

It is important to note that the probability distribution of possible events expresses the organizer's subjective beliefs. Also the benefit function associating a numerical benefit with each event-action pair depends not only on facts of technology of production, markets, and so forth, but also on the organizer's own tastes. To be sure, in the investment fund example, benefit may be identified with profit, a single, objective numerical criterion although even in this simple example, the organizer's subjective risk aversion and long-term rate of time discount may be involved. More generally for nonprofit organizations in particular, the benefit depends on the bundle of criteria in a manner that may vary from one organizer to another, and some of the subtler criteria are themselves evaluated subjectively. Yet the ideal organizer's stated duty cannot be evaded; it is like the duty of any maker of inevitable complex choices under uncertainty. The difficulty is mitigated if the organizer's probability beliefs are based on previous extensive experience and his tastes do not differ too much from those of any member. He also hopes that his choice of the preferred network is not too sensitive to variations of the assumed event probabilities and benefit functions. He remembers Pascal's proof that the inevitable immortality wager is insensitive to assumed probabilities and utilities, provided the utility of eternal bliss and the disutility of eternal damnation are very large, compared with temporal joys and sorrows. To be sure, sensitivity is greater when the concerns are temporal only. Yet the organization must be designed. The organizer goes to work, adding clarity of analysis to as much knowledge and judgment as he can command; not unlike any other designer of complex structures.[4]

The organizer's knowledge of the costs associated with possible processors of messages also involves subjective judgment. More precise or accurate processors, while possibly more beneficial, involve greater cost. Its objective technology is much better known in the case of computers and telephones than in the case of humans.[5]

Optimal Incentives

Physical and physiological laws may teach us how best to fuel and lubricate a motor or feed an animal, but they cannot bargain. In the case of humans, incentive functions can be agreed upon that are organizationally optimal. A processor's output (a message or an action) optimal to the member is also optimal to the organizer if such an incentive function is applied. As the simplest case, suppose the organizations's benefit is a smooth increasing function of a single member's action, the latter being a continuous numerical variable: his effort. (See figure 8.2). Let the disutility effort also increase smoothly with the effort. Suppose the difference between the organization's benefit and the member's disutility—call it total gain—has a maximum somewhere within the range of efforts considered. (This is the case if, but not only if, the marginal organizational benefit is decreasing and the marginal disutility is increasing with member's effort). At the amount of effort that maximizes the total gain, the marginal organizational benefit equals marginal disutility to the member. Let the member's compensation (incentive) be a function of effort that is some weighted averge of the benefit and the disutility functions. Then the marginal compensation to the member at the amount of his effort maximizing total gain is equal to both the marginal organizational benefit and the marginal disutility to the member. Hence both the difference between the organizational benefit and the compensation, and the difference between the compensation and the member's disutility are maximized by the same amount of his effort. The suggested incentive function is, in this sense, optimal for both the organization and the member.

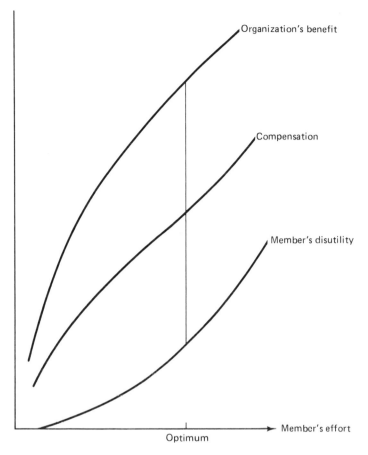

Figure 8.2 Optimum effort

This is just one of the possible incentive functions whose curve is a weighted average of the benefit and the disutility curves. Which of the many such in-between curves is applied is subject to bargaining about the shares of the total gain: a nonzero sum gain. With the reasoning extended to a several-members organization with possible coalitions, the core is to be explored: the set of all agreements such that no coalition is able and willing to improve its share.[6] The problem still needs extending to our general case: the network of stochastic processors.

Nonpurposive Organizations

The existence of an efficient organizational design assumes that the organization is a purposive one. However, parts of the reasoning can be also of some use in understanding nonpurposive organizations. To begin with, we have to ask, given the result-relevant event fed into a given network of tasks, what is the probability that a given member will take a given action? This question obviously arises in any organizations, purposive or not. But in a nonpurposive organization no single utility function is defined on the set of possible results of events and actions, and moreover the members may disagree on the probabilities of possible events—some members being, for example, more pessimistic than others. Therefore the evaluation of alternative networks will generally vary from member to member. But it is useful for each of them to know the probabilities of their joint action, given each event.

Another question that can be stated for both purposive and nonpurposive organization is that of informativeness of a network compared with some others. Call penultimate messages those that are responded to by actions. Depending on what the probabilities of these messages are, given the events, a network may be more informative (more precise or else more accurate) than another. It is as if the penultimate messages of the less informative network were obtained by garbling those of the other. Such characterization of a network is useful to each member regardless of the differences in their utilities and beliefs.

Still the difference from one member of a nonpurposive organization to another in their evaluation of alternative networks remains essential. In particular the bargaining about incentive functions is not constrained by the set of organizationally optimal ones, as this concept loses its meaning.

Notes

1. For some concepts and results common to our problem and that of statistics,

see Morris H. DeGroot, *Optimal Statistical Decisions* (New York: McGraw-Hill, 1970).

2. See, for example, Claude Berge, *The Theory of Graphs and Its Applications* (New York: John Wiley, 1966), and F. Harary, *Graph Theory* (Reading, Mass.: Addison-Wesley, 1971).

3. The computation of the overall transition matrix involves conventional multiplication of matrixes for coupling in series and a modified direct multiplication of matrixes for coupling in parallel. A direct product of two matrixes has as its elements the products of all pairs of their elements. See, for example, Taylor L. Booth, *Sequential Machines and Automata Theory* (New York: John Wiley, 1968). The direct product must be modified by deleting some of its rows whenever the inputs of two tasks coupled in parallel are related (for example, when messages have overlapping contents or are even identical commands) so that not all input pairs can occur.

When a deterministic function can be expressed by a transition matrix of few dimensions, this representation, and the use of conventional and direct matrix products, is computationally useful. I owe much to Professor Rudolph Drenick of New York Polytechnic Institute and to UCLA graduate students Igor Roizen and Masao Tsuji. Their working papers of the Western Management Science Institute are available.

4. See also pp. 313–324 in J. Marschak and R. Radner, *Economic Theory of Teams* (New Haven: Yale University Press, 1972).

5. For psychological facts about simple message-processing operations, see W. R. Garner, *Uncertainty and Structure as Psychological Concepts* (New York: Wiley, 1962), and D. E. Broadbent, *Decision and Stress* (New York: Academic Press, 1971).

6. See Jacob Marschak, "Optimal Incentives in Organizations," in *Quantitative Economics, Essays in Honor of Wilhelm Krelle*, Anton Hain, 1977 (in press). In this essay the threats of not concluding the contract, and thus the bargainers' "reservation prices," are also taken into account, reducing the set of admissible incentive functions.

Chapter 9

Ezra J. Mishan

Does Perfect Competition in Mining Produce an Optimal Rate of Exploitation?

In response to assertions by conservationists of wanton destruction of natural resources, economists invariably invoke the notion of a rising price of a depleting resource as a proper rationing device.[1] Indeed a widespread impression among economists is that under standard textbook conditions of perfect competition—at least in the absence of externalities—the time path taken by the price of the depleting resource over the future would be socially ideal.[2]

In fact two distinct issues are raised by this notion of an ideal time path of resource depletion: (1) whether the classical efficient time path of depletion associated with Hotelling (1931), defined as one that maximizes the discounted present value of net prices over time, tends to be generated by a perfectly competitive market, and (2) whether such an allocation of the finite resource over generational time is indeed Pareto optimal.

The answer to each of these two questions, which will be the subject matter of the sections on intrageneration and intergeneration efficiency respectively, are unambiguously negative. The main purpose of this essay is explicitly to establish these conclusions beyond doubt, for at the time of writing there is little more than occasional qualifications of the Hotelling thesis expressed in a broad context. For instance, Arrow's perceptive paper (1974) places the first issue in the general theoretical framework of uncertainty and information. He makes the essential observation that information about future commodity prices is not available from futures markets: only expectations of future prices are available (pp. 5–6). Yet he attributes "the failure of markets for future goods" to the heavy enforcement costs of contracts and to the costs arising from the uncertainties about the future (pp. 7–8).

Be that as it may, the popular belief that, provided prices of exhaustible

I am deeply indebted to Richard Jackman for his criticisms of the first part of this paper.

resources are rising at a rate about equal to the market rate of interest—
as would be the case in well-functioning markets—intertemporal allocative
criteria are being met and that, therefore, there is no cause for alarm, is
one that is too ingrained in the economics profession to disappear at an
affirmation of the obvious; that we cannot really know future commodity
prices.

Indeed, Solow's excellent address (1974b) still discovers in Hotelling's
article "the fundamental principle of the economics of exhaustible resources," one that requires as a condition of equilibrium that "net price"
(or royalty) rise exponentially at a rate equal to the market rate of interest
(pp. 2–3). Nonetheless in connection with the first issue raised above, he
touches on the possible instability of equilibrium using an example in
which the elasticity of price expectations exceeds unity. Notwithstanding
this surmise, he concludes that although the market is "vulnerable to
surprises," instability for long periods is implausible on the grounds that
producers have "some notion" of the long-run prospects as determined by
technological and demand conditions (pp. 6–7).

In fact the closest Solow comes to the categorical denial of this paper
to the first question—whether the classical (Hotelling) path is realized by
perfect competition—is this: "Many patterns of exploiting the exhaustible
resource pool obey Hotelling's fundamental principle myopically, from
moment to moment, but are wrong from a very long-run point of view.
Such mistaken paths may even stay very near the right path for a long time
but eventually they veer off and become bizarre in one way or another"
(p. 12). From these loose-limbed reflections, he concludes that someone
should take "the long view" and "somehow notice in advance that the
resource economy is moving along a path that is bound to end in disequilibrium of some extreme kind." Thus he perceives a case for encourag-
ing organized futures markets for longer terms than are usual.

The above remarks are suggestive. But as they stand they cannot substitute for an explicit analysis even of the first specific issue raised; whether,
or under what conditions, can the operation of perfectly competitive markets produce a Hotelling-efficient time path of resource exploitation.

Intrageneration Efficiency

Significance of the Analysis
In the first part of this essay the analysis is restricted to the first issue
mentioned above: namely, whether perfectly competitive markets generate
Hotelling-efficient consumption paths of depletable resources, such paths

being Pareto optimal for a given generation assumed to remain alive over the period in question. In order to guard against misunderstanding, let us recall the standard features of the ideal of perfect competition: free entry into the industry producing a single good (or combination of goods), an industry composed of so large a number of firms that no firm alone can influence the prices of the relevant good(s) and factors. In the absence of externalities, the Pareto ideal allocation of resources toward which the economy, it is believed, would tend if all economic goods were produced in perfectly competitive markets is a useful point of reference for economists.

As Demsetz (1971) observes, however, the fact that conditions for ideal perfect competition do not prevail, and the fact therefore that actual competitive markets do not realize an ideal allocation, do not of themselves warrant government intervention. For such intervention to be justified on economic grounds there must be expectations of net social gains arising therefrom after taking into account the calculable transactions costs and the less tangible social costs arising from the propensities of bureaucrats and bureaucracies. In the light of postwar experience at least, a presumption in favor of government as against private activity is not easy to establish.

Such a consideration would be valid if the point of the analysis to follow were to reveal the existence of actual market failures which, by reference to the hypothetical ideal, produces a suboptimal allocation. For the hypothetical ideal allocation cannot be realized either by government action. Although it is conceivable that government intervention brings the economy closer to the required marginal conditions, the additional costs incurred by government arrangements designed to fulfill these conditions can substantially exceed the gains involved in the marginal adjustments themselves. In short, the so-called total conditions of the economic change from the private to the public sector, requiring that net social gain be effected, may not be met even though the marginal conditions are. Thus for all practical policy purposes, the pertinent comparison is that between the actual market outcome and the actual "government-corrected" outcome.

What is at issue here, however, is not the suboptimal situation arising from some actual "market imperfection" compared with a hypothetical ideal competition. We are concerned with pure theory only, with the time path theoretically generated by a theoretically perfect market in a depletable resource. If we can show that, when all the standard features of perfect competition are built into the simplified model of a depleting resource, the required efficient time path associated with Hotelling's thesis does not result, we may reasonably infer that in actual competitive markets there is no tendency either for such an efficient time path to be produced.

A Simplified Model of Resource Consumption over Time
The following simplifications will be maintained throughout the present essay on the argument that if, as it transpires, the perfectly competitive model does not generate an efficient time path, neither will their removal enable it to do so:

1. The discovery at some moment in time of all the deposits of some mineral or metal ore, after which time no further discoveries occur.

2. No technological change occurs over the depletion period.

3. The appropriate social rate of discount r is operative and remains constant over the period in question.[3]

4. There are no relevant externalities.

5. All the mines produce a uniform grade of ore.[4]

Under these simplifications the efficient price-and-output path over time of the ore is given by the mathematically derived and intuitively plausible condition that, at any point of time t, the discounted present value of the net marginal social benefit be the same.

In fact a perfectly discriminating monopolist, intent on maximizing profit, would adopt the same condition and would therefore follow the same time path. The excess of marginal social value, or (since we exclude externalities) demand price, over marginal resource cost, which excess is the measure of marginal social benefit, appears to the perfectly discriminating monopolist as the marginal royalty on the ore being mined. Clearly he will seek that pattern of outputs over time such that no possible rearrangement can increase the discounted present value of the aggregate royalties. Contemplating this requirement, he can infer the necessary condition that the discounted present values of the marginal royalties be the same for all periods.[5]

The economic sense of this rule is illustrated in the three-dimensional geometry of figure 9.1 for the simple case in which the cost of ore extraction is assumed invariant to the amount extracted and to the rate of extraction,[6] and in which time, measured along the horizontal axis Ot,

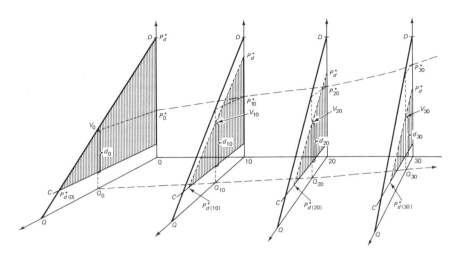

Figure 9.1

is divided into discrete units, say years, with the demand schedule DQ remaining unaltered from one year to the next.

With price (and marginal cost) per ton of ore measured vertically and, starting from any point along the time axis Ot, with the quantity of ore per annum measured along any of the Q axes, the demand curves for four different years, year 0, 10, 20, and 30, being the same, are all labeled DQ. Since it is the net price, or royalty, that has to be discounted, the rate of discount r has to be applied to the difference between each of the constant marginal cost curves and the corresponding demand curve. The resulting schedules of discounted net prices for each of the four years shown by the shaded vertical distances between $P_d^* P_{d(i)}^*$ and constant CC for $i = 0, 10, 20,$ and 30.

For a positive and constant rate of discount r, the required condition, that the discounted marginal royalty be the same, is met when the amounts of ore produced in selected years 0, 10, 20, and 30, are such that discounted net prices in these years, $d_0, d_{10}, d_{20}, d_{30}$, are all equal. Since marginal cost CC is assumed constant over time, the vertical distances $Q_0 V_0, Q_{10} V_{10}, Q_{20} V_{20},$ and $Q_{30} V_{30}$ are all equal also as in the figure. Corresponding to these discounted net prices $d_0, d_{10}, d_{20}, d_{30}$ we have the successively higher market prices $P_0^*, P_{10}^*, P_{20}^*,$ and P_{30}^* that have to prevail in these four years, and therefore also the quantities $Q_0, Q_{10}, Q_{20},$ and Q_{30} (each measured from the OT axis) respectively, required to clear the market at those prices.

Since each of the discounted net benefit curves $P_d^* P_{d(i)}^*$ is declining with respect to output, it should be clear from the figure that no rearrangement of outputs over time can raise the aggregate discounted present value of the given stock of ore above that indicated above: for the net gain from an additional ton of ore extracted in year i is smaller than d_i while the net loss from extracting a ton of ore less in year $j(i \leq j)$ is larger than d_j. Since $d_i = d_j$ any such rearrangement can only reduce the aggregate discounted present value of the stock of ore.

It should be emphasized that, along the efficient price path $P_0^*, \ldots,$ P_{30}^*, the market price P_t^*, in any year t, is above P_{t-1}^* not by the full rate of discount r (unless the marginal cost is constant at zero) but by a proportional discount factor q_t that is smaller than r according as the net price $(P_t^* - C)$ is smaller than the market price P_t^*. If, for example, the market price of a ton of ore in the initial year were 100 and the marginal cost were 75, the net price would be 25. With a discount rate of 20 percent per annum, the discriminating monopolist would be indifferent as between producing the marginal ton of ore this year at a net price of 25 or producing it next year at a net price of 25(1 + 0.2), or 30 and therefore at a market price of 105. In this case q_t, the proportional discount factor to be applied to the market price P_t, is 5 percent, or one quarter of the rate of discount r[7].

A mathematical derivation of the optimal time path of market prices can also be easily derived if we begin with the above mentioned requirement that the discounted net royalties at any two points of time, say i and j, be the same: $R_j \cdot e^{-rj} = R_i \cdot e^{-ri}$.[8] Where marginal cost C is invariant to the mount and rate of ore extracted, this condition can be written as $(P_j^* - C)e^{-rj} = (P_i^* - C)e^{-ri}$, from which equation we can infer the formula for the efficient price path, $P_t^* = (P_0^* - C)e^{rt} + C$,[9] which path is represented in figure 9.1 as $P_0^*, \ldots, P_{30}^*$ for an unchanged demand curve through time. In the figure, the initial market price is P_0^*, and the ultimate price P_T^* (not shown) is realized in the final year T and is, therefore, equal to $(P_0^* - C)e^{rT} + C$.

The Equilibrium Time Path for a Perfectly Competitive Market
As indicated above, the perfectly discriminating monopolist will maximize profits by following the efficient price $P_0^*, \ldots, P_T^*$, and therefore producing annual outputs over time described by the locus $Q_0 Q_{30}$ in figure 9.1. A moment's reflection suggests that the ordinary nondiscriminating mo-

nopolist guided, as he will be, by (discounted) marginal revenue rather than by (discounted) demand price, will underexploit the stock of ore. His initial rate of extraction, that is, will be less than OQ_o in the figure, and therefore less than optimal. But what can be said of the rate of extraction over time generated by a perfectly competitive industry?

On first thoughts it might seem that an equilibrium rate of price increase over time, suited to a competitive extraction industry, is also consistent with the efficient rate of price increase. Thus, following our previous example, if the per annum price differential required by the efficient path is 5 percent, this same annual 5 percent price rise also describes the equilibrium price path of the competitive industry. For given the rate of discount r, the competitive firms will be indifferent as between selling additional ore this year or selling it next year if next year's price is expected with certainty to be 5 percent more than this year's price.

Moreover, the general belief has it also that there is a tendency for the required 5 percent differential in these circumstances to maintain itself. To illustrate, if the price rise next year is expected to be more than 5 percent, the competitive firm, it is alleged, will have an incentive to defer production of ore until next year. For a ton of ore produced this year brings a royalty of 25 which, if invested at an r of 20 percent, amounts to no more than 30 next year compared with an expected market price of more than 105, and therefore a net price of more than 30, next year. However, as firms, in response to this price expectation, begin to withhold production of ore this year the price of ore this year starts to rise, so acting to restore the required 5 percent price differential.

Per contra, if the price rise next year is expected instead to be less than 5 percent, competitive firms, it is alleged, have no incentive to produce ore next year. For if a ton of ore is sold this year and the royalty of 25 invested at an r of 20 percent, it will amount to 30 in a year's time. In contrast, a ton of ore produced and sold next year is expected to realize a market price of less than 105 and, therefore, a royalty of less than 30. Again, however, in response to this loss of confidence in the expected future price, competitive firms expand output and sales this year; which action tends to lower this year's price and so restore the required 5 percent price differential.[10]

Allowing that there can be a 5 percent equilibrium price path over time—which concession, however, does not imply a necessary coincidence of this equilibrium path with the efficient path—under what conditions will it be stable? This is obviously a question of dynamics, one for which the concept of the elasticity of expectations is relevant.

If, for whatever reason, P_t, the current market price of ore at time t, moves up to P_t' but the elasticity of expectations, E, is zero, the market price expected to rule next year, P_{t+1}^e, remains unchanged—as tacitly assumed in the example above. Thus, if the required differential between P_t and P_{t+1}^e is 5 percent, then the upward revision of P_t to P_t', which narrows the expected price differential to less than 5 percent, provides an inducement to the extractive firms to sell more ore currently until, in consequence of their action, the revised current price P_t' sinks back to its original value P_t. However, this is the limiting case.

If (a) $0 < E < 1$, then although next year's expected market price will now also be revised upward to $P_{t+1}^{e'}$, its upward revision will be proportionally less than that of the current price. Consequently, it will exceed P_t' by less than the required 5 percent and, as in the limiting case above, firms will start to produce and sell more ore in the current year. This action lowers the current price which, in turn, lowers the expected future price—though by a smaller proportion—and so on until, given plausible time intervals of response, a return to the equilibrium price path is made.

On the other hand, if (b) $E > 1$, the exogenous rise from P_t to P_t' causes a proportionally greater upward revision from P_{t+1}^e to $P_{t+1}^{e'}$. The differential between P_t' and $P_{t+1}^{e'}$ is, therefore, more than 5 percent. Consequently firms now begin to reduce production of ore in the current year, which further raises the current price—as long as E exceeds unity—so raising the price expected next year in greater proportion, and so on in a process of positive feedback. It may reasonably be supposed that after some period (not exceeding a few years), a sense of the norm comes to prevail with E falling below unity and approaching zero. What cannot reasonably be assumed, however, is that when this occurs the resulting current market price and the expected price of the following year are those corresponding to the original equilibrium time path. These resulting prices will, in general, belong to a new equilibrium path.

Indeed, in the other limiting case (c) of $E = 1$, an exogenous upward revision of P_t to P_t' implies a proportional revision of the expected price P_{t+1}^e to $P_{t+1}^{e'}$. The revised expected price $P_{t+1}^{e'}$ is therefore exactly 5 percent greater than the revised current price P_t', the equilibrium price path being shifted upward at that point.

We conclude that only for price expectations having an elasticity of less than unity is the equilibrium price path unaltered by exogenous changes in the current price. This elasticity condition can be extended to exogenous revisions in the expected price next year since such revisions also affect the current production of ore and, therefore, cause the current price to change in the same direction as next year's expected price.

Finally, even if E remains below unity, or if there are no autonomous revisions either of present or of future expected prices, the equilibrium price path will coincide with the efficient price path over time only if the initial price P_0 happens to be equal to efficient price P_0^*. But what mechanisms are there consistent with a competitive extractive industry which make it plausible to believe that any of these conditions will tend to prevail?

Before developing the analysis any further, some provisional skepticism may be aroused by considering the special case for which perfect competition in the extractive industry cannot conceivably generate an efficient output and price path over time regardless of what responses we assume. This is the case in which the appropriate rate of discount r is zero.

The efficient output path for the constant demand over time we have assumed, and the one that would be followed by the omniscient perfectly discriminating monopolist in the case of zero discount rate, requires a minimal of physical output to be produced each year. If this minimum output is defined as one unit, the consumption in any year of two or more units involves an irrevocable loss of the aggregate ore value. Clearly, then, the requirement of a perfectly competitive industry, that a large number of price-taking firms be simultaneously and efficiently engaged in production, precludes the possibility of a physically minimal output being produced annually.[11]

A Perfectly Competitive Commodity Market with Perfect Foreknowledge

Let us now return to the normal case of a positive rate of discount and focus again on the competitive extractive firm. Such a firm cannot perceptibly influence the price of the ore by the scale of its operations. It seeks only to maximize the discounted present value of expected profits guided simply by the current price and expected prices in subsequent years. The preceding analysis suggests that there are no forces arising simply from the operation of a competitive mining industry which act to bring the resulting price and output path into harmony with the efficient path over time. Nor may it be supposed that (in the absence of new discoveries) the general belief, that the price of the ore must eventually rise, of itself, offers competitive mining firms any specific guidance from one year to the next—an allegation that becomes clear as the conditions necessary for specific guidance are examined below.

We now show that exact knowledge of the shape of the Hotelling-efficient consumption path, either by mining firms or by speculators, is a necessary component of the response mechanism required to generate a stable equilibrium time path coincident with the efficient path. Exact knowledge of this time path by mining firms, however, presupposes complete knowledge by them of the relevant supply and demand conditions over the future, and of the means of utilizing them. In general, such knowledge consists of changes in future technology, of the time rate of discovery over the future of new sources, of the changing demand schedules over the future (and therefore knowledge of changing substitution and recycling opportunities over time) plus, of course, the requisite intelligence for calculating the efficient path from such data.

If these wholly unrealistic assumptions are made for the purpose of the analysis, however, then all firms in the industry—or, rather, a fraction of them large enough to exert a predominating and significant influence on the market price—would know, at any point of time, whether or not the aggregate production of ore was "on target" by reference to the efficient path. Where it was not, they would know the direction and extent of the deviation. How does such knowledge ensure a return of the actual path to the efficient path?

Let us start with a point of time at which there is some deviation from the efficient path. Our knowledgeable firm now has two additional and valuable bits of information: the extent of the current deviation from the efficient path and the magnitude of P_T^*, the efficient market price in the final or Tth year. In order to act on such information so as to increase its profit, the firm has to take account of the effect of any deviation of the current price from the efficient price on the length of time—in the absence of subsequent deviations—before the ore is exhausted and the ultimate efficient price, P_T^*, is reached.

Thus, if at time t the rate of ore consumption happens to exceed the efficient rate, the resulting market price P_t falls below the efficient price P_t^*. The excess output of ore at time t ensures (in the absence of subsequent deviations) that total ore deposits will be exhausted and therefore that P_T^* will be reached, before T, say at T'. Since, by assumption, each firm at time t knows that P_T^* will not be reached at T', before T, then whatever the actual path to be taken by the price of ore after year t (about which actual path the firm is uncertain) the firm can be sure of adding to its profit simply by (a) leaving the ore it would otherwise have mined in the ground for as long as T' if necessary[12] rather than (b) selling that ore at the market price, P_t. (The alternative of mining the ore but not selling it will always be rejected by the firm since the storing of the ore after it has been mined incurs positive costs compared with the alternative of the ore under the ground at no cost.)

For at T', the profit per unit on the ore held over by the firm with the (a) option, R_a, will amount to $(P_T^* - C)$, which (as we know from the section on resource consumption over time) is equal to $(P_t^* - C)e^{r(T-t)}$. In contrast, the profit per unit under the (b) option, R_b, will amount at T' to $(P_t - C)e^{(T'-t)}$. Since, at t, $P_t^* > P_t$, and $T > T'$, it follows that $R_a > R_b$. Hence the (a) option is chosen by the competitive firms, a choice that acts at once to reduce the ore available on the market at time t and so raise the market price. The incentive for firms to act in this way continues until at some later date, $t + i$, the market price P_{t+i} is, once more, equal to the efficient price P_{t+i}^*.

The analysis is symmetric for a rate of consumption of ore at time t that happens to be below the efficient rate and, therefore, the market price P_t is above the efficient price P_t^*. For the resulting deficiency in the output at t ensures (in the absence of subsequent deviations) that total ore deposits will be exhausted—and therefore price P_T^* will be established—at T'', later than T. Since each firm knows this, then again, whatever the actual path to be taken by the price of ore after t (about which the firm is uncertain), it can be at least certain of one thing: it can add to its profit by (c) extracting more ore at t at the expense of (d) ore extracted at the later date T''.

For at T'' the profit per unit of the ore that was mined and sold at t under the (c) option, R_c, will have amounted to $(P_t - C)e^{r(T''-t)}$ whereas under the (d) option, the profit per unit, R_d, will be $(P_T^* - C)$ which, again, is equal to $(P_t^* - C)e^{r(T-t)}$. Since $P_t > P_t^*$ and $T'' > T$, it follows that $R_c > R_d$. The (c) option is then chosen by all the competitive firms, a choice that acts to increase the ore mined and sold at t and so reduce the market price. The incentive for firms to act this way, however, will continue until, once again, at some later date $t + i$, the market price P_{t+i} is no longer above the efficient price P_{t+i}^*.

Thus the special assumption of accurate foreknowledge by competitive firms ensures that deviations from the efficient time path immediately generate forces that act to return prices and output to their efficient paths.

An obvious corollary of this conclusion is that the existence of a futures market in metal ore, or in any other depletable material, is a sure indication—if one is needed—that perfect foreknowledge of future demand and supply conditions cannot be at the disposal of mining firms.

It is tempting now to enquire whether, if such knowledge were instead

available to private speculations, which in practice is hardly more likely,
it would alone suffice to guide the rate of ore extraction along the efficient
path. The answer is yes provided we ignore the differential between q_t and
r, and also the transactions costs associated with making futures contracts.
The larger such transactions costs are, the greater is the margin for deviations from the efficient time path.

Since the analysis of a competitive futures market in metal ore under
the assumption of perfect foreknowledge is similar in all essentials to the
preceding analysis it would inflict unnecessary tedium on the reader to
include it here. The analysis is relegated to the Note at the end of this
essay where, for heuristic reasons, it is expressed somewhat differently.

The Unavailing Virtues of Perfect Competition
Now the assumption that competitive firms or speculators have detailed
and accurate knowledge of the relevant demand and supply conditions is
not only alien to the conventional model of perfect competition. The very
absence of this sort of knowledge has always been regarded by the proponents of decentralized competition as a factor of crucial significance.
For one of the great virtues claimed for a well-functioning decentralized
price system is that the costs incurred by some central authority in collecting and processing the masses of data necessary for the calculation of
efficient outputs   assuming the tasks are physically possible, which not all
economists will concede—can be dispensed with. The required solution in
all markets is achieved in a decentralized enterprise economy without
reference to detailed knowledge of the underlying conditions of demand
and supply. Each competitive consumer, that is, need only know his own
consumption function. Each competitive firm need only know its own
production function. For the rest, maximizing consumers and producers
simply respond to the relevant product and factor prices—informational
goods that are inexpensively produced by well-functioning markets.

However, once the focus of concern shifts from an efficient allocation
of a given flow of resources at a given point of time toward an efficient
allocation of a given stock of resources over time, the knowledge that
would be required by a central planning authority is not only more costly
to collect and process; it is simply not available. If it is not possible to
forecast future patterns of demand and of new discoveries and technological developments, the efficient time path—even in the presence of the
simplifying assumptions introduced earlier—cannot be charted and, in
consequence, the efficient price at any point of time, including the present,
cannot be known. And if an all-powerful central authority cannot hope

to know the shape of the efficient time path, certainly no competitive firm can hope to know it.

There are, of course, other factors that exert an influence on the actual time paths of extractive industries, such as excise taxes, depletion allowances, and, of course, the existence of external diseconomies. It is therefore not inconceivable that such autonomous and unrelated factors should combine to produce, at least for a time, a path of consumption that closely follows the ideal. But the possibility of such coincidences cannot vindicate the belief that, in the absence of externalities and fiscal intervention, the operation of competitive markets tends to produce an ideal rate of exploitation of finite resources.

There may, finally, be good reasons for the suspicion that a competitively organized mining industry would tend initially to use up the ore in question at a rate faster than the ideal rate. But the exact relation of a competitive price path over time to the ideal time path cannot be determined within the familiar set of assumptions.

Intergeneration Efficiency

The Defenses of Complacency
The analysis of the second part of this essay is directed to answering the question: is the standard Hotelling time path of consumption of a finite resource also one that is Pareto optimal between generations. This Hotelling-efficient time path, we recall, has been defined as that time path of consumption of the given resource that yields the highest present value when discounted at a (constant) rate of interest—one which, ideally, should equal the common rate of time preference and the opportunity yield on new investment. The problems that arise when there are divergences, for any number of reasons (for example, the existence of income an corporation taxes), between the yield on new investment and the common rate of time preference are familiar and important in the literature on public investment criteria. They are only of secondary interest for present purposes, for however successful we may be in choosing devices to deal with such divergences for public investment purposes, such devices cannot be used to solve the intergenerational problem. In order therefore to show why the efficient time path of consumption is not Pareto optimal as between generations, we may as well continue to simplify the exposition by maintaining the fiction of a single rate of discount r, which reflects both time preference and opportunity yield.

Before demonstrating this intergenerational Pareto inefficiency of the

standard ideal time path, it may be as well to say a few words about the
contrary belief expressed in the common view that, provided a well-
functioning price system exists, no collective provision need be made by
the current generation for future generations either in respect of wealth
generally or of finite resources in particular. The reasons given for this
view rest on propositions that seem plausible only when vaguely adum-
brated.

It is sometimes argued, first, that in a private enterprise society each
person chooses freely either to leave assets to his children or to sell his
assets at the market price to members of the new generation, which is as it
should be. But if the freedom of individuals to dispose of their capital in
this way is defined as an "optimum" provision for the future, or otherwise
believed to be just and proper, it is so only by reference to the welfare of
the existing generation. Depending upon one's belief about the importance of "exogenous" technical progress and of future scarcities of natural
resources, future generations will be supposed to have either a lower or a
higher per-capita real income than that of the present generation in the
absence of individual or collective provision for the future.[13] Without
resolving this question of fact, it can be agreed that individual and collective provision of man-made capital and natural resources make a
significant difference to the standards of consumption of future generations, a difference that has to count if an optimal —or even an ethically
acceptable—time path of consumption has reference to the welfare also of
future generations, and not to the welfare only of the existing generation.
In this connection, it should be borne in mind that the classical ideal time
path of a scarce resource might well require that the whole, or at any
rate the bulk, of the resource be consumed within the life span of the existing generation. After all, the formulation of this efficient path of consumption makes no reference to the level of real incomes expected to be
enjoyed by future generations.

Related to this view is the contention that the exploitation over time of
a depletable resource is not to be thought of in terms of consumption. The
net return or royalties, say, from the current extraction of oil might be
regarded as a form of current investment, so that although the oil itself
may be wholly used up within a generation or two, the proceeds from
investing these net returns in plant and equipment leave future generations
an additional amount of capital that is equal in value to the compounded
future stream of net returns (or net benefits) released by extracting the
oil.

That such an altruistic arrangement is possible cannot be denied. But there is nothing in the ideally functioning market that conspires to ensure such a result. Indeed, the ideally functioning market is compatible with the draining of all the earth's oil wells by the present generation entirely for its own consumption and without any increase in its current investment.[14]

Finally, there is the argument that a corporation, whether public or private, does not limit its horizon to the present generation but extends it to the far future. If therefore it owns the property rights to a depletable resource—whether a mine, a forest, or the earth's ozone mantel—it is at all times aware of the future demands of generations yet to come and, consequently, of the higher prices that will come to rule as the resource in question becomes scarcer. Such a corporation would then have an incentive to use the resource more sparingly during the present, which is just what conservationists would wish it to do.

However, only a moment's reflection in needed to perceive that such an argument unwarrantably extends the rationale of a rising resource price over time to an intergenerational context. For the best to be expected from the corporation is a policy, again, of using up the scarce resource at a rate that will maximize its present discounted value. If it acts as a perfectly discriminating monopolist with perfect knowledge, but only if it does, the time path of consumption will be Hotelling efficient, as described in the first part of this essay. But the question being raised in this part of the paper is precisely whether this classical efficient time path is also Pareto optimal in an intergeneration context.

The Concept of Pareto Optimality in an Intergeneration Context

Let us first agree on the definitions of Pareto Optimality and of a potential Pareto improvement within a generation and between generations.

The common definition of a Pareto optimum used with respect to an existing community having given resource endowments, technology, and tastes, is one for which no conceivable economic rearrangement exists that—in the presence of costless transfers—can make everyone better off.[15] Put differently, an optimum exists if, at the given set of goods prices, no economic rearrangement can add to the aggregate net value of the output. As a corollary, a potential Pareto improvement exists where economic rearrangements can—in the presence of costless transfers—make everybody better off. Put differently, such an improvement is possible if economic reorganization can add to the aggregate net value of output at the given set of goods prices.[16]

Costless transfers within any existing economy are, for all practical purposes, impossible. However since the definition of Pareto optimality, and that of a potential Pareto improvement, do not envisage transfer payments taking place—indeed such payments are properly recognized as purely hypothetical—it is as well to interpret either criterion as involving an algebraic sum of losses and gains resulting from any proposed change in economic organization. Thus a potential Pareto improvement—which is a more precise term for an allocative improvement or a more efficient allocation—is met if the sum of individual gains exceeds that of individual losses. And a Pareto optimum obtains if no conceivable economic change can produce a potential Pareto improvement.

In an intergeneration context, costless transfers are impossible also for another reason; time moves in only one direction. Future generations cannot transfer income or wealth to generations that have passed into history. All the more reason, then, if we are to extend the nation of Pareto efficiency to the intergeneration context, so as to enable us to examine the claim made for the efficient time path of the previous part, should we think of it in terms of an aggregation of individual gains or losses, these being now spread over generational time.

The Intergeneration Nonoptimality of the Efficient Consumption Path

In order to show that the so-called efficient consumption path associated with the Hotelling model is not in fact Pareto optimal as between generations, it is convenient to assume that all mining costs remain constant at zero, in addition to maintaining all the simplifying assumption introduced in the section on resource consumption on time. None of them are necessary, however, in a more general analysis.

Now within a generation for which every person accepts, say, the r rate of discount, the efficient time path—that with a pattern of consumption over time yielding the highest present value—is indeed one for which no rearrangement of the consumption pattern over time can effect a potential Pareto improvement as defined. But, under the above simplifications, there is no difficulty in showing that, if this sort of efficient time path is extended over two generations, it is not Pareto optimal.

Let the two generations occupy two successive 50-year life spans, T_1 and T_2, respectively. All the individuals in the T_1 generation are conscious of benefits and/or losses only for the first 50 years, $y_1, y_2, \ldots, y_{50}$. We could say that all the T_1 persons are born in year y_1 and all die in year y_{50}. The same number of different individuals live their lives over the T_2 span; that is, for the second 50 years, $y_{51}, y_{52}, \ldots, y_{100}$.

If the value of the marginal ton of ore at y_{50} is \$350, its value at y_1 (at the r discount rate) is, say, \$100. At these prices it makes no difference whether the marginal ton of ore is consumed at y_1 or y_{50}. For the individuals of the T_1 generation are all indifferent as between receiving $350 at y_{50} and receiving $100 at y_1. There is then clear warrant for using the discount rate r to determine equivalent values over the years of the T_1 period inasmuch as by doing so we conform to the economist's basic principle of using only those valuations that the individuals themselves adopt.

What has been said of the T_1 generation applies equally to the T_2 generation. Assuming the T_2 generation adopts the same discount rate r, all members of it are also indifferent as between a sum $100 at y_{51} and the sum $350 at y_{100}. There is, however, no warrant for maintaining that $100 at y_{51} is equivalent in value to $100 (1 + r)^{-50}$ at y_1, for the simple reason that no individual of the T_1 generation is alive at y_1. Indeed, he is only born at y_{51}.

(I should add in parentheses that it is, of course, entirely possible for some individuals of the T_1 generation to value at y_1 the $100 to be received at y_{51} by members of the T_2 generation at any sum, X. But this would only mean that some individuals of T_1 are indifferent as between themselves receiving $X at y_1 and some members of the T_2 generation receiving $100 at y_{51}. This semblance of altruism has, of course, to count also, though its inclusion will somewhat encumber the analysis since we must take into account, in addition, the worth of the $100 to the T_2 recipient in year y_{51}. However, it seems sensible to ignore this complication here since, in any event, it has never been alleged that the optimal property of the Hotelling-efficient consumption path hinges on the altruism of the first or any other generation.)

Now the Hotelling-efficient consumption path which maximizes the discounted present value (at rate r) over the 100 years of T_1 and T_2 is one having a declining rate of consumption over that time. Thus if the marginal ton of ore is worth $100 at y_1, it is to be worth $100 (1 + r)$ at y_2, $100 (1 + r)^{50}$ (say $400) at y_{51}, and $100 (1 + r)^{99}$ (say $2,000) at y_{100}.

It is clear that each and every T_1 individual is, in this model, indifferent as between receiving an additional $100 at y_1 and an additional $100 (1 + r)$ at y_2 or, for that matter, an additional $100 (1 + r)^{49}$ at y_{50}. It is also clear that every T_2 individual will be indifferent between an additional $400 at y_{51} and an additional $400 (1 + r)$ at y_{52} or, for that matter an additional $2,000 at y_{100}. However T_2 individuals are not indifferent between an additional $400 at y_{51} and an additional $100 at y_1, for no T_2 person is alive at y_1. Indeed, there is no earlier year at which a T_2 person would accept a sum smaller than $400 for a sum of $400 at y_{51}, in which year he is born. And if such direct time comparisons of sums of money along the T_1-T_2 generational spectrum are not possible, then the Hotelling-efficient consumption path cannot be shown to be Pareto optimal.

Indeed we might go further. If, with respect to intragenerational time, we agree to compare like with like for the different generations—for instance, to compare present discounted value for generation T_1 at birth with present discounted value for generation T_2 at birth—we can show that a potential Pareto improvement can be effected, from which it follows that the Hotelling-efficient consumption path is Pareto suboptimal for the T_1-T_2 society. Thus, we can subtract one ton of ore from the amount consumed in any year by the T_1 generation and add one ton of ore to the amount consumed in any year by the T_2 generation. The consequent loss of welfare by the former, T_1, is equivalent to a loss of \$100 on its birthday, y_1. The consequent gain of welfare by the latter, T_2, is equivalent to a gain of \$400 on its birthday, y_{51}. The potential Pareto improvement from this deviation from the Hotelling-efficient consumption path is \$300; the excess of T_2's gain over T_1's loss.

In fact on this Pareto criterion, the optimal consumption path would require an exact division between the generations of the total stock of ore and, for any given r, an identical consumption path for each generation. It is a solution that, on the face of it at least, looks to be more ethical than the Hotelling-efficient consumption path, which could, especially for a high discount rate, leave very little ore for future generations. Moreover, it is a solution that has obvious affinities with the constant per-capita real-income (or consumption) generational time paths produced by intergenerational models as familiar as those of Ramsey (1928), Solow (1974a), and Page (1976).

Conclusion

We conclude that the Hotelling-efficient path is Pareto optimal only for a single generation or, more generally, for individuals who remain alive over the time span in question. Such a Hotelling path is no longer Pareto optimal when the time span is extended to cover more than one generation.

To put the matter informally, a rate of discount r would value a marginal \$1,000 of benefits to be enjoyed by some n^{th} generation in the future at, say, 10 cents today. Members of this n^{th} generation might well be indifferent between \$1,000 at, say y_{250} and \$500 at an earlier date, say y_{230}, at which time they are still alive. But in the nature of things they cannot be indifferent between \$1,000 at y_{250} and 10 cents at y_1, a time long before they are born. A neoclassical or Hotelling-efficient consumption path that reckons this \$1,000 at y_{250} as equivalent, for the whole society T_1- . . . .

$-T_n$, to 10 cents today clearly violates the traditiona leconomic principle of abiding by the individuals' own valuations, either at a point of time or through time.

Put otherwise, it is economically correct to reduce to any point of time within the generation the aggregate value of relevant gains and losses occurring over the intragenerational period, in particular to discount them to that generation's initial year. In our two-generation model, the aggregate value of the ore consumed within the first generation (years 1 to 50) can be discounted to year 1, and the aggregate value of the ore consumed by the second generation (years 51 to 100) can be discounted to year 51. But it is economically incorrect to extend this process to intergenerational time; to discount back to year 1, not only the valuations through time of generation 1, but also those of generation 2 (already, we may suppose, discounted back to year 51). In short, whereas the use of the discount rate r for generating time-equivalent valuations is an economically valid device within a generation (within a community whose members remain alive over the relevant time span), its use for the same purpose between generations has to be rejected.

Note

In this Note we enquire whether, in addition to a perfectly competitive current market in the ore, a perfect futures market tends to produce an efficient consumption path. It does so, of course, if we define a "perfect futures market" as one that succeeds in generating an efficient consumption path over time. But even if we accept such a definition, we are still constrained to ask whether this perfect futures market can, indeed, come into being under competitive conditions. There are semantic advantages then of conceiving a perfect futures market as a perfectly competitive market for speculation in the good in question, one having the standard features of free entry, and of numbers large enough that no single speculator can influence the present or futures price by his own transactions.

The question to be asked is what factors influence the formation of price expectations in this perfect futures market. As with the individual mining firm, the individual speculator can be sure only that the price of the metal will tend to rise over time. Unless he has access to more precise information as to time and magnitude, this broad expectation cannot be of much help to him in his day-to-day transactions.

Although of incidental importance here, it is generally recognized that an organized futures market puts limits to the immediate rise in the price of futures. For, bearing in mind the option open to speculators of buying the metal at the current price and storing it for three or six months, the quoted futures price P'_{t+1} cannot exceed the current price P_t by more than interest charges r and transport and storage costs s — though, as emphasized in the section on the equilibrium time path, the price P^*_{t+1} along an efficient consumption path is above the current market price P^*_t by less than r and, therefore, a fortiori, by less than $(r + s)$.

In the absence of complete knowledge of future demand and supply conditions, the production plans of competitive mining firms are being met when, at any time t, the price P_{t+1} is expected to be above the current price P_t by some fraction q (less than r) —whether or not P_t and P_{t-1} are efficient prices for t and $t + 1$. Thus at any moment of time, equilibrium in the competitive mining industry exists when the firms are indifferent as to producing ore this year or next year, as they will be if, when the current price is P_t the futures price for next year, P'_{t+1}, is equal to $P_t(1 + q)$.[18] Following any exogenous change in this price relationship, we can assume that the reaction of competitive firms—reducing current output if P'_{t+1} exceeds $P_t(1 + q)$ and increasing current output if the reverse relationship prevails—is such as to restore this equality.

We shall now show that (1) if marginal extraction costs are zero, so that $q = r$, and (2) if speculators are aware of this behavior, and (3) in addition, they have special knowledge of all future demand and supply conditions, and therefore of the shape of the efficient time path of consumption, their search for profits will act to maintain prices and outputs along the efficient path.

Thus, if at time t equilibrium exists—with the futures price P'_{t+1} equal to the expected price P^e_{t+1}, which is equal to $P_t(1 + r)$—but the current price P_t is below the efficient price P^*_t, there is scope for speculative gains. For each speculator will now know that the remaining price path cannot continue to rise at r, and so maintain itself until time T. Clearly an equilibrium price path below the optimal price path implies that amounts of ore in excess of optimal are being extracted. Therefore at some future time T', earlier than T, total available supplies of ore will be exhausted. And this in turn implies that the ultimate optimal price P^*_T will be reached at T', earlier than T. It follows that at some time $(t + i)$ after t, though not later than T', the actual market price P_{t+i} will have to rise above the corresponding efficient price P^*_{t+i}.

The speculator can be sure of making a profit by buying long provided transactions costs (including down payments) are zero. For at t he can buy futures at a price of P'_{t+1}, which in equilibrium is the fraction r above the current price P_t and sell them at time $t + 1$ at $P_t(1 + r)$ and, there-fore, without loss. He can renew this contract time and again, if necessary, until eventually at time $t + i$, not later than T', the actual price P_{t+i} will be above the equilibrium price $P_t(1 + r)^i$ which, in turn, will be above the efficient price P^*_{t+i}. The speculator can therefore anticipate an eventual profitable sale for the futures he buys at time t.

If each speculator can be sure of profit by buying futures whenever the current price of ore P_t falls below its efficient price P^*_t, his purchases of futures, along with those of all other speculators, will raise the price of futures P'_{t+1} above the equilibrium price for $t + 1$, $P_t(1 + r)$ correspond-ing to the current market price P_t. This differential between the current price P_t and futures price P'_{t+1} offers a sure way for mining firms to increase profit by reducing output at t in favor of more output at $t + 1$. The resultant action of all firms, however, raises the current price P_t and brings it closer to the efficient price P^*_t, an action that continues until the current price is equal once more to the efficient price.

Symmetrical analysis reveals that the reverse process takes place if at any time t, the current price P_t exceeds the efficient price P^*_t. Thus the assumption of complete knowledge by speculators of the efficient con-sumption path, plus their recognition of the required differential r between current and expected prices will suffice to maintain actual outputs and prices along the efficient consumption path. However, the larger are the transactions costs and the more r exceeds q, the larger is the margin for deviation of the actual path from the efficient path.

Notes

1. For recent examples, see W. Beckerman (1972) and Harry Johnson (1973).

2. Borne out by a number of passages in the paper by Nordhaus and Tobin (1971).

3. The problems of public project evaluation arise, inter alia, from the plausible assumption that ρ, the yield in the private investment sector, exceeds r, the social rate of time preference. If ρ were to equal r, it would be a matter of indifference, in calculating the Hotelling-efficient time path of consumption, whether the net benefits from the ore being mined were being consumed or invested. However, so long as ρ exceeds r, it is more efficient not to consume the net benefits but instead to invest them in the private investment sector at ρ. For the terminal value of the net benefits so invested would yield a sum in the terminal period which (discounted to the present at r) would exceed that if, instead, all or some of the net benefits were consumed as they occurred.

Thus with a ρ greater than r, the effective discount rate for rationing the mineral over time is ρ and not r. For society, and the perfectly discriminating monopolist, will then be indifferent between a net benefit R at time t and $R(1 + \rho)$ at time $t + 1$.

4. If there is more than one source of the mineral and marginal costs are constant, then—as indicated by Solow (1974b)—the lowest-cost source will have its entire output exhausted first. For example, if there are only two sources, the lower-cost source yields a higher royalty to the firms mining it, and therefore it alone is mined first. During this first period, the market price of the mineral along the equilibrium path must be rising at a rate equal to the interest on this higher royalty. Consequently, this rising market price would yield on the smaller royalties of the inferior source a rate of return that exceeds the rate of interest r on it. It is more profitable, therefore, for the owners of this more expensive source to leave the mineral in the ground until the superior source is exhausted, and the cost of extraction rises to the more expensive level.

5. Necessary conditions alone suffice for our analysis.

6. In the more general case, total cost $C = C(\dot{x}, x)$, so that unit cost varies both with the rate of extraction and with the total amount of ore, x, already extracted. The rule for the efficient path is, of course, the same, but—since the minimum average cost will now rise over time—the efficient path requires that extraction in the earlier years be greater as compared with the case adopted in the text in which unit cost is invariant to the amount extracted.

7. The required discount factor q_t that is less than r (when marginal cost is positive) is determined by setting $q_t = r(P_t - C_t)/P_t$ where C_t is the marginal cost of extraction at time t, and is here assumed to remain constant at C. With P_t rising over time and with C constant, q_t becomes larger over time. Since $Q_t = r - r(C/P_t)$, q_t approaches r as C/P_t approaches zero.

8. The formulation here closely follows that used by Herfindahl (1967).

9. Since $dP_o^*/dt = r(P_o^* - C)e^{rt}$ is positive, we confirm that for a positive r, the efficient price P_t^* rises over time.

10. The argument of these two paragraphs, from which a belief in the tendency of a competitive extractive industry to move along the efficient consumption path seems to be inferred, has to be modified when firms are faced with U-shaped average cost curves. For example, starting with a required 5 percent price differential at which outputs this year and next are at their minimum average cost points, any short-period expansion this year at the expense of next year's output (or vice versa) in response to a change in this price differential runs into rising marginal cost and, therefore, reduces marginal profit, so putting limits on the extent of the expansion for any change in the price differential.

11. Indeed, what theory there is of the competitive firm in the extractive industry does not throw much light on the question at issue. Assuming, for brevity, that each firm owns but one extractive plant and all plants are of equal efficiency, Scott (1967) correctly points out that if the discount rate were zero, the competitive firm would seek to produce an output corresponding to the lowest average cost in all years irrespective of the market price—in contrast to that output for which marginal cost is equal to price in the conventional (nonextractive) analysis. The reason for this is that the private mining firm owns a fixed amount of ore. If it produces ore in excess of the minimum average cost output in one year, the

marginal cost of the additional units will be higher, and therefore total profits lower, than if instead the minimum-average-cost output is produced every year.

The point is touched on here simply to indicate that once a positive discount rate is introduced the competitive mining firm, facing the same set of prices each year, will shift its production pattern forward (toward the present) in response to the magnitude of the marginal user cost—this being the marginal opportunity cost of extracting additional output during the year as measured by the discounted present value of profit such units would fetch if, instead, their extraction were distributed over the future in the most profitable way.

Although valid, the argument need not be invoked so long as the production of ore by the industry follows the efficient time path. It finds a place only as part of the disequilibrium mechanism. Thus, if next year's price happens to fall below the required 5 percent increase over this year's price, the concept of user cost serves to remind us that the consequent attempt to expand output this year is limited by rising unit cost.

12. For in order that P_T^* should, once more, be reached at T (or later), it would be necessary that, at some time $t + j$ after t, an output that is smaller than the efficient output be extracted at the market price P_{t+j}, which price must therefore be above the efficient price P_{t+j}^*. But if this happens, the firm's additional profit will be realized at time $t + j$, earlier than T'.

13. The concept of exogenous technical progress is misleading inasmuch as it is hard to conceive of technical (or even managerial) improvements that are not the result of effort and inputs. In particular, investment in research programs, facilities, and personnel is hardly a random factor in the economy. It is undertaken by large organizations in expectation of a return to the funds placed in research activity, bearing in mind opportunities for placing the funds instead in other yielding assets. In some ideal economy, the same (riskless) returns would accrue to investment in all forms of physical capital, human capital, environmental capital, and research and development.

14. However it is reasonable to suppose that inasmuch as the consumption of more oil raises real income, some fraction of the additional income is saved and invested so as to add to the stock of physical or human capital.

15. I follow my usage in writing "every one better off" as a shorthand for "at least one person better off and no one else worse off."

16. The possibility that the value ranking of two collections of goods will vary with the price set adopted, and in particular that the rankings will be reversed by adopting in turn the price sets corresponding to the distributions associated with each collection, is by now familiar enough in the literature. The allocative paradox it appeared to pose, however, has been resolved in my 1973 paper. (In order to guard against misunderstanding, I should add that any waiving of this objection or any disregarding of the possibility of self-contradiction is to be understood as a concession to the belief in the normative value of the efficient consumption path.)

17. The choice of a year is, of course, not only arbitrary but in this context implausible. A more realistic unit of time would be three or six months.

References

ARROW, K. J. "Limited Knowledge and Economic Analysis," *American Economic Review* 64(1) (March 1974): 1–10.

BECKERMAN, W. "Economists, Scientists and Environmental Catastrophe," *Oxford Economic Papers* 24 (November 1972).

DASGUPTA, P. and HEAL, G. "The Optimal Depletion of Exhaustible Resources," *Review of Economic Studies*, 1974.

GAFFNEY, M., ed. *Extractive Resources and Taxation*, University of Wisconsin Press, 1967.

HERFINDAHL, D. C. "Depletion and Economic Theory." In Gaffney, M., ed. *Extractive Resources and Taxation.*

HOTELLING, H. "The Economics of Exhaustible Resources," *Journal of Political Economy* 39 (April 1931): 137–175.

JOHNSON, HARRY. *Man and His Environment*, British-North American Committee, 1973.

NORDHAUS, W. and TOBIN, J. *Is Growth Obsolete?*, Cowles Foundation Discussion Paper, No. 319, 1971.

SOLOW, ROBERT M. "Intergenerational Equity and Exhaustible Resources," *Review of Economic Studies*, 1974a.

SOLOW, ROBERT M. "The Economics of Resources or the Resources of Economics," *American Economic Review* 64 (2) (May 1974b): 1–14.

SCOTT, A. "The Theory of the Mine Under Conditions of Certainty." In Gaffney, M., ed., *Extractive Resources and Taxation.*

PAGE, T. "Equitable Use of Resource Base," *Environment and Planning* (June 1976).

RAMSEY F. "A Mathematical Theory of Saving," *Economic Journal* 38 (1928): 543–59.

Chapter 10

Robert A. Mundell

Abba Lerner and the Theory of Foreign Trade

In 1930, when Abba Lerner began his career in economics at the London School of Economics, the theory of foreign trade was in the doldrums. The classical school fathered by Mill and formalized by Marshall (his foreign trade diagrams were worked out in 1871) and Edgeworth, two German bankers, Auspitz and Lieben, the Italians Pantaleoni (who published an exposition of Marshall's analysis) and Barone, and then Bickerdike, peaked by 1910. Not much new had been added by the publication of Marshall's *Money, Credit and Commerce* in 1922. Marshall's three students, Keynes, Pigou, and Robertson, were active but in policy, public finance, or money rather than in pure trade theory. There seemed to be no way to develop the insights of Marshall's appendixes in *Money, Credit and Commerce* further, and Marshall's school consequently seemed to have reached a dead end.

Then suddenly after 1930, a new generation brought the field to life. Lerner played a leading role. Between 1932 and 1935, he produced four papers on the theory of foreign trade that advanced the subject to a new plateau. The first paper, published in *Economica* in 1932, showed how opportunity cost schedules could be used in the theory of foreign trade, upon suggestions by Haberler and possibly Viner. His next paper was the famous unpublished proof of factor-price equalization given at the London School of Economics in December 1933. Next came his article on demand conditions in *Economica* in August 1934. Economic policy was then explicitly introduced with his famous "Symmetry of Export and Import Taxes" published in *Economica* in August 1936, in which he corrected a mistake of Edgeworth and gave a definitive treatment of the importance of the differences between the commodity *on* which the taxes were supposed to be imposed, the commodity *in* which the taxes were collected, and the commodities *on* which the proceeds were *spent*.

These four gems constitute the core of Lerner's contributions to foreign trade theory; and they are reprinted in his *Essays in Economic Analysis* (London, 1953). Nevertheless they do not represent his entire work in the field. He also had a hand in reviving Bickerdike's proposition about optimum tariffs, already hinted at in 1934 in his article on demand conditions in international trade, in which he related the effect of tariffs on the terms of trade to monopoly pricing. The relation is not exact, however, because monopoly equilibrium differs from the optimum tariff equilibrium in that it does not discriminate between home and foreign consumer prices.

Lerner's fame in the theory of foreign trade also rests, though not comfortably, on the so-called Marshall-Lerner condition. Marshall and Lerner of course never wrote anything together (Lerner was twenty-one when Marshall died in 1924 at the age of eighty-two), and the "condition," that the sum of elasticities of reciprocal demand and supply exceeds unity, has been misapplied in modern practice. Marshall would have rejected the application of his barter theory pseudostability condition to the condition for a change in the exchange rates to improve the balance of payments; he did in fact explicitly recognize the fallacy in mixing up a real condition with an essentially monetary problem (*Money, Credit and Commerce*). Marshall did not make the mistake of equating the exchange rate and the terms of trade, and even the stability condition attributed to him does not correspond to the condition of convergence of his second order dynamic system.

It is equally unfair to inculpate Lerner in the misuse of the "Marshall-Lerner" elasticity term. The term is often applied to the Bickerdike-Robinson-Brown-Metzler arrangement of partial equilibrium elasticities that emerges from the differentiation of the balance-of-payments equation with respect to the exchange rate. But the elasticities of the offer curves of Marshall and Lerner are general equilibrium elasticities resulting from changes in the terms of trade and cannot be identified with money price elasticities, which have no place in a barter model.

Lerner's symmetry proposition and its implications for exchange rate theory also must be qualified for a monetary economy. In a monetary economy, the central bank's assets have to be considered. Symmetry in real terms can hold in a monetary model only if the national composition of (domestic versus foreign) assets are unaltered, both at home and abroad.

To prove symmetry it is necessary to show that the imposition of a tariff combined with the removal of an export tax (for imposition of an export subsidy) will leave equilibrium unaltered. Lerner proved that proposition in the barter exchange model, but not for a monetary economy. In a monetary economy, however, the two differ by a price level adjustment since, at given foreign prices, a tariff raises the import price level by the amount of the tariff and an export subsidy similarly raises the domestic price of exportables. The domestic price level thus rises relative to the foreign price level, leading to an increase in domestic money requirements, and, if the foreign price level falls, a decrease in foreign monetary requirements. Under a full-scale gold standard the tariff-imposing country would experience a temporary balance-of-payments surplus. Under a flexible exchange rate system, on the other hand, the home country would experience an appreciation of the exchange rate.

In order to reach an exact result, however, it is necessary to establish the main factors determining the relative changes in the home and foreign price levels. Remember that we are not dealing with changes in the terms of trade, which will be constant if the rest of the world produces both import and export goods at constant costs. The basic theorem of price level adjustment is that the price level falls in the rest of the world relative to the increase in the price level at home in proportion to the relative changes in the money supplies. Thus if the tariff-imposing country accounted for 10 percent of the world production and money holdings, the shift, from, say, a 20 percent export tax to a 20 percent tariff would cause an 18 percent rise in prices at home and a 2 percent fall in prices abroad, assuming that gold (or foreign exchange) reserve ratios were the same in the two countries. The higher the reserve ratio at home, compared to that abroad, the greater the burden of price level adjustment on the foreign country.

This analysis suggests that the symmetry theorem Lerner proved applies strictly to the barter world of two commodities on which his proof rests. Even the above propositions have to be qualified in cases where capital movements or tourist services are involved since the money demand functions in those cases will depend not only on domestic prices but also on the foreign price level. Exchange rate changes in general cannot be analyzed outside an explicit monetary framework; a fortiori, tariff-cum-subsidy combinations have monetary effects and/or exchange rate effects.

In fairness to Lerner, it must be said that his work on monetary aspects of international trade theory was undertaken before the monetarist revolution in the 1960s. The *Economics of Control* was an attempt to bring economic theory to bear on problems of economic policy. It is remarkable that he could do as much as he did without an adequately developed integration of real and monetary theory. It is nevertheless necessary to say that his enduring contibutions to the theory of international trade lie in his exact analysis of the pure theory of exchange and comparative advantage rather than in his applications of propositions derived from the pure theory of trade to the real world.

This still leaves five contributions that Lerner made that ensure him a high standing in the future history books of the theory of international trade. They are all included in four essays. In the first, Lerner takes up a suggestion made by Haberler (in the 1930 *Weltwirtschaftliches Archiv*) to amend Enrico Barone's diagrams and develop a way of depicting increasing and decreasing opportunity cost curves for each nation. This he did with a flourish and an elegance that makes the 1932 *Economica* paper worth reading today, complete with a discussion of "projecting points" that arise from different conditions of increasing and decreasing costs; they are raw material for applications today. Lerner did not invent the convex transformation curve; Fisher had used it in his *Theory of Interest* (1930) applied to exchange over time, and Viner and Haberler had developed early applications in the theory of trade. But Lerner developed the first *global* production possibility schedule formed by combining national output possibilities at equal marginal cost ratios.

Lerner's second published contribution, "Demand Conditions in International Trade" was published in *Economica* in 1934. (Between Lerner's 1932 and 1934 articles Leontief had published a succinct exposition of demand and supply conditions, which was reprinted in the Ellis-Metzler volume of *AEA Readings*.) He analyzed the conditions of demand in the case of satiety and over-satiation and related the problems of tariffs and export monopolies (perhaps too closely since the optimum tariff result differs from that of export monopolies).

I have already commented on Lerner's symmetry paper, but further mention is needed of his development of the criterion for a tariff to reduce protection of the tariff industry, a result that can occur if the terms of trade improve by more than the tariff; the foreigner pays more than the whole of the tax. This occurs when the foreign elasticity of demand for imports plus the domestic marginal propensity to import is less than unity, a criterion Metzler needed in his celebrated article relating tariffs to the terms of trade and the internal distribution of income.

Lerner's 1933 paper on factor-price equalization contained the first exposition of the factor box diagram, the conditions for factor-price equalization, and an analysis of the significance of factor intensity reversals.

The proof of the conditions for factor-price equalization requires an integration of the theory of internal income distribution with the terms of trade, the theory of comparative advantage and factor endowments, and the corresponding conditions of international demand and supply. Proof of the conditions requires a knowledge of Euler's theorem and the marginal productivity theory of distribution as applied to a two-sector model. It implies also a full understanding of the conditions under which marginal productivities are proportionalized along the efficiency loci of box diagrams representing different endowment ratios.

The factor endowments theory of international location of industry or comparative advantage was already in the air in 1930. What is not generally recognized, however, is that it was first advanced, in a sophisticated form, in the nineteenth century by Dr. Stuart Wood, America's first Ph.D. in economics, who wrote articles published by the *Quarterly Journal of Economics*, a publication of the American Economic Association, and the *Annals of the American Academy of Political and Social Sciences*, between 1888 and 1890. Wood received his degree from Harvard in 1875, at which time he probably talked at length with Alfred Marshall on his visit to Harvard on the subject of international trade and protection (the subject of Wood's dissertation).

Stigler called attention to Wood's work in his *Production and Distribution Theories* (1941) and developed the theme of Wood's priority (before Clark, Wicksteed, and Flux) in connection with the marginal productivity theory of distribution in an article in 1947. Stigler correctly noted the importance of Wood's priority in developing the Heckscher-Ohlin or endowment theory of trade. However, Wood's pioneering contribution is even more remarkable than Stigler's enthusiastic commendation suggests. Stigler could not have been aware, in 1947, of the breakthrough by Samuelson or, of course, Lerner, in factor-price equalization theory.

The next step in the development was Ely Heckscher's now-famous article published in Swedish in 1919, following on the stimulus of a review by Wicksell of an earlier book of Heckscher's. But it was Ohlin's work on interregional and international trade that brought the endowment theory into public prominence. Heckscher's work was not translated into English until 1949, and the printing of the translation in the Ellis-Metzler *Readings in the Theory of International Trade* was the outstanding ornament of that volume.

Lerner's 1933 unpublished work gave the first formal geomathematical analysis of the Wood-Heckscher-Ohlin model. The Lerner-Samuelson formalizations of the subject taken together provided the technical apparatus for a deeper view of economic theory. The partial equilibrium approach to economics that had dominated applied economic theory since Marshall could now gradually give way to general two factor, two com-

modity, two (or more) region simplifications. These models were emphasized in Cambridge, Massachusetts under the influence of Samuelson and
his colleagues, and at the London School of Economics under the influence
of Meade. The year 1955 sticks out as the date of what must be termed a
new perception in modes of thought. After that date all economists
thought in terms of the new technology of economic theory, not only in
the theory of international trade, but in the theory of growth, and even,
to some extent, monetary economics.

Subsequent developments in the theory of the subject have concentrated on the problem of generalization. Free trade equalized commodity
prices (allowing for place utilities) and the global price vector (p) equalizes
relative marginal costs between places where the goods are produced. In
all zones where the same ordering of factor intensities prevails, equal
factor rewards imply equal factor proportions in the same industries and
therefore equal marginal costs (and prices). In other words, factor-price
equalization is *one* equilibrium solution. It is the *only* equilibrium solution
if the price-wage relationship is unique. Uniqueness is assured if the schedule of production possibilities is convex. Mathematically, the requirement
is that the vector function $p = f(w)$, relating prices (p) to factor rewards
or wages (w) is invertible into $w = f^{-1}(p)$, the condition for which is that
the Jacobian $\partial/p\partial w$ does not vanish. This is a convexity condition. Nonconvexity can be ruled out by specific assumptions about technology. For
example, production functions with differential factor shares but identical
elasticities of substitution cannot reverse factor intensity ranking. More
interesting, however, is the possibility of reversals at critical national
factor endowment ratios at which the convexity conditions break down
and production possibilities collaspe to a hyperplane. Groups of countries
with factor endowments between critical ratios equalize factor prices, but
not countries in different areas. The possibility arises, therefore, of groups
of countries between which factor mobility would not alter real wages or
interest rates, but only change the distribution of industrial production.

The real world is characterized by factor-price equalization zones rather
than a single worldwide zone where universal factor-price equalization can
be achieved. Such zones often become candidates for free trade areas or
customs unions since they disturb historical real income standards to a
lesser extent than do unions between countries in different factor-price
equalization areas. Countries in such zones achieve equalization of real
factor returns but not per capita incomes. The latter depends also on differences in national factor endowments within the critical range. For countries born on the wrong side of the vanishing Jacobian, factor-price equali-

zation will not be achieved solely by joining a rich man's club like the EEC. The sunbelt regions of the northern shore of the Mediterranean present particularly interesting examples.

The dust has not settled on the empirical, theoretical, and policy implications of the factor-price equalization theorem. Indeed we may be just approaching the level of knowledge at which the theorem can be readily utilized in applied subjects like systems of customs unions and optimum currency areas. We hope that the occasion of Abba Lerner's Jubilee will enlist his continuing interest in a subject he pioneered.

Chapter 11

Don Patinkin

The Development of Keynes's Policy Thinking

Among the major review articles that greeted the appearance of Keynes's *General Theory* was the perceptive and characteristically lucid one that Abba Lerner, then a young instructor at the London School of Economics, published in the *International Labour Review* (1936). In the years that immediately followed, Abba was also one of the most active participants in the process of clarifying the major theoretical issues raised by the *General Theory*. His valuable contributions to this clarification have been most conveniently included in his *Essays in Economic Analysis* (1953). But surely no less important than Abba's contribution to Keynesian theory was his analysis of the implications of this theory for economic policy. It was here that he developed his celebrated notion of functional finance, to which he devoted a significant part of his well-known *Economics of Control* (1946). And so it is most appropriate that my contribution to this volume be concerned with Keynes's economic policy, albeit largely for the period preceding the *General Theory*.

Since my concern is with economic policy, I must begin with a brief description of the economic situation in Britain during the period in

This a slightly modified translation of a paper presented before a conference in Jerusalem in spring 1976, which marked the foundation of the Israel Economic Association. The original paper was published in Hebrew in the proceedings volume of that conference and is reprinted with permission.

All references to the writings of Keynes are to the new edition of his *Collected Writings*. For simplicity, I shall refer to the two volumes of his *Treatise on Money* by the short titles *Treatise* 1 (2) or *TM* 1 (2), respectively. The *General Theory* will sometimes be further abbreviated to *GT*. Specific volumes in Keynes's *Collected Writings* will be referred to as *JMK* plus the volume number (for example, *JMK* 9).

This paper draws freely on the material in chapter 12 of my recent monograph on *Keynes' Monetary Thought* (1976). It is part of a larger study undertaken at the Maurice Falk Institute for Economic Research in Israel and financed in part by a grant from the Ford Foundation, received through the Israel Foundation Trustees.

question: 1920–1935. Figure 11.1 shows that significant unemployment prevailed throughout the 1920s and, as a result of the Great Depression in the United States, became even more severe in the beginning of the 1930s. But despite this continued unemployment, the nominal wage rate in Britain declined very slowly, and this together with the sharper decline in the price level meant that the real wage rate actually rose. This should be contrasted with the situation in the United States, where the nominal wage rate declined sharply, but not as sharply as the price level, so that there too there was an increase in the real wage rate, though much less so than in Britain.

There are two additional crucial events of the period, and both have to do with the gold standard. The first was Britain's return to this standard at prewar parity in April 1925, a decision that according to Keynes (1925), created deflationary pressures and hence a worsening of the unemployment. The second event was Britain's departure from gold in September 1931, which was followed by the collapse of the international gold standard as a whole.

You will note that in my description of the economic developments of this period, I have not made use of what would seem to be the most relevant macroeconomic statistics for this purpose: national-income statistics. The reason is simple: my desire is to present the economic picture as it was seen by the economists and policy makers of the period; and official annual national-income statistics were not then available. (Indeed they did not become available in Britain until World War II, several years after their appearance in the United States. Similarly I have not presented any figures on the money supply for, surprising as it may seem, such data were not published in Britain until the early 1960s, a full quarter-century after they began to be published in the United States (Patinkin 1976(b), pp. 1107–1111, p. 1116, fn. 54).

Against this background I will discuss the puzzle (for it is one) of the changes in Keynes's thought as represented in his major monetary writings of the interwar period: the *Tract on Monetary Reform* (December 1923), *Treatise on Money* (October 1930), and last and, of course, most important, *General Theory* (February 1936). In his first book, Keynes recapitulated the quantity theory of money as he had inherited it from his teachers at Cambridge, Alfred Marshall and A. C. Pigou. In his second book, Keynes developed what he presented in his preface as a "novel" theory (*TM* 1, p. xvii), which took the form of his famous fundamental equations. And in his third book he developed the $C + I + G = Y$ macroeconomic theory, which we continue to teach today.

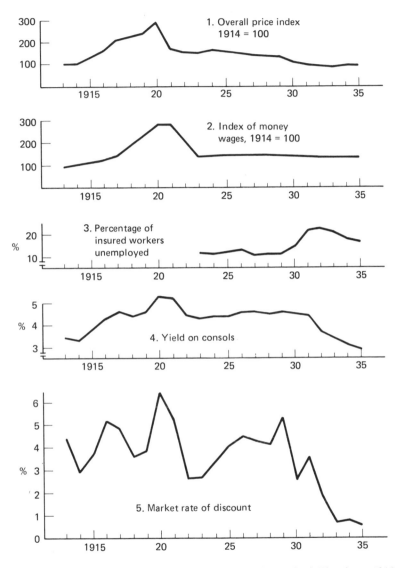

Figure 11.1 Major economic developments in the United Kingdom, 1913–1935. Source: Mitchell, B. R., and Deane, D. (1962). For chart 1, pp. 474–475; for chart 2, pp. 344–345; for chart 3, p. 67; for chart 4, p. 455; and for chart 5, p. 460.

A central problem that concerned Keynes in all three of these books was unemployment. As I have already noted, Britain suffered from unemployment in the two years that preceded the publication of the *Tract*. It continued to prevail throughout the five years that Keynes was writing the *Treatise*, and even more seriously throughout the five years that he was writing the *General Theory*. A common characterisic of all three of these books is Keynes's opposition to attempts to combat unemployment by reducing the nominal wage rate. At the same time, it seems to me that there is a difference between the *Treatise* and the *General Theory* on this point, for my impression is that in the *Treatise*, Keynes believed that such a reduction could theoretically help but practically could not be carried out; whereas in the *General Theory*, he opposed it on theoretical grounds as well. In part this difference may have stemmed from the fact that Keynes in 1930 was writing under the influence of the inflexibility of British money wages in the years that had preceded, whereas in 1936 he also had before him the U.S. experience of the sharp reduction in money wages during 1929–1933 that had not succeeded in solving the unemployment problem (note Keynes's allusion to this experience on p. 9 of the *General Theory*).

I will not, however, discuss this question further here, for what interests me is not the similarity between these two books but the difference between them with respect to the policies they advocated to reduce unemployment. The commonly accepted view is that whereas in the *Treatise* Keynes advocated the use of monetary policy, in the *General Theory* he advocated fiscal policy instead. By the latter I obviously mean a policy that makes use of variations in the level of government expenditures and/ or tax receipts in order to affect macroeconomic behavior. But in order to avoid any possible misunderstandings, I must emphasize that the meaning of "monetary policy" in this context does not correspond to its meaning today; for under the influence of Milton Friedman, this term has come to denote a macroeconomic policy that makes use of variations in the money supply; when applied to Keynes of the *Treatise*, however, it denotes a central-bank policy that attempts to affect macroeconomic behavior by variations in the rate of interest. Indeed, as I have already noted, at the time Keynes wrote, there did not even exist official statistics on the money supply. Correspondingly when in his *Treatise*, Keynes wished to provide an empirical description of the changes in the supply of money in Britain, he had to construct the estimates himself (*Treatise* 2, chap. 23).

This is the accepted version of the change in Keynes's policy views. And though in its broad lines it is correct, it does not properly describe what was in fact a much more complex development. The simplest and most concrete indication of this fact is that Keynes's advocacy of public-works expenditures preceded the *General Theory* by many years. In particular he had already advocated such expenditures in 1929 in his famous tract *Can Lloyd George Do It* which he wrote with Hubert Henderson in support of the Liberal party's platform in the British elections of that year. Here Keynes advocated "a positive policy of national development" (*JMK* 9, p. 86) as a necessary one for solving the serious problem of unemployment that then beset the country. Indeed he even went on to say that public-works expenditures would achieve this purpose not only because of the 'direct employment' that they provided but also because of the 'indirect employment' generated by the need to supply the necessary raw materials and the like for these works. And yet further employment would be generated by the fact that "many workpeople who are now unemployed would be receiving wages instead of unemployment pay would mean an increase in effective purchasing power which would give a general stimulus to trade. Moreover, the greater trade activity would make for further trade activity; for the forces of prosperity, like those of trade depression, work with a cumulative effect." (*JMK* 9, p. 106). In brief, the beginnings of the multiplier, but that is another story. What concerns me instead is the following question: Did Keynes advocate fiscal policy in 1929, change his mind and advocate monetary policy in his 1930 *Treatise*, and then change his mind once again in his 1936 *General Theory*?

Merely to describe such a quick double-reversal is enough to indicate its implausibility. This is particularly true in light of the well-known fact that Keynes spent several years writing and rewriting the *Treatise* and was indeed so engaged at the very time that he wrote *Can Lloyd George Do It*. Correspondingly one must ask why the strong advocacy of public works that characterizes the latter is not reflected in the *Treatise*.

One might contend that Keynes changed his mind about public works at too late a stage in the writing of the *Treatise* to reflect it there and that indeed this advocacy was one of the things that he had in mind in his preface to the *Treatise* when he said that were he to write the book again, he would do it differently. In my opinion, however, this can at best explain only a very small part of the puzzle, for it does not fit in with what is now known about the chronology of the writing of the *Treatise*. In particular, Keynes wrote *Can Lloyd George Do It* in May 1929, whereas in August 1929 we find him writing his publisher that a one-volume edition of the *Treatise* was more or less ready in proof, but that he had come to the realization that he must "embark upon a somewhat drastic rewriting" (*JMK* 13, pp. 117–118; Patinkin 1976(a), p. 78). And indeed as a result of this "rewriting" the book expanded to two volumes, which appeared only after another fourteen months. We also know that at the time that Keynes advocated public works in his "private evidence" before the Macmillan Committee in February 1930, he was still working on the proofs of the *Treatise*. It is clear, therefore, that even after May 1929, Keynes had the opportunity to introduce changes into the *Treatise*, had he so desired. And so the puzzle of the apparent inconsistency between Keynes of *Can Lloyd George Do It* and Keynes of the *Treatise* remains.

As a preliminary to solving this puzzle, let me add two more pieces of background information—two characteristics of Keynes that are essential to our story. The first is that Keynes did not live in the world of academe. He was not a professor. Indeed in the interwar period, he was not even a university lecturer. For Keynes first achieved fame not as a professional economist but as a publicist. In particular his sweeping criticism of the Versailles Treaty in his 1919 book, *The Economic Consequences of Peace*, turned him overnight into a worldwide figure. And from then on Keynes devoted a good part of his time to journalistic activities, which throughout the interwar period were his main source of income. Thus during this period Keynes wrote more than three hundred articles that appeared primarily in such sophisticated periodicals as the *Manchester Guardian, New Statesman and Nation*, and the like (Johnson 1977, pp. 90–92). At this time Keynes was also extremely active in the political sphere. He not only wrote political tracts, but also advised prime ministers and ministers of finance—sometimes informally, sometimes even formally. Thus Keynes was the central figure of three major government committees which, each in its own way, were charged with dealing with the problem of unemployment: the Macmillan Committee (1929–1931), the Economic Advisory Council (1930–1939), and its related Committee of Economists (1930).

The scope and intensity of these activities are attested by the simple fact that throughout the period in question, Keynes's regular schedule was one in which he spent most of the week in London, coming to Cambridge only on Friday evening for a long weekend. On Monday mornings of each autumn term, he gave (not because of any university obligation but because he was interested in doing so) a series of lectures on monetary economics; that evening he would lead a meeting of his famous Political Economy Club; and the following morning he would be back in London.

The second of Keynes's characteristics that I would like to emphasize is that, with the exception of his largely descriptive *Indian Currency and Finance* (1913), the *Treatise* was his first scholarly work in economics. Indeed it seems to me that after Keynes in the 1920s had won world acclaim as a public figure, he attempted by means of the *Treatise* to win similar acclaim as a professional economist. This was to be his magnum opus that would firmly establish his reputation in the academic world as a whole. And when Keynes first published the *Treatise*, there was no doubt in his mind that he had accomplished this purpose. This is evident from his very choice of the term "fundamental equations" to denote what he considered to be the book's primary theoretical contribution. Similarly his faith in the significance of the *Treatise* is exemplified by the fact that in order to provide Ralph Hawtrey with what Keynes thought would be a proper basis for his (Hawtrey's) testimony before the Macmillan Committee, Keynes supplied him with a set of proofs of the book (*JMK* 13, p. 126). At roughly the same time (May 1930), Keynes also wrote to the Governor of the Bank of England that he based his analysis of the *Treatise* on the "difficult theoretical proposition" embodied in his fundamental equations, and went on to say that it was "very important that a competent decision should be reached whether it [the proposition] is true or false. I can only say that I am ready to have my head chopped off if it is false" (cited by Howson and Winch, 1977, p. 48). And a year later, in June 1931, Keynes participated in the Harris Foundation Conference in Chicago on "Unemployment as a World Problem" and presented a paper that was essentially a song of praise to the *Treatise*. Thus he began with a reference to his fundamental equations and then went on to say: "This is my secret, the clue to the scientific explanation of booms and slumps (and of much else) which I offer you" (*JMK* 13, p. 354). Keynes apparently knew the Bible— and on various occasions (e.g., the "widow's cruse") even alluded to it—but the verse "Let another man praise thee, and not thine own mouth" (Proverbs 27: 2) does not seem to have been one of his favorites.

I have elaborated on this background material because it seems to me that it contains half the answer to our puzzle. For let us turn to the relevant pages of the *Treatise*, namely those of chapter 37 of volume 2, *The Applied Theory of Money*. Here we find what at first might seem to be an unqualified advocacy of monetary policy in the form of compensatory central-bank variations of the interest rate. Thus Keynes writes that if a given reduction in this rate does not suffice to establish full employment, the central bank need only continue vigorously with yet further reductions:

... circumstances can arise when, for a time, the natural rate of interest falls so low, that there is a very wide and quite unusual gap between the ideas of borrowers and of lenders in the market on long-term. . . . How is it possible in such circumstances, we may reasonably ask, to keep the market rate and the natural rate of long-term interest at an equality with one another, *unless we impose on the central bank the duty of purchasing bonds up to a price far beyond what is considered to be the long-period norm.* (*Treatise* 2, p. 334; italics in original)

So how surpising it is to find Keynes, just one page later, referring to "the insuperable limitation on the power of skilled monetary management to avoid booms and depressions" that has its source in "international complications"; more specifically, in a gold-standard world, reduction of the interest rate by one central bank acting in isolation will lead to the outflow of gold and hence to a dangerous loss of international reserves.

But for this too Keynes has a solution, international cooperation: that is, cooperation among all the central banks of the world to lower their rates of interest together. But what if such cooperation cannot be achieved? Then and only then does Keynes mention public works. In brief, when all else fails, when it is impossible to carry out a monetary policy of reducing the rate of interest, only then is Keynes ready to advocate public works as a means of combating unemployment.[1] In Keynes's words:

Finally, there remains in reserve a weapon by which a country can partially rescue itself when its international disequilibrium is involving it in severe unemployment. In such an event open-market operations by the central bank intended to bring down the market rate of interest and stimulate investment may, by misadventure, stimulate foreign lending instead and so provoke an outward flow of gold on a larger scale than it can afford. In such a case it is not sufficient for the central authority to stand ready to lend—for the money may flow into the wrong hands—it must also stand ready to borrow. In other words, the Government must itself promote a programme of domestic investment. It may be a choice between employing labour to create capital wealth, which will yield less than the market rate of interest, or not employing it at all. If this is the position, the national interest, both immediate and prospective, will be promoted by choosing the first alternative. But if foreign borrowers are ready and eager, it will be impossible in a competitive open market to bring the rate down to the level appropriate to domestic investment. Thus the desired result can only be obtained through some method by which, in effect, the Government subsidises approved types of domestic investment or itself directs domestic schemes of capital development.

About the application of this method to the position of Great Britain in 1929–30 I have written much elsewhere, and need not enlarge on it here. Assuming that it was not practicable, at least for a time, to bring costs down relatively to costs abroad sufficiently to increase the foreign balance by a large amount, then a policy of subsidising home investment by promoting (say) 3 per cent schemes of national development was a valid means of increasing both employment today and the national wealth hereafter.

The only alternative remedy of immediate applicability, in such circumstances, was to subsidise foreign investment by the exclusion of foreign imports, so that the failure of increased exports to raise the foreign balance to the equilibrium level might be made good by diminishing the volume of imports. (*Treatise* 2, pp. 337–338)

What is particularly interesting for our present purposes is Keynes's reference at the beginning of the second paragraph of this passage to the fact that he has "written much elsewhere" about his support of public-works expenditure for Britain at that time, undoubtedly an allusion to *Can Lloyd George Do It*. And, indeed, if we go back and read this tract more carefully, we will find that there too, at the end (*JMK* 9, pp. 118–119), Keynes explains that in the situation that then prevailed in Britain, one could not combat unemployment by reducing the rate of interest: for whereas Britain at that time was suffering from serious unemployment, the United States was in the midst of a great boom, which the Federal Reserve was attempting to keep under control by raising the rate of interest. Correspondingly, Keynes in *Can Lloyd George Do It* contended that a reduction in the rate of interest in Britain would simply generate an outflow of capital and a consequent dangerous loss of gold reserves (*JMK* 9, pp. 118, 123–124).

There is one further point that is relevant here: note how in the foregoing passage from the *Treatise* (and similar passages can be found in *Can Lloyd George Do It* (*JMK* 9, pp. 118–119)) Keynes presented public-work expenditures not as we would do it today (that is, not as an increase in the government component of aggregate demand that directly increases employment), but—in accordance with the analytical framework of the *Treatise*—as a reduction in the rate of interest. The crucial point is that it is not a uniform reduction but a discriminatory one, which reduces the rate of interest to a certain domestic borrower (the government) who will use the funds in order to finance public works at home and which keeps the rate at its originally high level with respect to any potential foreign borrower, who would (if induced to borrow by a lower rate of interest) simply cause an outflow of gold.

Let me also note in passing that in both *Can Lloyd George Do It* and the *Treatise*, Keynes overlooked the gold outflow that is generated by any expansionary development in the economy, whether due to monetary or fiscal policy. For such an expansion causes an increase in imports and hence a deficit on current account. It is as if in Keynes's mind gold flows were generated in the balance of payments only by changes on capital account, and not by those on current account. This is a puzzling point that deserves further study. In any event, this is the same "blind spot" that characterized Keynes's position in the famous German-reparations debate that he was carrying on at roughly the same time (1929) with Ohlin. For in that debate, too, Keynes effectively ignored the influence on the demand for imports of the change in "buying power" generated by the reparations, whereas Ohlin assigned this influence a crucial role.[2]

Thus, to return to our main question, there is no real contradiction between the *Treatise* and *Can Lloyd George Do It*. In both Keynes advocated a reduction in the rate of interest as a means of increasing employment; and in both he said that if restrictions imposed by the international gold standard render it impossible to make much of a reduction, then the government should instead carry out public-works expenditures. But whereas in the *Treatise* the primary message is the advocacy of interest-rate policy—with public-works expenditures barely mentioned at the end as a special case—in *Can Lloyd George Do It*, the opposite is true: the primary message is the advocacy of public-works expenditures, with only some passing remarks at the end to explain why interest-rate reductions are not feasible. And it seems to me that this difference in emphasis is a reflection of what I have described above about the different roles that Keynes was simultaneously playing during this period of his life.

More specifically, in the *Treatise*, Keynes was the distinguished man of science, presenting to the world as a whole the definitive work on money, the work in which he revealed the secret of the fundamental equations. Correspondingly the policy that he emphasized in that book is the one based on the universal truth embodied in these equations: a policy for all people and for all times. For that reason it is also a policy with a universal orientation: in principle the way to stabilize an economy is by means of monetary policy, and if perchance a specific economy is prevented by "international complications" from carrying out the interest-rate reductions called for by this policy, then the appropriate solution is "international cooperation."

But even in the *Treatise*, Keynes could not forget that in addition to his role as a scientific economist of international repute, he was also Britain's leading independent political economist with a unique influence on the formulation of its economic policy. Hence even in a *Treatise* addressed to the world as a whole, he could not escape the responsibility of saying something relevant to contemporary British problems. For that purpose he could not suffice with an ineffective appeal for "international cooperation" as a means of solving these problems. Correspondingly, in a still, quiet voice—as if out of a sense of obligation—he included at the end of the *Treatise* the passage cited above about public-works expenditures. On the other hand, Keynes's role in *Can Lloyd George Do It*, was exactly the opposite: here he was participating in a strictly domestic debate about the proper policy to pursue at that moment of time; hence only the existing British situation was of relevance.

Much the same pattern characterizes the "private evidence"—or, in effect, series of seminars—that Keynes gave before the Macmillan Committee in February 1930. Here in a manner which reminds me of Cyrano de Bergerac's recital of the ten different ways of reaching the moon, Keynes described ten different ways of increasing employment. He did indeed begin his evidence with an exposition of the basic interest-rate policy of the *Treatise*, but he hastened to explain that because of the danger of loss of gold reserves, that policy could not be used in the existing British situation. Correspondingly Keynes then proceeded to a detailed discussion of the policies that could effectively be used, dwelling in particular on public-works expenditures. And only at the very end—as lip-service to a measure that would in principle be most desirable but that in practice was unattainable—did Keynes mention the possibility of international monetary cooperation as a way of avoiding loss of gold reserves.

An additional bit of evidence on this point comes from the last sentence of the previously cited *Treatise* passage where Keynes referred cryptically to "the only alternative remedy . . . to subsidise foreign investment by the exclusion of foreign imports." I can understand this sentence only as a veiled suggestion to stimulate employment by imposing a tariff on imports. For it is well known that at this time Keynes—to the great consternation and even wrath of his academic colleagues—began to consider the possibility of abandoning the century-old British doctrine of free trade and advocating a tariff instead. Indeed this was one of the possible remedies that he presented in his evidence before the Macmillan Committee, though at that time he added the reservation that he had not yet reached "a clear-cut opinion as to where the balance of advantage" lay between the long-run advantages of free trade and the short-run advantages of the stimulus to employment that a tariff would provide.[3] In any event Keynes's reference to this "remdey" in the *Treatise* is noticeably less explicit than in his evidence before the Macmillan Committee; indeed it seems to me that in the aforementioned sentence in the *Treatise* he even deliberately avoided the use of the term "tariff." In my view all this is simply a reflection of the fact that tariffs are a highly nationalistic measure and hence have no proper place in a *Treatise* written for the world as a whole. Correspondingly Keynes restricted himself in this book to a bare hint at the possibility of imposing them.

I cannot conclude my discussion of this point without returning to a question that I raised with reference to *Can Lloyd George Do It*: Is it reasonable to expect Keynes's discussion before the Macmillan Committee about the possibility of imposing a tariff to be fully reflected in the *Treaties*? For the publication of books takes time, and so is it not possible that Keynes's testimony before the Committee came at too late a stage to affect the final version of the *Treatise*? But just as my question is similar to the one I asked above, so is my answer: From the materials published in *JMK* 13, we know that at the same time that Keynes was testifying before the Macmillan Committee (February and March 1930), he was also engaged in correcting the proofs of the *Treatise* (*JMK* 13, pp. 123–132; see also Patinkin 1976(a), p. 134). Thus it would appear that if Keynes had really wanted to, he could have modified the discussion of the *Treatise* to reflect his testimony before the Macmillan Committee, or, at the very least, he could have made explicit use of the term "tariff".

Let me finally turn briefly to the *General Theory*. The first thing to keep in mind is the fundamental change that took place in the whole framework of British economic policy as a result of its abandoning the gold standard in September 1931. This act freed the Bank of England from the restrictions on its interest-rate policy that have been repeatedly mentioned above: for in the years immediately following the devaluation of sterling, Britain effectively had a floating exchange rate and hence no need for international gold reserves. And indeed, in accordance with this fact, Keynes (immediately after the 1931 devaluation) advocated a reduction in the rate of interest, thus laying the basis for the well-known "cheap-money" policy of subsequent years (Moggridge and Howson 1974, pp. 237–238). Correspondingly, as figure 11.1 shows, the long-run rate of interest steadily declined during those years.

Despite this decline, however (and this is also brought out by the diagram), the level of unemployment remained very high in Britain, with roughly 20 percent of the labor force out of work. As a result of this development, a fundamental change took place in Keynes's policy views. In particular, despite the fact that interest-rate reductions were no longer limited by the international gold standard, Keynes nevertheless came to the conclusion that such reductions would not suffice to eliminate unemployment, so that it would also be necessary to carry out public-works expenditures. In other words, Keynes at this phase supported public works not because of the "international complications" that would be generated by continued reductions in the rate of interest but because such reductions would not be adequate to the task. This shift in view was already reflected in Keynes's contribution to the 1931 Halley Stewart lecture in which, shortly after Britain's abandonment of the gold standard, he said:

I am not confident, however, that on this occasion the cheap money phase will be sufficient by itself to bring about an adequate recovery of new investment. Cheap money means that the riskless, or supposedly riskless, rate of interest will be low. But actual enterprise always involves some degree of risk. It may still be the case that the lender, with his confidence shattered by his experiences, will continue to ask for new enterprise rates of interest which the borrower cannot expect to earn. Indeed this was already the case in the moderately cheap money phase which preceded the financial crisis of last autumn.

If this proves to be so, there will be no means of escape from prolonged and perhaps interminable depression except by direct State intervention to promote and subsidize new investment. (Keynes 1932, pp. 72, 84–85)

This changed view was expressed even more vigorously in Keynes's later *Means to Prosperity* (1933), where he stated that if a state of employment has existed for a prolonged period, then even after the central bank has reduced the

long-term rate of interest [to a level which] is low for all reasonably sound borrowers. . . it is unlikely that private enterprise will, on its own initiative, undertake new loan-expenditure on a sufficient scale. Business enterprise will not seek to expand until *after* profits have begun to recover. Increased working capital will not be required until *after* output is increasing. Moreover, in modern communities a very large proportion of our *normal* programmes of loan-expenditure are undertaken by public and semipublic bodies. The new loan-expenditure which trade and industry require in a year is comparatively small even in good times. Building, transport, and public utilities are responsible at all times for a very large proportion of current loan-expenditure.

Thus the first step has to be taken on the initiative of public authority; and it probably has to be on a large scale and organised with determination, if it is to be sufficient to break the vicious circle and to stem the progressive deterioration, as firm after firm throws up the sponge and ceases to produce at a loss in the seemingly vain hope that perseverance will be rewarded. (*JMK* 9, pp. 353–354)

In my opinion, then, the change in Keynes's policy views between the *Treatise* and the *General Theory* stemmed less from the transition from the fundamental equations to the $C + I + G = Y$ equation than from British economic developments in the quinquennium between the appearance of these two books. For, as we have seen, Keynes advocated public-works expenditures as a means of reducing unemployment even in the *Treatise*, albeit as a second-best policy under certain conditions. And what brought him to advocate such expenditures as a "first-best" policy was the experience of five additional years of deep depression in the face of a continuously declining rate of interest.

Let me conclude with a more general lesson that can be learned from all this. Let us be skeptical about the simplistic view that sees changes in economic policy proposals as the direct consequence of developments in economic theory. And a prime example of the superficiality of this view is provided by the story I have just told, for clearly Keynes began to give greater stress to a policy of public-works expenditures even before he perfected the macroeconomic analysis that was to provide the accepted theoretical underpinning for this policy. It was like the Children of Israel at the foot of Mount Sinai proclaiming, "We shall do—and we shall listen."

Notes

1. This is the central point of the recent instructive article by Moggridge and Howson (1974).

2. See Keynes (1929), Ohlin (1929), and the subsequent replies and rejoinders in the 1929 volume of the *Economic Journal*. For further details, see Patinkin (1976a), pp. 129–131.

3. See Committee on Finance and Industry (Macmillan Committee), unpublished minutes, March 6, 1930, p. 2. Keynes did not come out publicly in favor of tariffs until March 1931. For details, see Howson and Winch (1977), pp. 57–58; see also Winch (1969), pp. 150–151.

References

HOWSON, SUSAN, and WINCH, DONALD. *The Economic Advisory Council 1930–39*. Cambridge: Cambridge University Press, 1977.

JOHNSON, ELIZABETH. "Keynes as a Literary Craftsman." In Don Patinkin and J. C. Leith, eds., *Keynes, Cambridge and the General Theory*, pp. 91–97. London: Macmillan, 1977.

KEYNES, J. M. *A Tract on Monetary Reform* (1923). Reprinted in *Collected Writings*, vol. 4.

———. *The Economic Consequences of Mr. Churchill* (1925). Reprinted in *Collected Writings*, vol. 9.

———. "The German Transfer Problem." *Economic Journal* 39 (March 1929):

1–7; "A Rejoinder." *ibid.* (June 1929): 179–182. First of these reprinted in The American Economic Association, *Readings in the Theory of International Trade*, pp. 161–169. Philadelphia: Blakiston, 1949.

———. *A Treatise on Money*, vol. I: *The Pure Theory of Money* (1930). Reprinted in *Collected Writings*, vol. 5.

———. *A Treatise on Money*, vol. II: *The Applied Theory of Money* (1930). Reprinted in *Collected Writings*, vol. 6.

———. *Essays in Persuasion* (1931). Reprinted with additions in *Collected Writings*, vol. 9.

———. "The World's Economic Crisis and the Way of Escape." In Arthur Salter et al., *The World's Economic Crisis and the Way of Escape*, Halley Stewart Lecture, 1931, pp. 69–88. London: Allen and Unwin, 1932.

———. *The Means to Prosperity* (1933). Reprinted in *Collected Writings*, vol. 9.

———. *The General Theory and After, Part I: Preparation*, ed. Donald Moggridge. *Collected Writings*, vol. 13.

———. *Collected Writings*. London: Macmillan, for the Royal Economic Society, 1971–1973.

———, and Hubert Henderson. *Can Lloyd George Do It? An Examination of the Liberal Pledge* (1929). Reprinted in *Collected Writings.*, vol. 9.

LERNER, ABBA P. "The General Theory." *International Labour Review* 34 (October 1936): 435–454. Reprinted in Robert Lekachman, ed., *Keynes' General Theory: Reports of Three Decades*, pp. 203–222. New York: St. Martin's Press, 1964.

———. *The Economics of Control.* New York: Macmillan, 1946.

———. *Essays in Economic Analysis.* London: Macmillan, 1953.

MITCHELL, B. R., and DEANE, P. *Abstract of British Historical Statistics.* Cambridge: Cambridge University Press, 1962.

MOGGRIDGE, D. E., and HOWSON, SUSAN. "Keynes on Monetary Policy, 1910–1946." *Oxford Economic Papers* 26 (1974): 226–247.

OHLIN, BERTIL. "Transfer Difficulties, Real and Imaginary." *Economic Journal* 39 (June 1929): 172–178. Reprinted in The American Economic Association, *Readings in the Theory of International Trade*, pp. 170–178. Philadelphia: Blakiston, 1949.

PATINKIN, DON. *Keynes' Monetary Thought.* Durham: Duke University Press, 1976 (a).

———. "Keynes and Econometrics: On the Interaction Between the Macroeconomic Revolutions of the Interwar Period." *Econometrica* 44 (November 1976): 1091–1123 (b).

WINCH, DONALD. *Economics and Policy.* London: Hodder and Stoughton, 1969.

Unpublished Materials

Committee on Finance and Industry (Macmillan Committee). Unpublished minutes for February 28, 1930, and March 6, 1930. In the Keynes Papers in the Marshall Library, Cambridge, England.

Chapter 12

Paul A. Samuelson

Land and the Rate of Interest

Can society be worse off from possessing something useful? Keynes believed a laissez-faire system might be permanently harmed from having land:

That the world after several millenia of steady individual saving, is so poor as it is in accumulated capital-assets, is to be explained, in my opinion, neither by the improvident propensities of mankind, nor even by the destruction of war, but by the high liquidity premiums formerly attaching to the ownership of land and now attaching to money. (*General Theory*, p. 242)[1]

The effect of land as displacing capital formation has a truth, I believe, beyond that glimpsed here by Keynes. One must bring to bear upon the problem the Modigliani life-cycle saving model, an hypothesis that seems to throw more light on the cross-sectional and historical facts of capital formation than any other single explanation.

For, as can be seen in the quotations and verified from the full passages out of which they are taken, Keynes based his case primarily or even exclusively, on the role of land in satisfying liquidity preference and thereby exacerbating the problem of ineffectual demand and job opportunity: when the marginal efficiency of capital is already so low that what is needed is interest rate reduction to coax out enough investment to sustain full employment, Keynes feared that the existence of storable money, of other liquid assets such as jewelry or old masters, *and of land* would inhibit the needed capital formation by keeping the market's money rate of interest

I owe thanks to the National Science Foundation for financial aid. As will be obvious, the ideas expressed here go back to work done long ago; but the few-period life-cycle model, so useful in writings of Diamond (1965) or Samuelson (1958, 1967, 1968, 1975a, 1975b), provides a simple way to explain a basic property of land. My debt to Franco Modigliani's seminal writing on the life-cycle model is obvious: cf. Modigliani (1954, 1963, 1970, 1974) and still unpublished writings.

too high (above zero, for example, rather than at zero or below zero by the differential needed to coax from risk-averse investors the requisite volume of capital formation).

As thus stated, Keynes's argument proves too much, and, more importantly, too little. The argument claims too much because it can be argued—Lerner and Kaldor[2] have so argued—that Keynes erred in likening land to money: he can be charged with forgetting that the price of land is a variable that can be bid up to whatever level is needed to bring the interest rate down indefinitely close to zero. But, as stated, Keynes's argument claims too much, quite aside from the Lerner and Kaldor attacks on the cogency of his syllogisms. If land starves productive investment of its needed finance *only when capital is already so abundant that liquidity traps threaten and Keynes's euthanasia of the rentier class is imminent*, then land has presumably *not* really made the world "so poor . . . in accumulated capital-assets," as Keynes has claimed.

Quite aside from depression periods of gross inadequacy of effective demand, it can be shown that land does have the effect, other things being equal, of keeping steady-state capital levels lower per head than would otherwise be the case.[3] By not noting this, Keynes's own argument claimed much too little. Even if profit rates and interest rates are high—say 15 and 8 percent—and employment is full, the existence of land has effects on the long-run interest rate. Moreover, land is not unique in this respect: slavery in the ante-bellum South, to the degree that it *merely*[4] gave white capitalists a new asset to hold in the form of capitalized human labor-earnings power, the present analysis can show, likewise reduces the level to which plant and equipment expenditures will be pushed! Land is in many ways not at all like money in creating these long-run effects. What land is like is a long-lived machine, indeed an infinitely-lived asset if it is "Ricardian land" that we envisage, the "inexhaustible (unaugmentable) gift of nature."

As will be seen, the effect of land in keeping the long-run interest rate higher in the steady-state than it would otherwise be is no different in kind from the effect of *any change in technology that could be recognized as involving "greater durability" of capital assets*—greater "wealth-to-income" ratio.

Planning versus Laissez-Faire

No one, and certainly not Keynes, believed that having more of something productive, whether it be land or anything itself, would be anything other than a *potential blessing* to a well-run society. Only under private property in land and laissez-faire market conditions might the blessing become a curse. It is well, at the beginning, to go through some welfare-economics analysis to see how truly optimal development will be aided rather than hurt by more plentiful productive land.

If private ownership in land induced private saving behavior that would result in less reproducible capital in the long-run than is needed in a golden-rule state, a planned society could (a) nationalize land ownership, or (b) tax it in Henry George fashion, or (c) offset its effects by socially determined thrift. Familiar Ramsey analysis of optimal control, applied to a stationary economy (at first assumed free of technical change), shows what is needed to bring the system ever nearer to the golden-rule state of maximum per capital steady-state consumption. A Ramsey labor-land-(heterogeneous) capital model can approach that state at an optimal rate—optimal in the sense of maximizing, from the initial stock of capital goods, the expected lifetime utility level of a representative person who might be born in *any* future generation. One can verify by straightforward analysis what is my essential common-sense point, that having a higher land supply, B, does raise and not lower this attainable expected lifetime well-being of the representative person.

Even under laissez-faire, could it be the case that salting *all* land would make people better off in the steady state? Certainly if zero land implies zero output and zero consumption, this could hardly be the case.[5] At most, Keynes and other writers who worried about the investment-reducing influence of land ownership intended to say only that people will not be as well off under private property in land as they *might be*.

On reflection, though, one must wonder whether that is saying anything interesting. Even in the absence of land—that is, if it were so plentiful as to be "free"—is there really any Schumpeterian presumption that laissez-faire will lead to long-run golden-rule equilibrium? Of course not. Nor was this claim made by Senior, Böhm-Bawerk, or Fisher. Quite the contrary. Their arguments were to show why the interest rate in a stationary society would be *positive* rather than at the golden-rule level of zero; and, often, why this was only proper.[6] Paradoxically, it was Marx, and also Kalecki, who envisaged a process in which the golden rule state might conceivably be attained—namely, the process in which all profits are saved and only the non-capitalists consume.

Keynes's point about land as an inhibitor of real capital formation can, however, be shown to be stating something meaningful. To see this, agree that rigorous life-cycle models—such as those in Modigliani (1954,

1963, 1970, 1974), Diamond (1965), Cass and Yaari (1967), or Samuelson (1958, 1967, 1968, 1975a, 1975b)—prove that laissez-faire leads to divergence from the golden-rule state of maximum expected lifetime well-being. We can then introduce land into such a model and deduce that private ownership of land well may[7] keep up the long-run interest and profit rate and lower permanently the level of permanent per capita consumption.

The following sections will give the needed analysis.

Life Cycle Analysis

Begin with the simplest model. All people are alike. Each lives two periods, consuming c_1 in his working period and c_2 in his retirement period. Inheriting nothing and bequeathing nothing, his budget equation under laissez-faire is

$$c_1 + [c_2/(1 + r)] = w \tag{12.1}$$

where w is the real wage and r is the interest rate.

Subject to (12.1) he acts to maximize his lifetime well-being $u(c_1, c_2)$. What he doesn't consume while working, $w - c_1$, he lives off when retired, then having c_2 consumption equal to $(w - c_1)(1 + r)$. The counterpart of his principal is society's stock of capital goods (inclusive of land, B, if land is not so plentiful as to be free).

The schedule of each generation's asset holding depends on w and $1 + r$, being derived as follows:

$$\operatorname*{Max}_{c_i} u(c_1, c_2), \text{ subject to } c_1 + [c_2/(1 + r)] = w$$
$$= u(c_1\{w, 1 + r\}, c_2\{w, 1 + r\}) \tag{12.2}$$

$$w - c_1 = w - c_1\{w, 1 + r\} \tag{12.3}$$
$$= a\{w, 1 + r\}, \text{ per capita life-cycle asset holding.}$$

Note that a curly-brackets expression, such as $f\{x, y\}$ denotes a function of the variables (x, y).

Long-run equilibrium comes when the total of assets that life-cycle savers want to hold, $L(t)a\{w, 1 + r\}$, is equated to the total of productive assets of society that enterprises find profitable to (bring and) keep in existence at the long-run interest rate $1 + r^*$. (There may be more than one such equilibrium rate that clears the market, some perhaps locally unstable.)

The simplest technology to try in our model is the Ramsey-Solow-Meade one-sector case with one capital good ("leets"). This postulates

$$
\begin{aligned}
Q(t + 1) &= C(t + 1) + K(t + 1) - K(t) \\
&= F[L(t), B(t), K(t)] \\
&= L(t)f[b(t), k(t)]
\end{aligned}
\tag{12.4}
$$

where $f[b, k]$ is a concave function, smoothly differentiable in the standard neoclassical case and strictly concave,[8] and where $[b, k] = [B/L, K/L]$.

We must stipulate something about the supply of labor. Thus, we might posit a given stationary supply, $L(t) \equiv L_0$. Or, provided land were permanently excessive in supply (if that were imaginable), we could have labor grow exponentially, like $L_0(1 + g)^t$, or with the proper choice of dimension to make $L_0 = 1$, like $(1 + g)^t = R^t$.[9] Or, instead of assuming a fixed labor supply, we might postulate a subsistence living wage[10] at which $dL(t)/dt = 0$, and above or below which labor grows or decays at prescribed rates.

Begin with a given labor supply, L_0, and arbitrary capital stock, $K_0 = k_0 L_0$. What must k be so that it represents k^*, an equilibrium ratio of capital, associated with a long-run equilibrium profit or interest rate r^*? The conditions for long-run equilibrium for k^*, r^*, w^*, and for β^*, the rent of land per unit, can be written down, when the price of capital and consumption goods is taken to be unity by our choice of such numeraire units.

$$\bar{b} = \bar{B}/L_0, \text{ a prescribed constant} \tag{12.5a}$$

$$r = \partial f[\bar{b}, k]/\partial k \tag{12.5b}$$

$$\beta = \partial f[\bar{b}, k]/\partial b \tag{12.5c}$$

$$w = f[\bar{b}, \bar{k}] - rk - \beta\bar{b} \tag{12.5d}$$

$$La\{w, 1 + r\} = K + (\beta\bar{B})/r \text{ or}$$

$$a\{w, 1 + r\} = k + (\beta\bar{b})/r \tag{12.5e}$$

Marginal productivity relations are given by (12.5b) and (12.5c), and for that matter, in view of Euler's theorem on adding up, by (12.5d). Our life-cycle saving condition is embodied in (12.5e), which says that at the long-term r^*, the cross-sectional total of what people of all ages have saved must equal the earnings assets of the firms in the economy, land plus capital goods. Land's value comes from capitalizing its perpetual income stream at the long-run interest rate; the equilibrium capital stock, $K^* =$

k^*L_0, is adjusted to the long-run interest rate; a simultaneous equation solution is, of course, needed to define this statical equilibrium, since in this paper I do not present in detail the dynamic transient paths by which, starting out from $K_0 < K^*$, the system evolved into K^* and r^*.

Equations (12.5a–12.5e) suffice to determine our 5 unknowns, β^*, r^*, w^*, k^*, b^*. Indeed, substituting (12.5a)–(12.5d) into (12.5e) gives us a single implicit equation in k, namely

$$a\{f[\bar{B}/L_0, k] - (k\partial f[\bar{B}/L_0, k]/\partial k) - (\bar{B}/L_0)(\partial f[\bar{B}/L_0, k]/\partial b),$$
$$1 + (\partial f[\bar{B}/L_0, k]/\partial k)\}$$
$$= k + (\partial f[\bar{B}/L_0, k]/\partial b)(\bar{B}/L_0)/(\partial f[\bar{B}/L_0, k]/\partial k). \tag{12.6}$$

So our system is "determinate"[11]: after solving (12.6) for a k^* root, we calculate r^*, β^*, and w^* from (12.5b)–(12.5d).

Turgot Vindicated

Before vindicating Keynes's dictum that land ownership tends to keep up the interest rate, we can set to rest the problem that Böhm-Bawerk wrestled with—namely, *Why* is there a positive interest rate?

It will be recalled that, prior to Marshall's 1890 *Principles*, Böhm-Bawerk was probably the world's best-known economist. From the mid-1880s until his 1914 death, he wrestled in three fat volumes with the puzzle of interest. In the volumes that preceded and followed his own *Positive Theory of Capital* (1888), Böhm engaged in tireless polemics, reviewing all old and new theories of interest and finding them all inferior to his own preferred version.

Thus, Böhm divided earlier theories into such categories as *productivity* theories (naive and otherwise), *exploitation* theories (Marx and all that), *abstinence* theories, and so forth. And, of course, he found each lacking: the productivity theories were naive, the exploitation theories begged the issue, etc., etc. Although he is painstaking and tireless, his logic chopping tends to be tedious and boring, besides being so often casuistical and sterile. I do not propose to review his merits and demerits here: it is enough to say that I agree with the general evaluation of Wicksell and Fisher that, for all Böhm-Bawerk's hooplah and merits, in the end he must do what he castigates others for doing—namely, he must "explain" interest in no other way than to point to the supply-and-demand forces that operate in consumption and production loan-assets markets of the world, involving (1) the desires of people to demand both future and present goods, and (2) the ability of businesses to find time-phased production operations that pay competitively at different market profit rates. In short, at his best, Böhm glimpses a Fisher model of intertemporal general equilibrium; and if he had extended to many an earlier writer the charity we extend to him, he could have spared us hundreds of pages.

What is relevant for my present analysis of land and the interest rate is Böhm's initial analysis of Turgot's so-called *fructification* theory of interest. Right at the beginning, after Böhm has warmed up by demolishing the amateurish strictures on usury and interest of the Bible, Aristotle, and the Church's Schoolmen, he turns to Turgot, "the greatest of the physiocrats," and "the first to attempt a scientific explanation of all interest on the fact that the owner of any capital employed in a fruitful field always has the option of a different field. That is to say, he can use it for the purchase of land which is then capable of yielding land rent."[12]

I shall not go into the question of whether the theory attributed to Turgot does that author full justice.[13] It is enough for us that Böhm attributes to Turgot the view that the permanent fertility of land is the source of a positive interest rate: for if one can buy land at 20 (or 30 or . . .) years purchase, then by competitive arbitrage all alternative opportunities to invest that are equally safe must also yield 0.05 or 5 per cent per annum (or $30^{-1} = 0.333$ or . . .).

Böhm seems to think that 20 year's purchase, or any finite n year's purchase begs the question by assuming what needs to be "proved" and "explained." Salty Edwin Cannan (1929, p. 280) did not at all agree, writing "If the question, Why is there a rate of interest? is put in the form 'Why is there a ratio between capital-value and income-value?' it looks rather silly, . . ." The only legitimate scruple that Böhm should have investigated (but hardly began), and that Cannan might have more humbly explored, is whether an acre of good land could in equilibrium have an *infinite* value relative to any finite bushel of grain or quantum of money purchasing power.

My old teacher, Joseph Schumpeter, with his quaint theory of zero interest rate in the stationary circular-flow general equilibrium, may have had some such infinity notion in mind.[14] Within the context of a reasonable life-cycle model, we can put the whole matter to definitive rest. We can provide for the "first scientific" writer on interest, Turgot, a perfectly plausible and consistent model for a positive rate of interest; so, even prior to Böhm-Bawerk's own 1888 "positive" solution, Böhm might better have conceded that truth had already been glimpsed.

Turgot's Purest Case

Forget for the present purpose about the existence of any produced inputs, K or $K_1, K_2, \ldots$. Let there be the labor of people, who like all men are mortal, and let there be permanent land in limited amount: as with Sir William Petty, labor sires out of land the progeny of annual product, $Q = Lf[B/L], f''[b] < 0$. Grant Turgot the reasonable supposition, which need not even have been explicit, that whatever are people's preferences about future and present, they will want to consume in their lifetimes *some finite* portion of the total principal that is theirs to consume or to bequeath. Then Böhm should have admitted the truth of the following Turgot-like Theorem.

If land has a perpetual net yield and at least one mortal wishes to enjoy a finite portion of the assets at his disposal rather than bequeath it, we have sufficient conditions for a necessarily positive steady-state interest rate.

To prove the obvious, rewrite (12.6) so that $a\{w, 1 + r\}$ has included in it the effects of whatever (finite!) bequests or inheritances people decide on; and suppose that K is absent from $F[L, B]$. We then have

$$L_0 a\{\partial F[L_0, \bar{B}]/\partial L, 1 + r; \text{inheritance}\} = \frac{\bar{B}}{r} \partial F[L_0, \bar{B}]/\partial B \qquad (12.6')$$

Equation (12.6') is the Turgot-Modigliani equation for the land-begotten positive interest rate, positive because at $r = 0$ the infinite right-hand side would have to exceed the left-hand side.[15] To be conciliatory, we can willingly admit that two of Böhm's three blades are here operative: along with his third "productivity" cause of interest (involving land's permanent observed yield, not "proved" or "explained" but accepted), Böhm can save face by claiming that his second cause of interest, "time preference" of some kind, is invoked by our assumption that men someday die and do not entail their land against any sale. Turgot could gladly agree to the emendation; and could point out that, putting some capital goods back into (12.6') would still leave its smallest r^* root positive, with nothing fundamental having been begged in the discussion.

Figure 12.1 illustrates the Turgot equilibrium of (12.6') in the simplest case of zero inheritance and bequeathal. The unknown interest rate, r, is on the vertical axis; on the horizontal axis is the total of per capita assets to be held, $a\{w, 1 + r\}$, which in this simplified Turgot case consists only of the land that workers buy when young and live off when old. Since the rent income of land per capita is determined by $\bar{b} = \bar{B}/L_0$ times land's marginal product, $\partial F[L_0, \bar{B}]/\partial B$, dd is a rectangular hyperbola. The "sup-

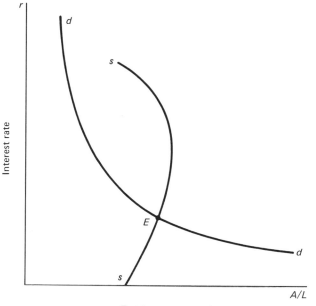

Figure 12.1 In the pure Turgot model, the constant amount of land rent is capitalized by $1/r$, giving dd as a unitary-elasticity demand by firms for assets that owners are to hold. From life-cycle saving considerations, the supply of asset holding by families is given by ss (being simply $\bar{w} - c_1\{\bar{w}, 1 + r\}$ in the two-period life-cycle model). The equilibrium interest rate is shown at r^*, what Böhm calls the first "scientific" demonstration of a positive interest rate. If the supply of land increases and if that raises total rent along an elastic marginal-product curve, dd shifts out to $d'd'$, raising r^* in the fashion alleged by Keynes.

ply schedule" of what people will want to hold for Modigliani life-cycle reasons is given by ss: at $r = 0$, it begins at a finite intersection on the horizontal axis to the west of dd; therefore, Turgot's model does provide a rigorous demonstration that the interest rate cannot fail to be positive.

An increase in the supply of land, in $\bar{B}$ and $\bar{b}$, could raise or lower the dd hyperbola; but, on the customary presumption that the marginal-product demand for land is *elastic*, it will shift dd upward and most likely raise r^* much as Keynes alleged would be the case.

Keynes Vindicated

Now we can demonstrate the germ of putative truth in Keynes's contention that the existence of private ownership in land serves to inhibit capital formation. It is his conclusion I support, though I jettison his liquidity-mechanism reason in favor of life-cycle reasons. The procedure to be followed is that involved in analyzing the incidence of a tax, or of the change in comparative-statical equilibrium values produced by a specified change in some parameter.

Subtracting the right-hand "demand side" of (12.6) from the left-hand "supply side," we rewrite it and its implied equilibrium changes in the short form:

$$H[k; b] = 0 \tag{12.7a}$$

$$\frac{dk^*}{db} = - \frac{\partial H[k^*; b]/\partial b}{\partial H[k^*; b]/\partial k} \tag{12.7b}$$

To evaluate (12.7b)'s algebraic sign, one usually applies dynamic stability analysis to a spelled-out short-run scenario of the system being described. Then, if this dynamic analysis establishes that the sign of (12.7b)'s denominator is positive, one can infer that Keynes alleged inhibition by land of the level of capital will follow from (12.7b)'s numerator being shown to be positive. This is not the place to pursue in depth such needed dynamic stability analysis.

It is enough to indicate an important warning or qualification. Even in a simple *leets* model, the land-incidence problem is a bit more delicate than was the public-debt-incidence problem for Diamond (1965). That is (1) because an increase in land, ΔB or Δb, must *directly* raise society's total output per capita, $f[b, k]$, and will thus generally have a *direct* effect on both the w and the r in $a\{\omega, 1 + r\}$, but in unknown directions or degrees. And (2) because the effect of Δb on total land rent per capita, βb in $\beta b/r$, has already been seen to be not necessarily positive in sign. Hence, the final sign pattern in (12.7b) need not be unambiguously definite, and Keynes's sweeping conclusion does have to be qualified.

Figures 12.2 and 12.3 indicate how the actual picture might look. These two-dimensional diagrams bear a vague resemblance to those of Tobin (1967, p. 234, Figure 1). However, two dimensions cannot capture all of the present story, since the W in $a\{w, 1 + r\}$ need not bear a systematic technical relationship to r once land complicates the simplest leets model. As footnote 16 discusses,[16] there is one singular case in which B/L or the land-rent rate does not affect the (r, w) factor-price frontier; my Figures 12.2 and 12.3 may be assumed to apply to that singular (and unrealistic!) case.

In Figure 12.2, the total demand relation of dd gives $k + (\beta b/r)$ as a function of r; note that $(\beta b/r)$ is added horizontally to the (sans-land) neo-

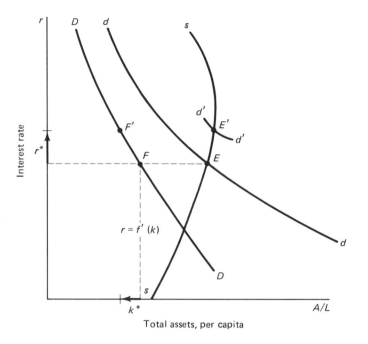

Total assets, per capita

Figure 12.2 Supply, *ss*, is as in Figure 12.1. But now *dd* is the lateral sum of *DD*, the reproducible *k* assets, and land's capitalized asset value—giving *dd* as shown. The intersection of *ss* with *dd* is shown yielding a higher *r** than would the sans-land intersection with *DD*—thus providing a confirmation of Keynes's conjecture.

classical *dd* demand relation that comes from inverting $r = f'(k)$. The *ss* supply relation plots $a\{\ ,\ \}$ against *r* alone, it being understood that each *r* gives rise to a unique *w* along the factor-price frontier $w = \omega(r)$.

The intersection at *F* defines the equilibrium point of (k^*, r^*) that is due west of *E*. Now note how an increase in land, *B*, and in its total rent βB, shifts equilibrium from *F* to *F'*, and shifts *E* to *E'*, confirming Keynes's hypothesis that land inhibits k^* and raises r^*.

Figure 12.3 shows some of the multiple equilibria that can occur when we go beyond the neoclassical 1-sector leets model (or, for that matter, recognize that the Modigliani *ss* locus can be twisty). Allowing for Wicksell effects, heterogeneous capital goods like $(k_1, k_2, \ldots)$ rather than scalar *k* alone, or more simply following Liviatan and Samuelson (1969, p. 456, Figure 1) and postulating the kind of "complementarity" that joint-production leets models may display, we can replace the monotone $f'(k)$ *DD* schedule of Figure 12.2 by the twisty *DD* shown in Figure 12.3. Adding land's rectangular hyperbola to *DD* gives the twisty *dd* locus. Note the

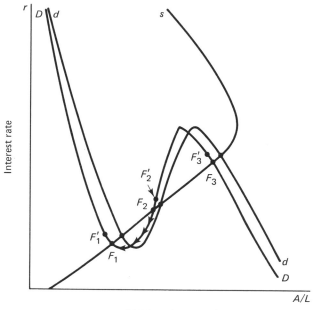

Total assets, per capita

Figure 12.3 Sans land, DD here reverses its direction because of Liviatan-Samuelson "complementarity" of joint production. Multiple equilibria occur at F_1, F_2, and F_3, with F_2 being "locally unstable." Adding land shifts DD out to dd. As Keynes claimed, k^* falls from F_1 to F_1'; and r^* falls from F_3 to F_3'. However, k^* does not rise from F_2 to F_2', but instead it falls "catastrophically" from unstable F_2 to stable F_1'—as shown by the dynamic arrows.

sans-land equilibria at F_1, F_2, and F_3; and how the addition of land leads to new equilibria points for (k^*, r^*) at F_1' and F_3'; but, perhaps surprisingly, the initial unstable F_2 point is shifted, not to F_2' in its neighborhood, but rather is shifted "catastrophically" all the way to F_1' in an extreme vindication of Keynes's conjecture. How dynamic stability affects the comparative-statics shifts in an r^* as a result of shifts in dd is briefly discussed in a footnote.[17]

Conclusion

What Keynes never successfully demonstrated by liquidity trap analysis —that the existence of private ownership in land serves to keep up the long-run interest rate—has been shown to be plausible in a model of life-cycle saving. However, certain exceptions were shown to require qualification in various complicated, but not impossible, cases. On the other hand, by introducing Hicks-neutral or Harrod-land-augmenting technical change, the analysis provided here for stationary population and zero-golden-rule states could be generalized to Harrodian exponential-growth systems: Keynes's presumption still holds, that existence of capitalizable land rent will help surfeit the life-cycle need for assets to support one's old age, and will thereby tend to keep the profit rate higher than it would otherwise be.[19]

How important is Keynes's point about land? From his portentous rhetoric, one must weigh this question seriously. Smith, Malthus, Ricardo, Wicksell, the Maynard Keynes of the *Economic Consequences of the Peace* (1919), and last week's Club of Rome, have all expected scarcity of land and natural resources to become increasingly important, with a presumed (but not logically inevitable) rising share in national income of pure rent. The historical facts seem, so far, to have been otherwise. The measurements in Denison (1974, pp. 57–59) of the separate sources of growth, the most careful estimates we have, seem to show pure land rent has a trend of declining relative share of NNP, now being less than 5 per cent of the total. Agricultural economists, such as Theodore Schultz and Gale Johnson of the University of Chicago, have stressed the cardinal importance of land-saving technical change, both in history and at the present time. If they are right, Keynes's point will continue to be of only moderate import, representing more a rhetorical flourish on his part than a pithy insight.

Notes

1. See also p. 241 and p. 358 in J. M. Keynes, *The General Theory of Employment, Interest and Money* (London: Macmillan, 1936) where he writes ". . . there have been occasions in history in which the desire to hold land has played the same role in holding up the interest rate at too high a rate which money has played in recent times. . . . As I have mentioned above, there have been times when it was probably the craving for the ownership of land, independently of its yield, which served to keep up the rate of interest."

2. See A. P. Lerner, "The Essential Properties of Interest and Money," *Quarterly Journal of Economics* 66 (1952): 172–193, particularly its penultimate section. Lerner observes, ". . . what is perhaps the most challenging and memorable part of the chapter [the famous Chapter 17 of the *General Theory* on own rates of interest] . . . is the assertion that '. . . land has played the same role in keeping up the interest rate. . . .'" Lerner goes on to argue: "This intriguing speculation seems, however, to fall to the ground. . . [since] there is nothing to stop the value of land from rising . . . as there is in the case of money . . . [and hence no reason] for keeping up the marginal efficiency of land (and, therefore, in equilibrium, the rate of interest)." N. Kaldor, "Keynes' Theory of the Own-Rates of Interest," an essay not published until it appeared as Chapter 2 in his *Essays on Economic Stability and Growth* (London: Gerald Duckworth & Co., Ltd., 1960),

pp. 58–74, arrives at a critique of Keynes similar to that of Lerner. J. Robinson, "Own Rates of Interest," *Economic Journal* 71 (1961): 596–600, accepts Kaldor's criticism of Keynes, on the proviso that landowners display all the properties of the capitalist class. But, she goes on to argue, often landowning gentry have sold out to thrifty capitalists only in order to maintain consumption, acting in this respect like the rentier heirs to businesses who sell those businesses to conglomerates and other promoters of takeovers: thus, the thrift that might have gone to provide the finance for "productive investment" is diverted into offsetting consumption. Her 1961 lines were prophetic of what the pseudonymous Adam Smith wrote about in *Supermoney* (New York: Random House, 1972). The Robinson argument, as stated, is not incompatible with the Marshall classical view that Keynes was attacking: in the sentence on p. 242 that follows my original quotation from Keynes, Keynes wrote: "I differ in this from the older view as expressed by Marshall . . . : '. . . the accumulation of wealth is held in check, and the rate of interest so far sustained, by the preference which the great mass of humanity have for present over deferred gratifications, or, in other words, by their unwillingness to "wait." ' " But, if we suppose that widows and orphans and selling-out gentry have exceptional risk-aversion, they may favor gilt-edge and even "hoarding" and contribute some exacerbation of an effective demand problem in depressed periods of low interest rates, an effect not in Marshall's mind.

3. This is quite apart from any alleged "high liquidity-premiums formerly attaching to the ownership of land and now attaching to money." (Actually, land is not a liquid asset in the sense of offering a narrow spread between bid and asked and a stable, predictable mean of those limits; there is no reason to think it ever was liquid in this sense, except in made-up history. But, in any case, the issue is irrelevant for what follows.) Also, a possible willingness to hold land at lower yields than other assets—for social climbers or arrivers—has no particular relevance to the analysis that follows.

4. As stated, this argument has to be qualified if it is the case that investment in human capital—education and training of slaves, even number of Negro births—is itself pushed further under slavery's profit motive than under emancipation.

5. A less obvious case is one in which we destroy a little land, reducing B to $B - \Delta B$. Is the long-run steady-state interest rate that results a little higher or a little lower? The later analysis will show that the answer is ambiguous, depending inter alia on whether less land raises or lowers land's relative share in current product and what its effects are on labor's relative share and on capital's yield.

6. If the representative man lives forever (or is part of a self-reproducing clan, or plans vividly for his posterity), and if he applies systematic time preference to consumptions of a future date, the optimal solution to his Ramsey saving-consuming problem is to stay forever away from the golden-rule state of maximum per capital consumption. An ethical observer who regards such subjective time discounting as "myopic" will, of course, regard a closer approach to the golden-rule as more optimal: but, no matter what "reswitching" can occur, a move to the highest plateau of permanent consumption from a lower one cannot be feasible without incurring the need to "wait," "abstain," and "do without" something at one time in order to get something later. Much of Nassau Senior will have to go under socialism, but not that part based on irreducible technology.

7. The words "may well" are used here rather than "must" for at least two reasons: (1) It can be shown that laissez-faire can sometimes lead to interest rates

below the golden-rule rate; and then, like increments of public debt in Diamond (1965), more land may then improve the level of capital formation. (2) Multiple equilibria are always possible, and, as soon as one leaves simplest neoclassical capital models (one-sector "leets," etc.), we know that multiple equilibria are particularly likely: so, depending upon the branch that a laissez-faire system happens to end on, a new increment of land may have complex effects upon the displacement of equilibrium. This ambiguity is reduced if the change in land impinges on an equilibrium that is sufficiently near to the golden-rule state.

8. Ramsey (1928), Solow (1956), Meade (1961) are standard references. Ricardo (1817) is often presumed to be assuming that labor and capital must be applied to corn land in a fixed-proportions dose. In that case, which also has some attraction for modern economists like Robinson (1956), Kaldor (1955), and Pasinetti (1962), $F[L, B, K] = \phi[B, \min(L, K/k\dagger)] = L\phi[b, \min(1, k/k\dagger)$, where $k\dagger$ is a particular technical constant denoting the ratio of capital to labor in the fixed dose. If land is superabundant and free, $k\dagger$ is the "capital-output ratio" times "the product produced by one labor working with its requisite amount of capital." See Samuelson [1977] for an interpretation of Adam Smith along these lines. Even in this non-neoclassical case, long-run $r*$ may still be determined—as a unique or a multiple root. (Warning: with land limited and no technical change, and the wage needed for life being finite, we'll deduce that a positive $r*$ will emerge even if net investment and saving is ultimately zero: the $r* = g/s$ tautologies do not apply in this model, becoming at best the indeterminate form $0/0$.

9. Alternatively, suppose that land is limited in supply and useful: but suppose that when B/L is indefinitely small, a real wage can be earned that will support life. Then, we can have $L(t) = R^t$, $K(t) = k*R^t$, and $B/L(t) = b(t) \to 0$ in a golden-age exponential-growth state; however, with rent becoming negligible, Keynes's point evaporates in importance. As still another alternative, we can suppose that exponential technical change takes place to offset land's scarcity; then, provided that $u(c_1, c_2)$ is homothetic, we can still define exponential-growth states.

10. If workers must be paid their wage at the beginning of each period, we have to count advanced wages as capital assets along with B and K. To sidestep this complication I assume the wage is paid post-factum and the same for land rent.

11. Uniqueness of a solution for $k*$ is not assured. To see this, denote by $a_i\{\ \}$, $f_i[\ ], f_{ij}[\ ]$, the partial derivatives of the relevant function with respect to the indicated argument. Then the Jacobian of the difference between the two sides of (12.6) is given by

$$J = a_1\{\ \}(-kf_{22} - bf_{12}) + a_2\{\ \}(f_{22}) - 1 - (bf_{12}/f_2) + (f_{22}f_1b)/(f_2)^2$$

Even though a one-sector leets model cannot involve reswitching or perverse "Wicksell-Swan" effects, J need not be one signed. However, it is easy to show that the smallest $r*$ root must be positive; and it will be unique if various strong restrictions are placed on $u[c_1, c_2]$ and on $f(b, k)$.

In the Ricardo case of fixed-dose of L and K, we replace (12.5c) by $\beta = \partial f[b, \min(1, k/k\dagger)]/\partial b$, and replace (12.5b)'s marginal-productivity condition by $k = k\dagger$. Then (12.6) becomes a single equation for $r*$:

$$a\{f(b, 1] - rk\dagger - b\partial f[b, 1]/\partial b, 1 + r\} = k\dagger + (b\partial f[b, 1]/\partial b)/r.$$

The sign of its relevant Jacobian depends on $-a_1\{\quad\}k\dagger + a_2\{\quad\} + b\beta/r^2$, which can be ambiguous and yield multiple r^*: if however, $a_2\{\quad\}/a_1\{\quad\}$ is sufficiently large, r^* will be a unique positive number.

12. Turgot is discussed in Chapter 4 of Böhm-Bawerk (1884 and 1959). These quotations are taken from pp. 39–40. Turgot's chief relevant work is given as his 1769 *Réflextions sur la formation et la distribution des richesses*, particularly Sec. 57, 58, 59, 61, 63, 68, and 71.

13. Marshall, in a letter to Wicksell—for which see Gardlund (1958, pp. 339–345) —seems to deny that it did; and Marshall may be right even though Wicksell ended not thinking so; in any case, since Marshall is often not at his best when reading sense into safely-dead economists, we can here leave the matter moot. I might add that Turgot's instincts seem to lead him beyond the pieties of the Physiocratic system; periodically he guiltily pays lip service to the overimportance of land.

14. I must write "may" since Schumpeter would neither abandon his theory nor cogently defend it; indeed it was hard to get him to talk on the subject, and perhaps more than mere modesty was involved. In various *Festschrift* and obituary writings on Schumpeter, I have adverted to the problem of infinite land value at a zero interest rate, as in Samuelson (1943, 1951, 1972).

15. All this is not so obvious as to make proof unnecessary. For reversing the argument to remove land from the production function and to put K back into it, we can specify a case in which $r^* = 0$ *is* the long-run root. Thus, let people (or the planning unit for the state) live forever and have zero subjective time preference. Then, as with Ramsey (1928),

$$\text{Max} \sum_0^\infty U[C(t)] \text{ s.t. } C(t) = F[K(t), L_0] + K(t) - K(t+1)$$

leads, from any $K(0)$, provided $\partial F[K^*, L_0]/\partial K = 0$ has a finite K^* root, to $K(t) \to K^*$, $r = F[K, L_0]/\partial K \to r^* = 0$ as $t \to \infty$. So it is permanent land that is needed to assure that a zero or negative root is *never* possible for the laissez-faire market's supply-demand equation.

16. For a three-factor Solow-Meade function, $Lf[K/L, B/L]$, we have a three-dimensional factor-price frontier, $w = \omega[r, \beta]$. However, $\partial\omega[r, \beta]/\partial\beta \equiv 0$ when $f[k, b] = f(k) + \bar{\beta}b$, the singular case where there is a unique (w, r) tradeoff.

17. The Liviatan-Samuelson joint-production technology is defined by $C_{t+1} = F[L_t, K_t; K_{t+1} - K_t]$, with the steady-state relation between the profit rate and the per capita K/L, given by the rate of partial derivatives, $r = -F_2[1, K; 0]/F_3[1, k; 0] = \delta(r)$. With the proper "complementarity," away from $r = 0$, $\delta'(r)$ can change sign shown by dd in Figure 12.3. To avoid ambiguity, let me spell out the (somewhat arbitrary) "dynamics" assumed here. Let $r_t = \partial f(b, k_t)/\partial k$, $\beta_t = \partial f(b, k_t)/\partial b$, $w_t = f(b, k_t) - r_t k_t - \beta_t b$; and denote $a\{w_t, 1 + r_t\} - k_t - (\beta_t b/r_t)$ as $H[k_t]$. Then our posited dynamics adjustment is guided by $k_{t+1} - k_t$, a function of $H(k_t)$, with the property $0 < [k_{t+1} - k_t]/H[k_t] \ll 1$.

Near stable equilibria, F_1 and F_3, aa shift in dd can be expected to raise r^* in the Keynes's manner. How does unstable F_2 get shifted? Toward lower rather than higher r^*? However, as indicated in Samuelson (1971, p. 343, Figure 153) one must avoid such a fallacious interpretation of the *correspondence principle* linking perverse comparative-statical shifts with dynamically unstable fixed points a system that begins precariously at unstable F_2 will be shifted by the slightest jarring of *dd* to the vicinity of F_1 and not to the new intersection near F_2; thus, even in this "unstable" case, a "global correspondence principle" yields concordance between dynamics and comparative statics.

18. Since life-cycle saving can lead to r^* *below* the golden-rule level of the system's natural growth rate, readers of Keynes should realize that what he called a curse could in such cases as these be a blessing!

References

BÖHM-BAWERK, E. VON, *Capital and Interest*, vol. I. (South Holland, Illinois: Libertarian Press, 1959).

CANNAN, E., *A Review of Economic Theory*. (London: P. S. King and Son, Ltd., 1929).

CASS, D., and M. YAARI, "Individual Savings, Aggregate Capital Accumulation and Efficient Growth," In K. Shell, ed., *Essays on the Theory of Optimal Economic Growth*, (Cambridge, Mass.: The MIT Press, 1967), pp. 233–268.

DENISON, E. F., *Accounting for United States Economic Growth, 1929–1969*. (Washington, D.C.: The Brookings Institution, 1974).

DIAMOND, P. A., "National Debt in a Neoclassical Growth Model," *American Economic Review* LV (December 1965): 1126–1150.

FISHER, I., *The Rate of Interest: Its Nature, Determination and Relation to Economic Phenomena*. (New York: Macmillan, 1907).

GARDLUND, T., *The Life of Knut Wicksell*, trans. Nancy Adler. (Stockholm: Almquist and Wicksell, 1958).

KALDOR, N., "Alternative Theories of Distribution," *Review of Economic Studies* 23 (1955): 83–100; reprinted in *Essays on Value and Distribution*, pp. 228–236. (London: Gerald Duckworth and Company, 1960).

KALDOR, N., "Keynes' Theory of the Own-Rates of Interest," 1955; reprinted in *Essays on Value and Distribution*, chapter 2.

KEYNES, J. M., *The Economic Consequences of the Peace*. (London: Macmillan and Company, 1919).

KEYNES, J. M., *The General Theory of Employment, Interest and Money*. (London: Macmillan and Company, 1936).

LERNER, A. P., "The Essential Properties of Interest and Money," *Quarterly Journal of Economics* 66 (1952): 172–193; reprinted in *Essays in Economic Analysis*. (London: Macmillan and Company, 1953).

LIVIATAN, N., and P. A. SAMUELSON, "Notes on Turnpikes: Stable and Unstable." *Journal of Economic Theory* 1, No. 4, (December 1969): 454–475; reprinted in R. C. Merton, ed., *The Collected Scientific Papers of Paul A. Samuelson*, vol. III. (Cambridge, Mass.: MIT Press, 1972), chapter 141.

MEADE, J. E., *A Neoclassical Theory of Economic Growth*. (New York: Oxford University Press, 1961).

MODIGLIANI, F., and R. BRUMBERG, "Utility Analysis and the Consumption

Function: An Interpretation of Cross Section Data." In *Post Keynesian Economics*. (New Brunswick, New Jersey: Rutgers University Press, 1954).

MODIGLIANI, F., and A. ANDO, "The 'Life Cycle' Hypothesis of Saving: Aggregate Implications and Tests," *American Economic Review* 53 (March 1963): 55–84.

MODIGLIANI, F., "The Life Cycle Hypothesis of Saving and Intercountry Differences in the Saving Ratio." In *Induction, Growth and Trade: Essays in Honor of Sir Roy Harrod*, W. A. Eltis, M. F. Scott, and J. N. Wolfe, eds. (Oxford: Clarendon Press, 1970).

MODIGLIANI, F., "The Life Cycle Hypothesis Twenty Years Later." In M. Parkin, ed., *Contemporary Issues in Economics*. (Manchester: University of Manchester Press, 1974).

PASINETTI, L., "Rate of Profit and Income Distribution in Relation to the Rate of Economic Growth," *Review of Economic Studies* 29 (1962): 267–279.

RAMSEY, F. P., "A Mathematical Model of Saving," *Economic Journal* 38 (December 1928): 543–549.

RICARDO, D., *On the Principles of Political Economy and Taxation*. (London: John Murray, 1817, 1819, 1821; Dent and Sons, Ltd, 1912, 1957).

ROBINSON, J., *The Accumulation of Capital*. (Homewood, Illinois: Richard C. Unwin, Inc., 1956).

ROBINSON, J., "Own Rates of Interest," *Economic Journal* 71 (1961): 596–600.

SAMUELSON, P. A., "Dynamics, Statics, and the Stationary States," *Review of Economics and Statistics* XXV, No. 1 (February 1943): 58–68; Essays in Honor of Joseph Schumpeter, reprinted in J. E. Stiglitz, ed., *The Collected Scientific Papers of Paul A. Samuelson*, vol. I, (Cambridge, Mass.: The MIT Press, 1966), chapter 19.

SAMUELSON, P. A., "Schumpeter As A Teacher and Economic Theorist," *Review of Economics and Statistics* XXXIII, No. 2 (May 1951): 98–103; reprinted in J. E. Stiglitz, ed., *The Collected Scientific Papers of Paul A. Samuelson*, vol. II (Cambridge, Mass.: The MIT Press, 1966), chapter 116.

SAMUELSON, P. A., "An Exact Consumption-Loan Model of Interest With or Without the Social Contrivance of Money," *Journal of Political Economy* 66 (1958): 467–482; reprinted in J. E. Stiglitz, ed., *CSP*, vol. I, chapter 21.

SAMUELSON, P. A., "A Turnpike Refutation of the Golden Rule in a Welfare-Maximizing Many-Year Plan." In K. Shell, ed., *Essays on the Theory of Optimal Economic Growth*. (Cambridge, Mass.: The MIT Press, 1967), chapter XIV, pp. 269–280; reprinted in R. C. Merton, ed., *The Collected Scientific Papers of Paul A. Samuelson*, vol. II (Cambridge, Mass.: The MIT Press, 1972), chapter 137.

SAMUELSON, P. A., "The Two-Part Golden Rule Deduced As the Asymptotic Turnpike of Catenary Motions," *Western Economic Journal* VI, No. 2, (March 1968): 85–89; reprinted in R. C. Merton, ed., CSP, vol. III, chapter 138.

SAMUELSON, P. A. "On the Trail of Conventional Beliefs About the Transfer Problem." In J. Bhagwati et al., eds., *Trade, Balance of Payments, and Growth: Papers in International Economics in Honor of Charles P. Kindleberger*. (Amsterdam: North-Holland Publishing Company, 1971), chapter 15, pp. 327–351; reprinted in R. C. Merton, ed., CSP, vol. III, chapter 163.

SAMUELSON, P. A., "Paradoxes of Schumpeter's Zero Interest Rate," *Review of Economics and Statistics* LIII, No, 4, (November, 1972): 391–392; reprinted in H. Nagatani and K. Crowley, eds., *The Collected Scientific Papers of Paul A. Samuelson*, volume IV (Cambridge, Mass.: The MIT Press, 1978), chapter 217.

SAMUELSON, P. A., "The Optimum Growth Rate for Population," *International Economic Review* 16, No. 3, (October 1975a): 531–538; reprinted in H. Nagatani and K. Crowley, eds., *CSP* IV, chapter 221.

SAMUELSON, P. A., "Optimum Social Security in a Life Cycle Growth Model," *International Economic Review* 16, No. 3, (October 1975b): 539–544; reprinted in H. Nagatani and K. Crowley, eds., *CSP* IV, chapter 220.

SAMUELSON, P. A., "A Modern Theorist's Vindication of Adam Smith," *The American Economic Review* 67, No. 1, (February 1977): 42–49.

SCHUMPETER, J. A. *Theorie der wirschaftlichen Entwicklung.* Munich: Duncker and Humblot; English trans. R. Opie. *The Theory of Economic Development.* (Cambridge, Mass.: Harvard University Press, 1961).

SMITH, A. (G. J. W. Goodman), *Supermoney.* (New York: Random House, 1972).

SOLOW, R. M., "A Contribution to the Theory of Economic Growth," *Quarterly Journal* LXX, (February 1936): 65–94.

TOBIN, J. "Life Cycle Saving and Balanced Growth." In W. Fellner et al., eds., *Ten Economic Studies in the Tradition of Irving Fisher*, (New York: John Wiley and Sons, Inc., 1967), chapter 9, pp. 231–256.

TURGOT, A. R. J., *Reflections on the Formation and the Distribution of Riches.* (New York: A. M. Kelley, 1963).

Chapter 13

Hans W. Singer

Environmental Factors in Project Analysis: A Conceptual Note

A realization of the problems involved gains from some historical perspective. In classical economics, the predominant strands of thought were an emphasis on resource limitation and a derived emphasis either on appropriate policies or acceptance of zero growth. This is clear in the cases of Malthus, Ricardo, Jevons (*The Coal Question*), and John Stuart Mill. However, with John Stuart Mill and John Maynard Keynes, the forecast of a stationary state for advanced economies shifts the projection of zero growth away from the natural environment to the social environment. In the case of Keynes, the main emphasis is on the interaction of a falling marginal efficiency of capital with liquidity preference. The concept of the stationary state in the thought of John Stuart Mill and Keynes is not a gloomy one as it is with Malthus and Ricardo but a positive concept: the stationary state goes hand in hand with an emphasis on the arts, leisure, and a general raising of the quality of life. These clearly are forerunners of some of the current environmentalists. What all these thinkers have in common is a discussion of the environmental factors in terms of macrostrategy or macroprospects rather than in terms of individual projects. The projects are determined by the macropicture rather than the other way round.

This offering to Abba Lerner deals with a subject in which he has shown interest and, as always, has made his distinctive contribution: "Environment—Externalising the Internalities?" *American Economic Review* 67 (March 1977): 176–179. His discussion there with Jerome Stein goes back to an earlier discussion of the same subject, also in the *American Economic Review* (September 1971). My own contribution probably goes more under the conventional heading of "Internalizing the Externalities," but I hope Abba will accept it, all the same, as an extension of the discussion in which he has been engaged.

It was only after having written this contribution that I came across the chapter on the same subject by E. J. Mishan (who is also a contributor to this volume) in the new edition of his book, *Cost-Benefit Analysis* [New York: Praeger, 1976]. There is some overlapping of ideas, but this is not surprising.

It is in turning to Alfred Marshall and his pupil Pigou that we get an emphasis on individual projects and other microelements. Marshall gives great attention to the environmental impact of the actions of individuals and individual firms, even though he does not use the particular term. Pigou further developed and refined this analysis. The economic box into which the environmental impact of individual projects or activities was placed by Marshall was the concept of externalities. There are three major points of interest to note.

1. Marshall's discussion seems conducted mainly in terms of external economies, that is, favorable external (environmental) impacts. Although formally and conceptually this does not matter since the argument can easily be reversed for external diseconomies, or unfavorable impacts, it is nevertheless of some significance. It fits into the picture of an expanding world in which, through interlocking and the development of social infrastructure, expansion feeds upon itself and can be continued for a very long time, if not indefinitely. Since the current discussion of environmental impact is conducted almost exclusively in terms of diseconomies or unfavorable impacts, Marshall's main paradigm of a falling social cost curve as industries expand can serve as a useful reminder that there are many productive activities with a favorable impact on the environment. This applies most generally to activities that help to reduce the pollution of poverty. Second, many agricultural activities such as tree planting, terracing, and training, can be said to improve the environment, natural and social.

A third category of external economies would be activities undertaken specifically to correct an initial unfavorable impact, such as environment protection works or pollution control resulting in additional expenditures. In some sense, it is still true that part of the answer to environmental damage could be not zero growth or less production but more production, although differently composed. This is, of course, less true of environmental diseconomies arising from the depletion of resources as distinct from pollution or noise; but even in the case of depleted resources, different technologies, quite possibly resulting in higher GNP, may be the appropriate answer. It is notable that in the United States, for example, the need for environmental protection has given stimulus to a number of technological innovations rasing the GNP.[1]

Fourth, as Michael Lipton has reminded us, the shift of fertilizer production and application to the developing countries would at the same time increase overall agricultural production (since the output-to-fertilizer ratio is much higher in the developing countries than in the fertilizer-saturated richer countries) and reduce pollution (since the pollution threshold is further away in the developing countries).[2] Here again we have an association of increased output with less pollution (external economies).

2. Marshall deals predominantly with individual projects—the actions of private firms and individuals—that have an unintended and perhaps unknown external impact on others, and his general remedy is public action designed to internalize such external impact. Since Marshall in the neoclassical tradition is mainly concerned with a Pareto optimum in a freely competitive equilibrium situation, the main tools for such public action would be market-conforming measures such as education (to make the polluter aware of the impact insofar as this would affect his action), taxes and other forms of levies on the output or marginal output of the polluter, the establishment of a proper legal framework to make the polluter liable to compensation payments for his own action, subsidies to the producer for not producing polluting output, and so forth. All these measures would move the economy closer to the Pareto optimum within a framework of perfect competition. However, public action outside the framework of the Pareto optimum—for example, the establishment of binding noise or pollution standards, regulation, prohibition, and also the establishment of an overall strategy that rules out certain types of projects altogether before they can even be appraised—would not fit well into the conceptual picture of project analysis in the neoclassical framework.

Another remedy that would be ruled out by the neoclassical framework is to internalize, through mergers, externalities such as adverse environmental impact. If the polluting firm upstream a river merges with the pollution-suffering firm farther downstream, the damage to the latter would be added to the combined cost curve, and therefore output would return to its optimum level. But on the other hand, the merger remedy may be conceptually incompatible with a Pareto optimum within a perfectly competitive model.[3]

The point to emphasize here is that in this conceptual framework, the projects analyzed are assumed to be in the private sector, with the state or government appearing in the role of the wise adjudicator who corrects the actions of individuals, keeps the ring, and sees that the rules of the Pareto game are observed, thus moving the economy nearer to its Pareto optimum.[4] This is in sharp contrast to the conceptual framework of current environmental discussion in which we seem to be mainly concerned with the impact of very large public sector projects (the building of airports, nuclear power stations, big dams, or irrigation projects) or with the action of very large private firms subject to public direction and regulation. In other words, we think of the state or public sector no longer as the adjudicator but as the main actor, and we treat it no longer as essentially wise and representing the public good. Instead we are very worried about the apparent difficulty and inability of the state, in the light of difficulties of administration and coordination and of conflicting political and vested interests, to take environmental factors properly into account.[5]

This shift in the role of the government and public sector reflects the move from an essentially private enterprise economy to a mixed and publicly regulated economy; but it is somewhat ironic that it should be accompanied by a change in the perceived role of the government from an intervening angel to that of a devil.

3. The analysis developed by Marshall and Pigou in the neoclassical framework conceived of the external (in our case, environmental) impact as essentially that of a single, separate, and quantitatively measurable impact. It would be either pollution, or noise, or bad air, or some other factor. By contrast we are now much more aware of the interlocking and cumulative nature of environmental damage. We think in terms of a balance of nature, which, when endangered, results in vicious circles of deterioration with cumulative effects over time. The best example is the interrelation of land fertility, forest cover, climate, water, and erosion. In addition to the impact's being confined to a single factor, the concept underlying neoclassical externalitics analysis and principles of project appraisal derived from it is that the impact is measurable. The obvious case of this is where the impact enters the market system itself—once again, where the action of a polluting firm upstream reduces the output of or imposes additional cost on another firm downstream.

Today, by contrast, we picture the external impact as essentially outside the market system. One reason is that, being aware of the interlocking and cumulative nature of environmental damage, we think of the impact on future generations yet unborn who cannot make their claims felt within the present market system.[6]

The neoclassical tradition would lead us to try to quantify the impact as much as possible, and this is certainly useful for any kind of project appraisal, even where the ultimate decision is political. For instance the neoclassical remedy would be that if people suffer from pollution, noise, or bad air, we could interview them and try to determine what kind of money payments would induce them to accept the problem. But here we are up against another problem, quite apart from the administrative difficulties and costs of organizing such interviews on a large scale. The interview tool clearly assumes that people are aware of the damage they suffer and that they are able to visualize what money payments would put them back into the prepollution optimum. Both assumptions are obviously unrealistic. What if people have suffered permanent brain damage as the result of noise and pollution, which makes them incapable of answering the questions asked by the interviewer? Moreover will it not be a natural tendency for people, when asked what money payments they would accept, to ask for a much higher figure than the sum that restores them to the previous situation, seeing a chance of a profitable transaction? No doubt there are neoclassical answers to some of these questions, but they will be only to indicate that you move out of the Marshallian Pareto world the moment you assume that the external impact is not directly measured within the current market system.

It is worth reflecting on the main reasons why our present concern with the environmental impact of projects differs so sharply from the Marshallian approach. Most obviously we are more concerned about environmental impacts because, since the days of Marshall, economic output and activity have multiplied many times over, and we now have a sense of approaching limits that was not present in Marshall's day. The problem of resource depletion, which the classical predecessors of Marshall and Jevons had much more clearly in mind than Marshall himself, has reasserted itself in our consciousness. We think of an environmental impact as typically adverse rather than beneficial, and, moreover, we think of environmental impact of any kind as the rule rather than the exception.

Related to the great increase in production, and as a main cause of it, we are now conscious of the tremendous impact of science and technology. Insofar as Marshall took this into acount, he conceived it as an almost entirely beneficial force. We, on the contrary, have realized that science and technology, if let loose without social or political controls, can also have tremendously destructive and dangerous consequences.

As a result of increasing wealth in the industrial countries, the priority given to environmental factors as against the production of goods has sharply increased, entirely in line with the predictions of John Stuart Mill and John Maynard Keynes when developing their benevolent version of the stationary state.

At the same time, we have also become much better informed and educated about environmental impacts. This incidentally illustrates one of the more beneficial impacts of the development of science in making us aware and better informed about environmental problems and of technology in giving us the potential means of controlling and correcting environmental impacts.

We no longer have the simple faith in the competitive equilibrium where all the units concerned have more or less equal size and equal political power and where, as a result, the sufferers from adverse impact have the same chance of making their interest felt as those causing the impact. We now think of those causing the impact as much more powerful and capable of inflicting damage on the community (big public projects and big transnational enterprises, for example), whereas the suffering community is too scattered and not sufficiently aware of its interests and able to identify the sources of the damage to make its countervailing views felt (as presupposed in the neoclassical analysis).

We are aware now that the environmental impact of projects has both international and intergenerational aspects. The international aspect means that the problem can no longer be dealt with by national adjustments under the aegis of a governmental adjudicator, at least not in the absence of world government. The intergenerational aspect means that the orthodox type of project analysis breaks down. One of the main instruments of orthodox project analysis is the social discount rate by means of which present net benefits and net costs are calculated and compared. However with the usual discount rate of 10 percent per annum or so, the costs (as well as the benefits) occurring after the lapse of a generation virtually disappear from the horizon. This in practice would be true even if the discount rate were much lower, in fact with any conceivable discount rate. Hence the concern about future generations should lead us away from treating environmental costs in the framework of ordinary project analysis. Rather it requires a strategy under which intergenerational concern is expressed through the exclusion of projects that have clearly harmful long-term effects of sufficient impact even before ordinary project analysis is applied.

We think of the environmental impacts as cumulative and mutually interacting. This makes the impact both more formidable and less easy to quantify.

Perhaps paradoxically, together with our increased knowledge and information about environmental factors, we also have a heightened realization of how much we do not know about environmental factors. This has given us a sense of incalculable and fearful risks and uncertainty, and in view of the incalculable risks, it seems to us safer to be pessimistic rather than run such risks. On the other hand, the incalculable nature of the risks creates the institutional danger of neglecting them. Both of these trends are currently clear in the case of nuclear technology.

Apart from the incalculable nature of the risks, we are also now thinking in different terms about the factor to which the risk applies. We no longer think of the risk simply in terms of discomfort, or possible bad health, or possible falls in production suffered as a result of environmental externalities. Rather we now feel that the risk may apply to the survival of the human race itself (this risk, of course, is attributable not only to the environmental impact of our activities but also to the arms race and the existence of nuclear weapons, another emanation of uncontrolled science and technology). The fact that the risk is seen to apply to survival itself removes it altogether from the realm of orthodox project analysis based on neoclassical externalities and instead moves it to the field of strategic policy formulation.

Finally one can add the redefinition of the objectives of economic growth and development, frequently now described as the "dethronement of GNP." While in the developing countries the objective is now defined as the elimination of poverty, in the industrial countries the redefinition is more in terms of creating the conditions for a good life. It is clear that such a reorientation of concepts directs our attention much more directly to environmental factors than the increase in GNP, even given all the Marshallian welfare corrections. In the Keynesian system, the increase in GNP was compatible with environmental priorities for two reasons: because it was linked with the reduction of poverty, caused by depression and unemployment (in the Britain of the 1930s there was still plenty of the "pollution of poverty") and because the increase in production would finally result in a stationary state.

Attention has also gradually shifted, as far as tools or instruments of correction for environmental externalities are concerned, from market instruments such as taxes and subsidies (the natural instrument in the neoclassical paradigm designed to maintain Pareto optimum) toward control and regulation (designed to establish acceptable tolerance levels for noise, pollution, and so forth in the absence of market forces capable of expressing a quantitative demand), and then further toward prohibitions, and finally to overall development and planning strategies in which the protection of the environment enters through the front door as a major objective instead of through the back door as a subsequent correction.

Another complication of which we have become increasingly aware is that there is not only a natural environment but also a social environment, and these two interact again in many ways that are often difficult to quantify or to predict. An obvious example is the equality or inequality of income distribution as an important element in the social environment.

It has become a commonplace to observe that people's standard of living is determined not only by their absolute income level but also by their place in the income scale relative to others (concept of "relative poverty"). Environmental control is bound to affect income distribution in one way or another, and the different instruments of environmental control will affect income distribution in different ways. Even limiting ourselves to the neoclassical kit, while conceptually there may be no difference between a tax on polluting output and a subsidy (or negative tax) for not produc- ing pollution, it will obviously make a considerable difference in terms of income distribution and final incidence of the burden of environmental control. It is not easy to generalize about the relationship of environ- mental controls and income distribution. On the one hand, if the priority for environmental protection is an increasing function of affluence, then environmental protection would benefit the rich more than the poor. On the other hand, the rich have better ways of avoiding the environmental impact, for example, to avoid air pollution, they can move to healthier suburbs or install expensive air-conditioning or air-purifying equipment in their houses. Similarly if the cost of environmental control falls on the government budget and has to be financed from taxes, a good deal depends on whether the tax system is progressive or regressive. Furthermore there may be a difference in this respect between the tax system in general and the additional or marginal taxation required to carry the cost of environ- mental control. If the environmental control consists of shifting the loca- tion of industries from congested areas to relatively undeveloped ones, the income of the congested areas will decline—along with their pollution —while the income of the areas to which location has been shifted will increase—but at the price of bringing them nearer to the threshold of pollution. The previous income level in the congested area may be initial- ly lower or higher than in the undeveloped area. But there are enormous obstacles in the way of measuring the effect on income distribution, even approximately. This problem has attracted much attention in the case of shifts from congested industrial countries to nonindustrialized develop- ing countries where, with proper safeguards, the effect on international income distribution can be presumed to be favorable, but the same prob- lem also exists for shifts of location within the same country.[7]

In the light of these increasing complications and in the light of the move from the correction of externalities toward environmentally con- scious development strategies, a new tool that is required is something in the nature of a refined and extended input-output matrix for the econ- omy as a whole with special emphasis on activities that threaten the environment. This thought seems to have occurred to various analysts recently, and the attempt has been made to develop a materials balance for the national economies—or even the world—as a whole. The existence of such information, combined with the technique of computer analysis, might enable us to cope with the complications discussed above. At least it seems that much of the need of future research lies in such directions.

Notes

1. See "US Informal Study Shows Less Smoke More Jobs," *Development Forum* (January–February 1977): 3.

2. Michael Lipton, *Why Poor People Stay Poor* (London: Temple Smith; Cambridge, Mass.: Harvard University Press, 1977).

3. If the merging firms are both very small and in different branches of production, perhaps the merger could still be accomodated within the perfect competitive framework.

4. This benevolent role attributed to the state would be modified by considerations of the cost of collecting taxes, administrative inefficiencies, or the possibility of unwise public action under the pressure of political interest. Ultraliberals (but not Marshall or Pigou) would attach great weight to such factors in their conceptual framework.

5. See "Planners Asked to Care for Environment," summary of a report by the Department of the Environment in *London Times*, February 12, 1977, p. 2: "Planners should pay more attention to the effects of big schemes on the environment. . . . Bad decisions sometimes led to large compensation payments having to be made from public funds.

"The report accused planning authorities of failing to examine proposals for large-scale development in sufficient depth. Important environmental questions were too often given an examination that was superficial, belated, hasty or nonexistent. . . .

"The report said that studies of the environmental impact of the steelworks were carried out only after the project's first phase had been approved. If the project now had to be halted, a great deal of abortive work would have been done."

6. Unless, of course, we assume that the present generation feels fully responsible for their unborn children and grandchildren and represents their claims in the same way as they themselves would. But this is a far-fetched assumption.

7. See Founex Report, *Environment and Development* (Paris: Mouton, 1972).

Chapter 14

Jan Tinbergen

Changing Factor Shares and the Translog Production Function

Changing Factor Shares: Some Estimates

Numerous estimates by various authors have shown that over long intervals (varying between a century and a few decades), the shares in national income obtained by various production factors—capital as well as various types of labor—are shifting. Table 14.1 shows some estimates of the share of income from assets (or capital income or unearned income) for six countries. In most cases over the fairly long periods considered, there has been a clear downward shift. Table 14.2 shows income shares of various types of labor; for Denmark and the Netherlands, incomes include income from capital; for the United States, incomes are earnings. For all three countries, income shares of independents are shown. In the two small European countries, independents are heads of establishments as defined in the continental censuses of production. For the United States three shares have been calculated: those of main occupational group A (professionals, technicians), main occupational group B (managers, administrators), and the sum of the two. The American shares show an increase (although small for group B), whereas in the two small European countries, the shares considered clearly fell over the last few decades. For the United States the two groups selected may be called the intellectual and the leadership elites. The choice has been influenced by my rather successful attempt to explain income of thirty-one occupational groups, characterized by various levels of education performance and by three levels of independence in decision making required by their occupational group. The regression equation obtained is

I want to thank Professor W. H. Somermeyer for a number of comments he made on a previous draft of this paper. Remaining errors are, of course, mine. Among them perhaps is my use of the translog production function. My defense is that, within certain intervals of its parameters, it constitutes an easily manageable approximation admitting changes in income shares.

Table 14.1 Percentage share of capital income in national income and capital per capita around 1954

	Germany	France	United Kingdom	Sweden	Netherlands	United States
Shares	1895 34.5 1913 31.5 1925–1929 16.5 1954–1960 25.0	1911 35.0 1954–1960 17.5	1864–1865 43.5 1954–1960 23.5 1910–1914 36.0 1960–1963 18.1	1950 13.3 1972 4.2	1913 24.1 1930 25.5 1968 15.9	1903–1904 27.5 1954–1960 20.5 1929 36.1 (gross) 21.4 (net) 1969 31.7 (gross) 15.9 (net)
Capital per capita around 1954	1.72	3.10	1.69	4.93	2.00	6.21

Sources: S. Kuznets, *Modern Economic Growth* (New Haven, 1966), p. 168; C. H. Feinstein, *National Income and Expenditure, 1870–1963* (Department of Applied Economics, University of Cambridge, 1964); A. Lindbeck, "Inequality and Redistribution Policy Issues (Principles and Swedish Experience)," in *OECD: Education, Inequality and Life Chances* (Paris, 1975), 2:229; J. Tinbergen, The figures for 1930 and 1968 of 33 and 21 percent respectively, for "income from capital and profits of unincorporated enterprises" shown in official statistics have been reduced by 7.5 and 5.1 percent respectively, to correct for labor income of the heads of these enterprises. Official figures are those of Central Bureau of Statistics (CBS). The 1913 figure has been derived from CBS: *Berekeningen over het nationaal inkomen van Nederland voor de periode 1900–1920* [Calculations of the national income of the Netherlands, 1900–1920] (The Hague, 1941); L. R. Christensen and D. W. Jorgensen, "U.S. Income, Savings and Wealth, 1929–1969," *Review of Income and Wealth* 19(1973):329; R. Goldsmith and C. Saunders, *The Measurement of National Wealth, Income and Wealth*, Series VIII (London, 1959).

Table 14.2 Percentage share in national income of some types of labor

	Types of Labor	Share	Source
Denmark			
1950	Independents	0.487	Bjerke c.s.
1974	Independents	0.280	Bjerke c.s.
Netherlands			
1930	Independents	0.33	Central Bureau
1963	Independents	0.21	of Statistics[a]
1930	University trained	0.051 ⎫	Tinbergen,
1962	University trained	0.064 ⎬	Bedrijfstellingen CBS
		⎭	(Censuses of Production)
United States[b]			
1949	A[c]	0.1136	Census 1950[e]
1949	B[d]	0.1693	Census 1950
1949	Groups A and B	0.2829	Census 1950
1969	A	0.2083	Census 1970
1969	B	0.1720	Census 1970
1969	A and B	0.3803	Census 1970

Sources: Kj. Bjerke and K. E. Vangskjaer, *Udviklingen i restindkomsten i perioden 1949–1965* [The development of residual income 1949–1965], complemented by figures obtained by courtesy of the authors; J. Tinbergen, *Income Distribution: Analysis and Policies* (Amsterdam, 1975), pp. 100–103.

a. Capital and unincorporated enterprises included.
b. Shares are shares of earnings in total earnings of male, white, nonfarm workers, 25–64 years of age, in experienced labor force.
c. Professionals, and technicians.
d. Managers and administrators.
e. Money incomes times ratio between earnings and money incomes for 1959; from 1960 census.

$$e = 1.531\,l - 0.643s + 0.0591s^2 + \text{const}, \tag{14.1}$$

where e: earnings in 1969, in \$1,000, white males, age 35–54

  l: level of independent decision making required ($l = 2$ for groups A and B, $l = 1$ for C, D, and E and $l = 0$ for groups F, G, H, and J)

  s: years of schooling, assumed to be ≥ 8

shows an $R^2 = 0.918$; $r_{el} = 0.618$; $r_{es} = 0.769$; and $r_{ls} = 0.25$.

This suggests that as a crude first approximation of the earnings structure (apart from race, age, sex, and a few other factors), it makes sense to distinguish the two elites just defined.

Table 14.2 shows an interesting difference between the European and the American figures: reduction of the share of independents in the two European countries, as against a rise of the share of both elites in the

United States; for group B, however, the rise is insignificant. For the top executives reported on by Burck (1976), earnings expressed in 1952 dollars did not change much between 1952 and 1976 (actually fell by 3 percent), whereas nonfarm wages in 1952 prices went up 39 percent. Our figures refer to all managers and administrators; their median earnings rose between 1949 and 1969 (in current prices) to about 285 percent as against a rise to 252 percent by the nonelite groups. (I am considering all managers and administrators as a homogeneous group. This is admittedly a crude classification of labor.)

Table 14.3 shows ratios in numbers belonging to the groups or types of labor defined. The denominator of the ratios shown here is not the total of both groups but the number of the other group. Hence the relative changes in income or in earnings per capita cannot be obtained simply by the division of the shares of table 14.2 through the corresponding ratios of table 14.3. A somewhat more complicated formula would be necessary. The ratio of independents of group B to the rest of the active (male, white) population has also fallen in the United States but much less than in Denmark and the Netherlands. The main conclusion to draw from tables 14.1 and 14.2 is that the various factor shares have changed considerably. This implies that an explanation of factor shares' behavior cannot be

Table 14.3 Quantity ratios of two types of labor

	Types of Labor	Ratio
Denmark		
1950	Independents/Dependents	0.3085
1974	Independents/Dependents	0.1679
Netherlands		
1930	Independents/Dependents	0.3120
1963	Independents/Dependents	0.1539
1930	University trained/Nonuniversity trained	0.0061
1962	University trained/Nonuniversity trained	0.0142
United States[a]		
1949[b]	A and B/C through J	0.2078
1949[b]	A/B through J	0.0768
1949[b]	B/A, C through J	0.1433
1969[b]	A and B/C through J	0.3854
1969[b]	A/B through J	0.1805
1969[b]	B/A, C through J	0.1121

Note: The definitions and sources cited in table 14.2 apply here also.

a. For meaning of letters, cf. definition of symbol l in equation (13.1).

b. Persons with income (white male, experienced labor force, 25–64 years old).

undertaken on the basis of Cobb-Douglas production functions with constant coefficients.

The Translog Production Function

The facts shown in tables 14.1 and 14.2 have been known for some decades now and have given rise to the CES production function (Arrow, Chenery, Minhas, and Solow 1961). Other alternatives have also been offered and checked. My purpose here is to apply the transcendental logarithmic (or translog) production function to the material in the simplest way conceivable. The translog production function has been introduced by Christensen, Jorgensen, and Lau (1973) and further analyzed and tested in a series of articles by Berndt and Christensen (1973a, 1973b, 1973c, 1974). I owe a great deal to their exhaustive analysis and their interesting applications to American manufacturing time series covering periods from 1929 to 1968. Twice (1973b, 1974) they considered three factors and once four (1973c). In the last study they split up both labor (into blue and white collar) and capital (into structures and equipment); in the 1973b study, labor constituted one factor and in the 1974 study capital. In all cases they used second-degree additive functions expressing the logs of production in terms of the logs of production factors; I do the same here. Using αs as the coefficients of the linear ("Cobb Douglas") and γs in the quadratic terms, one can show, as they do, that the γs are independent of units used (pure numbers) but the αs are not. While in the choice of the quadratic translog production function I follow the authors and greatly profit of their analyses, this study deviates from theirs in the following aspects:

1. Figures for the whole economy are used.
2. I do not apply regression analysis but simple algebra applied on a number of observations equal to the number of unknown parameters.
3. I do not add other demand or supply factors.
4. I restrict myself to the simplest conceivable choice of the number of coefficients, based only on the assumption of linear homogeneity (that is, no returns to scale).

My reasons for these simplistic choices follow. First it is interesting to have an impression of where our economies as a whole are heading for. Fourastié (1965) expected developed economies to move into services rather than manufacturing as their main sector. Second, I am interested in trend movements, and a trend series hardly contains more information than that given by the final observations (those at the beginning and those at the end). This looks like an inversion of my position defended against Keynes (Keynes 1939, 1940; Tinbergen 1940), but it is not. Between 1919 and 1932 there was an enormous cyclical component, but in most of the present material we can disregard this component. Third, it seems to be superfluous to add other demand factors to equations explaining the shares of total product. The parameters α and γ of the production function are already demand factors. Other demand factors such as possibly total demand is irrelevant for the shares in a linear homogeneous production process: larger total demand only means a repetition of the same process proportionally to that demand. This seems to be in contradiction to my insisting (Tinbergen 1975) on having demand factors added on discussing Bowles's (1969) and Psacharopoulos's and Hinchliffe's (1972) cross-section estimates of the elasticities of substitution between various types of labor. The reason why I insisted is that production functions for different geographical units need not have identical coefficients, if their industrial structures differ. And finally I feel justified to make the assumption of linear homogeneity because the overwhelming part of an economy is in sectors with an optimum-size plant unit far smaller than total demand in that sector. Many large enterprises, moreover, in fact are federations of a number of small units. I have also chosen on purpose the simplest translog production function since this study is meant to be a first reconnaissance of how shifts in shares can occur. Thus in my analysis with two factors, I need only one γ:

$$ln\ Y = (1 - \alpha)\ lnL_1 + \alpha lnL_2 + \tfrac{1}{2}\ \gamma ln^2(L_1/L_2), \tag{14.2}$$

where Y is national product and L_1 and L_2 are the quantities of production factors 1 and 2, respectively. From it I derive the share λ_2 of factor 2 by the following operation:

$$\lambda_2 = \frac{\partial ln\ Y}{\partial ln\ L_2} = \alpha + \gamma(lnL_2 - lnL_1) = \alpha + \gamma\ ln\frac{L_2}{L_1} = \alpha + \gamma lnL'. \tag{14.3}$$

Here L' stands for the quantity ratio of factor 2 to factor 1. In order to estimate α and γ, we need two observations of λ_2 and of L'. (In later sections F will apply this procedure to the factors labor and capital, to what I have called the academic elite and other labor in the United States, and to independent and dependent labour—the leadership elite and other labor—in Denmark, the Netherlands, and the United States.)

Similarly for the case of three production factors, I want to arrive at the simplest possible translog production function with three production factors. This is possible with the aid of two coefficients only, to be indicated by β and γ (apart from the linear terms) in a production function:

$$ln\,Y = \alpha_1 ln L_1 + \alpha_2 ln L_2 + (1 - \alpha_1 - \alpha_2)\,ln L_3$$
$$- \tfrac{1}{2}\gamma\{\beta ln L_1 + (1 - \beta)\,ln L_2 - ln L_3\}^2, \tag{14.4}$$

which can also be written as:

$$ln\,(Y/L_3) = \alpha_1 ln\,(L_1/L_3) + \alpha_2 ln(L_2/L_3)$$
$$- \tfrac{1}{2}\gamma ln^2\{(L_1/L_3)^\beta\,(L_2/L_3)^{1-\beta}\}. \tag{14.5}$$

In this expression β and $1 - \beta$ can be considered as the relative weights of the ratios of each of the two elites to the majority of workers L_3 in the term making for shifts in shares, whereas γ is decisive for the intensity of the shifting. Following Berndt and Christensen in their econometric set-up, the share equations, similar to (14.3), will now run:

$$\lambda_1 = \alpha_1 - \gamma\beta^2 ln L_1 - \gamma\beta\,(1 - \beta)\,ln L_2 + \gamma\beta ln L_3. \tag{14.6}$$

$$\lambda_2 = \alpha_2 - \gamma\beta(1 - \beta)\,ln L_1 - \gamma(1 - \beta)^2\,ln L_2 + \gamma(1 - \beta)\,ln L_3. \tag{14.7}$$

Since the unknown are four (α_1, α_2, γ, and β) we only need four observations for the application of the "trend reconnaissance" method, implying that we again need observations for two terminal years, on the shares and the L_i ($i = 1, 2, 3$).

Alongside the coefficients of the quadratic terms, the substitution elasticities between the factors considered will be calculated. On the basis of the general formula given by Allen (1938),

$$\sigma_{ij} = |G_{ij}|\,/\,|G|, \tag{14.8}$$

the only (Allen) substitution elasticity for the two-factor case is

$$\sigma_{12} = \frac{-\lambda_2^2 + \lambda_2}{-\lambda_2^2 + \lambda_2 - \gamma}. \tag{14.9}$$

The calculations, on the basis of (14.8), of the various substitution elasticities in the three-factor case are shown only numerically.

The main purpose of this study is to arrive at estimates of the changes in numbers needed in order to attain given reductions in income ratios w. For the two-factor cases, the general formula for relative demand L' as a function of relative factor prices w can be written:

$$w = \frac{1}{L}\,\frac{\alpha + \lambda ln L'}{1 - \alpha - \lambda ln L'}. \tag{14.10}$$

For the three-factor case, the numerical equivalents of (14.6) and (14.7) will be used to obtain some numerical results of a comparable character.

A somewhat fuller discussion of the meaning of production functions seems necessary. To begin with, it should be kept in mind that any production function, and more particularly a macroproduction function, reflects a number of elements. It reflects technology first of all, including changes in technology, and also the changing organization of production.

In this reconnaissance, two aspects of production come to the fore: the level of capital intensity K/L and the average size of production units measured by the size of their personnel. The latter is developing not only because of increases in knowledge but also changes in preferences of the labor force, which has gradually become more educated. Production functions also reflect variations in sector composition, over time as well as among countries, reflecting, in their turn, changes in consumption patterns. The estimation and application to planning of production functions then makes the heroic assumption that the joint effect of the elements summed up shows in constant coefficients.

A first cause for differences in both capital intensity and size of units among the countries and periods studied may be sector composition. Heavy industries, such as steel making, chemicals, and power, require large quantities of capital. This seems to be illustrated by the considerable differences in capital per capita between the countries shown in table 14.1. In addition, over time, countries first industrialize by switching from agriculture to manufacturing and later to relatively more services. The role of human capital becomes more important, and some substitution of physical by human capital can be expected. Among countries, especially small ones, differences in specialization may play a role.

A second cause for differences may be a difference in preferences with regard to the size of production units, possibly also implying differences in capital intensity. Various reasons may exist why in one country or period larger units are chosen than in another —for example organizational ability, working climate, concern for the environment, or for unnecessary megalomania, against which reactions are gaining momentum. Mammoth tankers or aircraft and trucks are beginning to pose their problems of pollution or of putting too heavy responsibilities on the shoulders of the crew. Preferences for large units have been typical for Anglo-Saxon as well as for communist countries, as is shown by the average size of industrial units.

A third reason for differences, mainly in capital intensity, may arise from political preferences, combined with savings behavior. High taxes in general, and on profits in particular, as well as inflationary policies, may reduce net yield on capital investment and lead to low real interest rates. These in turn may evoke various reactions: increased investment by public authorities or reduced growth of private investment together with a willingness to continue saving, as a safeguard against an uncertain future. This state of affairs has some similarity to the theoretical construct of a steady state in which there is no net investment, although investment in new enterprises goes on. This steady state situation may characterize the private sector but need not apply to the public sector also; it then constitutes a slow transition to a less capitalist structure. It may also apply to the economy as a whole and then seems to be close to Lord Kaldor's "premature maturity" (Kaldor 1966).

The first cause for differences in average size of production units, sector composition, may also be illustrated by a cross-section sample among countries as given in table 14.4.

With the aid of these figures a regression equation has been estimated (where dashed symbols represent logarithms):

Table 14.4 Average size of production units (x), percentage of active population in agriculture (y), percentage in services (z) and average size of production units in manufacturing (u), 1965–1970

Country	Year	x	y	z	u
Federal Republic of Germany	1970	8.6	9	52	19.7
Belgium	1969	5.4	5	63	11.5
Denmark	1965	4.4	15	56	11.2
France	1968	3.3	15	58	11.7
Great Britain		14.7	3	62	82.6
Ireland	1966	4.0	31	50	22.0
Italy	1969	3.3	21	49	5.1
Spain	1969	3.3	30	43	6.9
Algeria	1966	3.6	50	44	3.1
Canada	1970	8.6	8	71	45.4
United States	1969	10.7	4	70	81.6
Indonesia	1964–1965	1.1	67	27	1.2
Israel	1969	3.6	10	64	4.9
Japan	1965	4.2	24	52	9.1
Pakistan	1965	1.3	68	22	1.4

Source: *Statistisches Jahrbuch für die Bundesrepublik Deutschland* (Wiesbaden, 1971), pp. 44*, 45*.

$$x' = -10.6 - 0.53y' + 6.91z' - 0.87z'^2, \ R^2 = 0.905,$$
$$\quad\quad\quad (0.19) \quad (6.60) \quad (0.92)$$

and the figures in parentheses are standard deviations of the regression coefficients. Clearly the movement away from agriculture raises the average size of production units. The postindustrial development toward services is less clear because of the unreliability of the coefficients found, but they suggest that after an initial rise in size (for small values of z'), an inverse tendency may show up. This tendency may also be illustrated by the figures for the average size u of manufacturing units: even in the most industrialized countries, this size far surpasses average size of production units x'. Another feature is that of the three countries whose figures on average size of units I will analyze in the next few sections, Denmark shows still a rather large agricultural sector. Finally on the factor markets, the demand side is one of free competition. The supply side need not be competitive. In other words it is assumed that even though wage levels may have been fixed in a process of collective bargaining, individual employers will employ people up to the point where their marginal product equals the wage rate.

Two-Factor Production Functions for Capital and Labor

For the first step, I applied the translog production function in its simplest version in order to study the shift in the share of income from capital for the countries shown in table 14.1. For this application I needed trends in the capital-labor ratio. Figures about this ratio vary a good deal among the sources used and mentioned in table 14.5. In order to check the figures directly bearing on capital per capita, I also used indirect figures derived from the identity

$$K/M = (K/Y) / (Y/M), \tag{14.11}$$

where M stands for manpower, K for capital, and Y for national product (the last two are in constant prices). Since the years or periods for which figures have been estimated by the authors I consulted greatly vary, all figures have been expressed in terms of average annual percentage changes. As much as possible comparable periods have been used for checking the directly by the indirectly obtained estimates. Some of the earlier figures, such as my own about capital stock from 1870 to 1910 (Tinbergen 1959), are admittedly quite primitive. For labor in some cases simply population has been taken if no other figures were shown by the sources consulted.

Table 14.5 Estimates of average annual percentage growth of capital per worker K/L

Sources	Values A[a]	Values B[b]	Remarks on Estimation
Germany			
1853–1912 Gahlen	1.68		Direct
1873–1961 Kuznets (1)	1.36	1.52	{ Kuznets Y/L 1.66% pa
			{ Tinbergen K/Y 0.30% pa
1870–1910 Tinbergen	1.78		
France			
1852–1913 Clark	1.78		Direct
1870–1910 Tinbergen (2)	2.3	1.46	Population instead of labor force growth
1870–1910 Tinbergen (3)	0.3		Nondeflated capital figures
Great Britain			
1865–1933 Clark	0.88		Direct
1857–1958 Kuznets }	0.05	0.465	{ Kuznets Y/L 1.33% pa
1885–1927 Kuznets }			{ Kuznets K/Y 1.28% pa
Netherlands			
1913–1968 Tinbergen (1)	1.01	1.01	Direct
1930–1968 Tinbergen (1)	1.23	1.23	Direct
Sweden			
1896–1919 Clark }	2.24		Clark, direct 0.58% pa
1870–1910 Tinbergen (2) }			Tinbergen, 3.9% pa
1863–1961 Kuznets }			{ Kuznets Y/L: 2.52% pa
1900–1960 Goldsmith }	0.82	1.53	{ Goldsmith K 0.98 } K/Y
1900–1930 Lindahl }			{ Lindahl Y 2.7 } 1.7% pa
United States			
1879–1969 Clark and Christensen and Jorgenson	1.90		1879–1939 Clark 1.67% pa
			1940–1969 Christensen and Jorgenson 2.31% pa
		1.62	Average 1.90% pa
1839–1961 Kuznets }	1.34		Kuznets Y/L 1.80% pa
1850–1950 Kuznets }			Kuznets K/Y −0.26% pa
1929–1969 Christensen and Jorgenson		1.48	Private national wealth per capita % pa

Sources: L. R. Christensen and D. W. Jorgenson, "U.S. Income, Saving, and Wealth, 1929–1969," *Review of Income and Wealth* 19(1973): 329. Colin Clark, *The Conditions of Economic Progress* (London, 1951), p. 486. B. Gahlen, *Die Überprüfung produktionstheoretischer Hypothesen für Deutschland (1850–1913)* (Tübingen, 1968), tables A–1, 3–1. R. W. Goldsmith, *Financial Structure and Development* (New Haven, 1969), p. 294. S. Kuznets, *Modern Economic Growth* (New Haven, 1966), pp. 64, 76. E. Lindahl, E. Dahlgren, and K. Kock, *National Income of Sweden, 1861–1930* (London, 1937). J. Tinbergen: (1) calculations as shown in Table 14.1; (2): *Selected Papers* (Amsterdam, 1959), pp. 182ff; (3) *Economische Bewegingsleer* (Amsterdam, 1942), p. 43 [English version J. J. Polak and J. Tinbergen (Chicago, 1950) p. 37, table 9].

a. Direct estimates or indirect with the aid of growth rates of Y/L, minus those of K/Y, drawn from source indicated.

b. Mostly average of values A for same country.

As much as possible the figures for the average annual percentage growth rates of capital per worker have been estimated for about the same period for which figures on capital income shares were available (cf. table 14.1). A case of a glaring deviation seems to be Sweden, but various figures suggest that Swedish development has been remarkably stable, probably because it was not involved in either of the two world wars.

I followed some of the authors consulted in what could be called a quasi-uniformity in the choice of units by taking K/L equal to unity in 1949. This choice does not affect γ, but it does affect αs.

Table 14.6 summarizes the values obtained for γ. They cannot be very accurate, and their diversity could partly be seen as an illustration. Yet there may be some sense in the differences.

High negative values of γ indicate a tendency to a rapid reduction in capital share in national income. This tendency appears to be strongest in the United Kingdom and weakest in the United States and Germany in the 1950s. It seems to be the third reason mentioned earlier, the political preferences, which may give an explanation here, implying that British policies have been more socialist than American and than post–World War II German policies.

The results obtained enable us also to answer the question at what level of capital intensity K/L the share in national income of income from capital would be halved, assuming that the coefficients of the production functions estimated remain constant. Since the units used are such that for 1949 $K/L = 1$ the capital intensities necessary for halving capital share are intensities as compared with 1949. They are shown in table 14.7.

From these figures a similar conclusion might be drawn: it will take a considerably longer period for the United States and postwar Germany to reduce the share of national income derived from capital ownership than in Great Britain or interwar Germany and in this case Sweden. Such a conclusion about Sweden does not follow from table 14.6 however. Such incompatibilities again illustrate the uncertainties around this reconnaissance.

Two-Factor Production Functions without Capital

The Intellectual Elite versus Other Labor

The diminishing and low (especially for Scandinavia) capital income share makes it interesting to neglect capital as a (scarce) production factor and to consider production functions with labor categories only. One of the labor categories may be endowed with relatively much human (and

Table 14.6 Coefficients α_{10} and γ of simplest translog production function with capital and labor as production factors;

Period[a]	(K/L) 1954	Growth[b] K/L	α_{10}	γ	σ
Germany					
1895–1925/29	1.72	1.52	0.649	−0.373	0.270
1895–1954/60	1.72	1.52	0.428	−0.102	0.648
France					
1911–1954/60	3.10	1.46	0.205	−0.263	0.354
United Kingdom					
1864–65–1954/60	1.69	0.465	0.252	−0.466	0.278
1910/14–1960/63	1.69	0.465	0.226	−0.779	0.160
Netherlands					
1913–1968	2.00	1.01	0.236	−0.149	0.473
1930–1968	2.00	1.23	0.266	−0.207	0.392
Sweden					
1950–1972	4.93	1.53	0.129	−0.250	0.139
United States[c]					
1903/04–1954/60	6.21	1.62	0.215	−0.081	0.668
1903/04–1954/60	6.21	1.48	0.217	−0.089	0.600

Note: α_{10} Based on $\alpha_0 = 0$ and capital per worker $= 1$ in 1949; and corresponding values of Allen elasticity of substitution σ.

a. Period over which capital share in national income has been available (cf. table) 14.1.

b. Percentage growth per annum as shown in table 14.5, values B.

c. Figures based on L. R. Christensen and D. W. Jorgenson, "U.S. Income, Saving, and Wealth, 1929–1969," *Review of Income and Wealth* 19 (1973), gross property compensation share in gross private national income yield $\alpha_{10} = 0.339$ and $\gamma = -0.075$; if gross figures for property compensation as well as gross income are transformed into net figures by deducting from gross figures their depreciation and replacement figures, we obtain $\alpha_{10} = 0.187$ and $\gamma = -0.094$.

Table 14.7 Capital intensities K/L required to reduce to one-half the capital income share ($K/L = 1$ for 1949)

	Growth Rate of K/L	K/L Required
Germany		
1895–1925/29	1.52	1.25
1895–1954/60	1.52	3.40
France		
1911–1954/60	1.46	1.39
United Kingdom		
1864/65–1954/60	0.465	1.29
1910/14–1960/63	0.465	1.12
Netherlands		
1913–1968	1.01	1.70
1930–1968	1.23	1.47
Sweden		
1950–1972	1.53	1.09
United States		
1903/04–1954/60	1.62	3.54
1903/04–1954/60	1.48	3.16

some physical) capital, the other with relatively little. Here I will consider as the human capital group the intellectual elite. In table 14.2 such figures have been shown for the Netherlands, where only fully academically educated manpower constitutes group 2, with all other labor in group 1. Somewhat different figures have been shown for the United States, where the census group A represents group 2.

Table 14.8 shows that in both countries, income shares as well as quantity ratios increased during the periods shown. Table 14.5 accordingly shows positive values for γ. Values of Allen elasticities of substitution have been estimated with the aid of equation (14.9). Whereas the Dutch figure is stable and relatively low, the American figure is highly unstable. Several authors in differing attempts at estimating Allen elasticities of substitution between various types of labor have experienced how unreliable the results so far obtained are, among them Berndt and Christensen (1973, a, b, and c, 1974), Bowles (1969), Dresch (forthcoming), Dougherty (1972), Fallon and Layard (1974), Psacharopoulos and Hinchliffe (1972) and Ullman-Chiswick (1972), discussed in Tinbergen (1975).

Independent versus Dependent Labor
Choosing now the leadership elite, to constitute group 2 the figures for

Table 14.8 Factor share λ_2, quantity ratio L, and coefficients of simplest translog production function α_{10} and γ and Allen elasticity of substitution σ for intellectual elite versus other labor

	Share λ_2	Ratio L'	α_{10}	γ	σ
Netherlands					
1930	0.051	0.0061	0.13	0.0154	1.47
1962	0.064	0.0142			1.35
United States					
1949	0.1136	0.0768	0.398	0.1107	−10.1
1969	0.2083	0.1805			3.4

Denmark, the Netherlands, and the United States, are shown in table 14.9. All the figures for the Netherlands are crude approximations only, those for Denmark have been taken from a very careful study (Bjerke and Vangskjaer 1975), supplemented by data, obtained by courtesy from the Danish authors. The unreliability of the Dutch estimates shows itself in the values for σ. More remarkable, however, are the apparently much stabler, but in several respects opposite, results obtained for Denmark and the United States. The Danish figures clearly indicate a complementary character of the two types of labor,[2] whereas the American figures suggest substitution to be stronger. It should be admitted that group 2 constitutes a very heterogeneous group where small entrepreneurs are numerically by far the most important members. In 1950 the average size of enterprises $1/L'$ was three persons; this increased to about six in 1974. The American group B, managers and administrators, excludes farm managers and-craftsmen, who are included in the Danish "independents." In the United States the average number of employed (including the manager or administrator) decreased from nine to seven. Thus in Denmark concentration prevailed, whereas in the United States deconcentration was relatively stronger. The phenomena involved are both technological and organizational. With a rising service sector, postindustrial development may be one of deconcentration again. Evidently a subdivision of group 2 according to size of production units is called for if the development is to be studied more carefully. Unfortunately such a subdivision is not available in either country, although the Danish study provides a subdivision according to industry. An attempt is now being made to use the recent data of *Fortune* magazine on the five hundred largest American corporations in order to obtain a crude subdivision into levels of leadership and so to obtain a more differentiated model.

Table 14.9 Factor share λ_2, quantity ratio L', and coefficients of simplest translog production function and Allen elasticity of substitution σ for independent versus dependent labor

	Share λ_2	Ratio L'	α	γ	σ
Denmark					
1950	0.487	0.3085	} 0.887	0.340	−2.78
1974	0.280	0.1679			−1.45
Netherlands					
1930	0.33	0.312	} 0.528	0.170	4.33
1963	0.21	0.154			−40.5
United States					
1949	0.169	0.1433	} 0.193	0.011	1.08
1969	0.172	0.1121			1.08

Three-Factor Production Functions without Capital: Intellectual and Leadership Elite and Other Labor, United States, 1949–1969

The last element of reconnaissance will be a three-factor translog production function without capital, where I introduce the two elites, groups A and B, separately and all other labor as factor number 3. Using equations (14.6) and (14.7) for 1950 and 1970 census figures (male, white, experienced labor force, 25–64 years old, with earnings), where the 1949 figures have been transformed into earnings (see the notes to table 14.3), I found the results shown in table 14.10.

Written in the form of equations (14.6) and (14.7), this implies the following for all three shares:

$$\lambda_1 = 0.3748 + 0.1041 \; \ln L_1 + 0.0028 \; \ln L_2 - 0.1069 \; \ln L_3. \tag{14.12}$$

$$\lambda_2 = 0.1764 + 0.0028 \; \ln L_1 + 0.0001 \; \ln L_2 - 0.0029 \; \ln L_3. \tag{14.13}$$

$$\lambda_3 = 0.4488 - 0.1069 \; \ln L_1 - 0.0029 \; \ln L_2 + 0.1098 \; \ln L_3. \tag{14.14}$$

Since $\lambda_i = w_i L_i / (\Sigma w_i L_i)$, these three equations can be considered to be implicit demand equations, expressing L_i in terms of the ratios of the w_i.

Table 14.10 shows that the simplest three-factor model shows a low elasticity of substitution between intellectuals and leaders, a rather high elasticity of substitution between the former and all other labor, comparable to the 1969 figure for the United States in table 14.8 but considerably higher than the Dutch figures in that table. "Leaders" and "other labor" appear to be complementary, which is plausible. With the aid of Allen's formula for the simple demand elasticity and assuming for the elasticity of demand for total national product η alternatively the values 0 and +1,

Table 14.10 Factor shares, numbers, earnings, coefficients of translog production function, and Allen elasticities of substitution for a three-types-of-labor model, United States, 1949–1969

Year	Shares	Numbers (mln)	Earnings ($ 000)	Coeffs. γ		AES σ
1949[a]	$\lambda_1 = 0.1136$	$L_1 = 2.73$	$w_1 = 3.616$	11	0.1041	−11.23
1949[a]	$\lambda_2 = 0.1693$	$L_2 = 3.86$	$w_2 = 3.810$	22	0.0001	−4.82
1949[a]	$\lambda_3 = 0.7171$	$L_3 = 31.71$	$w_3 = 1.965$	33	0.1098	−1.50
1969	$\lambda_1 = 0.2083$	$L_1 = 5.88$	$w_1 = 11.716$	12	0.0028	0.76
1969	$\lambda_2 = 0.1720$	$L_2 = 4.82$	$w_2 = 11.807$	13	−0.1069	3.56
1969	$\lambda_3 = 0.6197$	$L_3 = 27.26$	$w_3 = 7.384$	23	−0.0029	−1.04

Note: 1 = professionals, technicians; 2 = managers, administrators; 3 = all other nonfarm labor. All are male, white, experienced labor force, ages = 15–64, with earnings.

a. Figures are earnings estimated from money incomes on basis of 1960 census ratios between earnings and money incomes.

we find for the simple demand elasticities of the three types of labor that the figures shown in table 14.11.

Demand for and Supply of the Factors Considered

Assuming the validity of the very simple translog production functions established and a behavior of free competition between the organizers of production in the factor markets, I am justified in considering equations (14.3), and (14.6) and (14.7), as demand equations for the factors considered. This does not necessarily apply if I doubt the validity of the production functions. This doubt may be in favor of alternative production functions but also in favor of alternative behavior of the organizers of production: either noncompetitive or expecting changes in production functions for the future (cf. Tinbergen 1975a and 1976). However using the assumptions just enumerated, the numerical results for equations (14.3) or (14.6) and (14.7) do indicate the price ratios that the organizers of production are likely to offer to the types of labor given the quantities supplied. For the latter, we can consider two alternative supply patterns. One may be called either the short-term or the inelastic supply behavior. It implies that all in the possession of the qualities required to take the jobs discussed (in a highly aggregative way, to be sure) actually offer themselves on the factor markets concerned. The other alternative implies

Table 14.11 Simple demand elasticities E for the three types of labor ($E_i = \lambda_i(\sigma_{ii} - \eta)$), United States, 1969

i	$\eta = 0$	$\eta = 1$
1	-2.34	-2.55
2	-0.83	-1.00
3	-0.93	-1.55

Note: For definitions of 1, 2, and 3, see table 14.10.

that the quantities of labor actually taking employment may differ from those who possess the qualities required; a certain proportion of the latter may stay out of the market. For married women one of the most recent inquiries by Rosen (1976) analyzes this well-known phenomenon very carefully. For men between 25 and 64 the former alternative is close to reality, and hence the first alternative is worth being pursued. Table 14.12 shows one possible application. It indicates how many additional persons with the required qualifications would, by entering the labor force, reduce the inequality of incomes to one-half. These estimates may be considered an alternative to a method I applied elsewhere (Tinbergen 1975a), when I described the "race between technological development and the expansion of education." Changing technology is supposed now to be incorporated in the production functions used, contrary to my previous treatment. Table 14.12 refers to the two-labor types approach, that is, on the numerical values for α and γ in equation (14.3). The leadership elite would have to be extended from 13 to 35 percent of the labor force in the Netherlands and from 12.5 to 14 percent (defined in the more restricted way as discussed) in the United States, but it would have to be reduced (that is, concentration be pushed) in Denmark from 14 to 11 percent. The intellectual elite in the Netherlands would have to be doubled (in the restricted definition adhered to for that country) from 1.4 to 2.9 percent and be raised from 15 to 22 percent in the United States. For both elites together, an increase of a similar size would reduce inequality (as measured here) to one-half.

The question must be asked why Denmark (and not the Netherlands and the United States) should reduce the relative number of independents or leaders. The answer might be that Demark has to industrialize somewhat further, whereas the United States and the Netherlands are already in the postindustrial phase.

Another question about the Danish figures is whether equation (14.10), notwithstanding its positive slope, provides the correct answer to my

Table 14.12 Relative earnings for two groups of labor w, and relative numbers L' for last year observed; inequality reduced to half: w values and necessary L' values

Types of labor	Last w	observed L'	Inequality halving w	L'
Denmark				
Independents/Dependents	1974	2.32	0.168	1.66	0.12
			(14.4)		(10.7)
Netherlands				
Independent/Dependents	1963	1.73	0.154	1.365	0.53
			(13.3)		(34.6)
Academy/Nonacademy trained	1962	4.51	0.0142	2.755	0.0295
			(1.42)		(2.87)
United States				
Two 'elites'/Rest	1969	1.59	0.385	1.30	0.68
			(27.8)		(40.5)
Independents/Dependents	1969	1.47	0.143	1.235	0.172
			(12.5)		(14.8)
Intellectuals/Others	1969	1.45	0.180	1.225	0.285
			(15.3)		(22.2)

question. This can be shown to be so: with $L_1 + L_2 = 2.28$, as in 1974, the value of L_2 maximizing profits appears to be the actual value 0.327 for 1974.

The three-labor types model for the United States requires a somewhat less simple treatment. Equations (14.12) through (14.14) can be used to calculate the changes in income shares that would result from given changes in the numbers L_1 through L_3; and from the new shares and the new numbers the earnings w_1 through w_3 would follow. This can be illustrated by a few examples.

If the number L_1 increases by 10 percent, the share λ_1 increases by $0.1041 \, ln \, 1.1 = 0.00992$, and the share λ_3 decreases by -0.01019. Per capita of each group this means a decrease in group 1 by 5.25 percent and in group 3 by 1.65 percent (101.9/61.97 %). Total income goes up by an amount that can be calculated from the production function (14.4), but what is important from the distribution point of view is that, relatively speaking, members of group 3 will, in comparison to those of group 1, advance by $5.25 - 1.65 = 3.6 \%$.

If the number L_2 increases by 10 percent, the share λ_2 increases by 0.0001 ln 1.1 = 0.0000095, and the share λ_3 decreases by −0.000276. Per capita this means a decrease by 9.99 percent of income of group 2 and a decrease by 0.04 percent of group 3. Their relative position vis-a-vis group 2 has thus improved by 9.95 percent.

So far I have assumed that supply was inelastic. This assumption can now be changed into one where supply shows some elasticity. Then I have to introduce a supply function linking L' and w with a supply factor. The most natural one would be (where w_o is w in the last observed year):

$$L' = L^0 \left(\frac{w}{w_0} \right)^{\rho},$$
(14.15)

where L^0 is the relative number of those trained for leadership and ρ the supply elasticity. The crucial problem will now be to find L^0, which is needed in order to attain a desired level of w; for $\rho > 0$, $L^0 > L$; that is, we would have to train more potential leaders than can actually find a corresponding job. For the w aimed at by the policy makers, a number of the potential independents will prefer to take a job as a dependent worker, a phenomenon observed frequently when relative incomes change. As long as this is their own free choice, I think one cannot raise as the only argument against such a deliberate policy to reduce income differences that it thwarts expectations. A final judgment on such a policy should be based on a joint consideration, in terms of social welfare of thwarted expectations, costs of the policy, and the advantage of having less inequality.

Provisional Interpretation of Findings

This paper should be seen as first reconnaissance of the possibilities to reduce income inequalities in mixed economies. The macroeconomic character of the study, the admittedly crude statistical material used, as well as the deliberate choice of the simplest version of the translog production, itself already a simple type of function, underline the character of a reconnaissance of only the problem area. The impression obtained is that further reduction of inequality by competing down high incomes through an enlarged supply of scarce factors of production constitutes a possibility of some importance. Reduction to one-half of existing income inequalities is not to be ruled out beforehand.

Notes

1. With these letters the main occupational groups of the U.S. Census for non-

farm occupations have been indicated: A: professional, technicians; B: managers, administrators; C: sales workers; D: clerical and kindred workers; E: craftsmen; F: operatives, except transport; G: transport equipment operators; H: laborers, except farm; J: service workers.

2. Implying a positive slope of the "relative demand curve" (14.10); even so it yields the L_2 maximizing profits for given values of $L_1 + L_2$ (cf. section on demand for supply of factors considered).

References

ALLEN, R. D. G. *Mathematical Analysis for Economists.* London, 1938.

ARROW, J. K., CHENERY, H. B., MINHAS, B. S., and SOLOW, R. M. "Capital-Labor Substitution and Economic Efficiency." *Review of Economics and Statistics* 43 (1961): 225.

BERNDT, E. R., and CHRISTENSEN, L. R. "The Internal Structure of Functional Relationships: Separability, Substitution, and Aggregation." *Review of Economic Studies* 40 (1973a): 403.

———. "The Translog Function and the Substitution of Equipment, Structures and Labor in U.S. Manufacturing, 1929–1968." *Journal of Econometrics* 1 (1973b): 81.

———. "The Specification of Technology in U.S. Manufacturing." Discussion Paper 73–17, University of British Columbia, Department of Economics, October 1973c.

———. "Testing for the Existence of a Consistent Aggregate Index of Labor Inputs." *American Economic Review* 64 (1974): 391.

BJERKE, K., and VANGSKJAER, *Udviklingen i restindkomsten,* Copenhagen, 1975.

BOWLES, S. *Planning Educational Systems for Economic Growth,* Harvard Economic Studies, vol. 133. Cambridge, Mass., 1969.

BURCK, C. G. "A Group Profile of the Fortune 500 Chief Executive," *Fortune* May 1976: 173

CHRISTENSEN, L. R., JORGENSON, D. W., and LAU, L. J. "Transcendental Logarithmic Production Frontiers." *Review of Economics and Statistics* 55 (1973): 28.

DOUGHERTY, C. R. S. "Estimates of Labor Aggregation Functions." *Journal of Political Economy* 80 (1972): 1101.

DRESCH, S. P. "Demography, Technology and Higher Education: Toward a Formal Model of Educational Adaptation." *Journal of Political Economy,* forthcoming.

FALLON, P. R., and LAYARD, P. R. G. *Capital-Skill Complementarity, Income Distribution and Output Accounting.* Higher Education Research Unit, London School of Economics, 1974.

FOURASTIÉ, J. *Les 40,000 heures.* Paris-Geneva, 1965.

KALDOR, N. *Causes of the Slow Rate of Economic Growth of the United Kingdom.* Cambridge, England, 1966.

KEYNES, J. M. "Professor Tinbergen's Method." *The Economic Journal* 49 (1939): 558.

―――. "Comment." *The Economic Journal* 50 (1940): 154.

KUZNETS, S. *Modern Economic Growth.* New Haven, 1966.

PSACHAROPOULOS, G., and HINCHLIFFE, K. "Further Evidence on the Elasticity of Substitution among Different Types of Educated Labor." *Journal of Political Economics* 80 (1972): 786.

ROSEN, H. S. "Taxes in a Labor Supply Model with Joint Wage-Hours Determination." *Econometrica* 44 (1976): 485.

TINBERGEN, J. "On a Method of Statistical Research: A Reply." *The Economic Journal* 50 (1940): 141.

―――. *Selected Papers.* Amsterdam, 1959.

―――. *Income Distribution: Analysis and Policies.* Amsterdam, 1975a.

―――. "Substitution of Academically Trained by Other Manpower." *Weltwirtschaftliches Archiv* 111 (1975b): 466.

―――. "The Demand-Supply Theory of Incomes Tested by 1970 Census Figures." *Review of Income and Wealth* 22 (1976): 199.

―――, and POLAK, J. J. *The Dynamics of Business Cycles.* Chicago, 1950.

ULLMAN-CHISWICK, C. "The Growth of Professional Occupations in the American Labor Force: 1900–1963." World Bank Summary of unpublished Ph.D. thesis, Columbia University, 1972.

Chapter 15

James Tobin

Deficit Spending and Crowding Out in Shorter and Longer Runs

Does expansionary fiscal policy fail because of the restrictive effects of the accumulation of nonmonetary debt? Are the direct effects of government spending on aggregate demand canceled or reversed with the passage of time as the public debt grows? Does explicit recognition of the government budget identity overturn standard Keynesian doctrine regarding fiscal policy? These questions have been much discussed in recent years.[1]

The main point I wish to make here is the following: Suppose it is agreed that the public's demand for money, given their total wealth, is negatively related to interest rates. Then it will also be agreed that the very short-run impact effect of increasing the rate of government expenditure is expansionary. Although the money supply is unchanged, its velocity will rise along with interest rates. This impact effect will be canceled or reversed only if the passage of time turns the negative response of money demand to interest rates into a zero or positive response. This in turn will happen only if wealth effects on demand for money come to dominate the substitution effect. Specifically the condition is that the public's demand for wealth, and their saving, are positively related to interest rates, and that part of the accumulation induced by higher interest rates on assets other than money is held in money.

Stock-Flow Problems in Interpretation of Keynesian Equilibrium

According to Keynes, his *General Theory* refers to a short run in which "the existing quality and quantity of available equipment," among other "elements in the economic system," are taken as given.[2] Yet the solution of the model determines a rate of net investment in capital equipment that

The research reported in this paper was in part assisted by a grant from the National Science Foundation. I am grateful to William Brainard, Willem Buiter, and Gary Smith for helpful discussions of the problems and issues under study, but I absolve them of responsibility for what I say.

is in no way constrained to be zero. In general it will not be zero, and with the passage of time, the stock of capital—one of the given or independent variables of the system—will change. But "the schedule of the marginal efficiency of capital depends partly on the existing quantity of equipment."[3] Therefore the investment function, one of the crucial equations, will shift as capital accumulates or decumulates. This is an obvious reason, though not the only one, why the Keynesian solution cannot be a steady state in time.[4] The solution contains the seeds of its own destruction.

Abba Lerner long ago recognized the confusion of stock and flow in the treatment of capital investment in the *General Theory*.[5] He proposed a model in which the marginal efficiency of *investment* depends, inversely, on both the stock of capital and the flow of investment. If equation of this marginal efficiency to the interest rate requires positive net investment, the capital stock will gradually increase, lowering the rate of investment induced by the same interest rate. Ultimately net investment will dwindle to zero, and the capital stock will be stationary. In this equilibrium the marginal efficiency of investment can be identified with the marginal productivity of capital, and both will be equal to the interest rate. This was one of Lerner's many brilliant clarifications of macroeconomic theory.

The investment-capital dynamic is not the only flow-stock relationship that makes the Keynesian "equilibrium" temporary. Saving adds to wealth; wealth affects the propensity to consume and possibly the demand for money. Government deficits add to public debt and thus to the outstanding stocks of nonmonetary and monetary government liabilities; changes in the supplies of these assets may change interest rates. It is this latter observation that has attracted so much attention in the literature of macroeconomic theory in recent years. Some authors claim to have discovered a fatal flaw in the Keynesian macro model as exemplified in the common IS/LM apparatus. The flaw is described as ignoring the government budget identity.

It is more accurate, however, to regard the failure to track the cumulation of deficits into debt as just one aspect of the model's temporary and short-run character. Investment is not cumulated into capital or saving into wealth. Keynes's excuse was that he was concerned with so short a time period that, whatever the rate of investment, its effects on the capital stock would be negligible. He refers to "factors in which the changes seem to be so slow. . . as to have only a small and comparatevely negligible short-term influence on our question. Our present object is to discover what determines at any time the national income of a given economic system."[6] Even though he was not explicit about other assets, the spirit of the approach is that there is not enough time for the flows to alter the stocks significantly. Deficits do add to public debt, but even a $50 billion per year federal deficit adds only $5 billion a month to a $500 billion stock. Curiously the latter-day discoverers of the government budget equation have confined to government debt their objection to the constant-stock assumption. Indeed they have generally been content to acquiesce in Keynes's assumption that the physical capital stock is constant. But if the time span of the model is to be extended enough to allow flows to affect stocks, all stocks should be tracked, not just government debts.

The only precise way to justify the Keynesian procedure is to regard the IS/LM model as determining the values of variables at a point in time. Then this model must be regarded as a slice, in time of measure zero, of a continuous-time dynamic model. Asset stocks are among the state variables of the model at that time; they are constant (independent of the solution of the model) insofar as they are completely inherited from the past. They change as time passes, moving the instantaneous IS and LM curves. The short-run model has a new solution each microsecond; whether and where it settles down requires dynamic analysis.

It is still possible to answer certain questions by comparative static analysis of the temporary solution: How will the solution at that moment be different if, for given values of stocks and other state variables, government expenditure is different? How will the solution be different if the government, by open-market transactions with the public that take zero time, instantaneously alters the supplies of its several liabilities? How would the solution be different if past history had been different and had bequeathed to the present different stocks of assets? But the relevance of these exercises is limited because the same changes in exogenous variables will affect subsequent temporary solutions as well.

Certainly, it must be admitted, the Keynesian model, particularly the IS/LM version, has not usually been acknowledged to be so evanescent. The equilibrium language of Keynes suggests that he had a more durable solution in mind. Moreover, since the *General Theory* and even before, the dynamics and stability of Keynesian equilibrium have been discussed on the tacit presumption that it is the steady state of a dynamic system rather than itself a momentary stage of a dynamic process. Examples of such discussion include the theory of the multiplier as an infinite series, Samuelson's application of his correspondence principle to the Keynesian model, and the analysis, pioneered by Hicks himself, of the stability of IS/LM "equilibrium."[7] Presumably such dynamic analysis would be unnecessary and irrelevant if the model itself determined the values of its variables at every moment of time. If it did so, its structural equations would allow for the adjustment lags that are considered in the stability analyses cited. To make the point another way, it is somewhat inconsistent to assume that the Keynesian "equilibrium" is the asymptotic result of a long process of behavioral adjustment while ignoring the changes in stocks that are bound to occur during the period of convergence.

Interpreting the Keynesian equilibrium as the momentary solution of a dynamic continuous-time process is subject to another class of objections. The model is, after all, a set of simultaneous equations. To be sure, looking at the economic interdependence in this way is one of the most useful and insightful abstractions of economic science. But it is perhaps an unusual strain on credulity to imagine that a new set of simultaneous equations, finding the prices and quantities that clear several markets at once, is solved every instant. The weight on that much burdened *deus ex machina*, Walrasian auctioneer, would be extremely heavy.

An alternative to the continuous-time abstraction is a discrete-time model. Time is broken into periods of finite duration, during which each of the simultaneously determined endogenous variables assumes one and only one value. Flows add finite amounts to stocks: saving during the period makes wealth larger at the end of the period, investment adds to the capital stock, government deficits add to public debt, and so forth. In deciding their consumption, investment, and asset demands, economic agents are determining their end-of-period stocks; their behavior takes this into account.[8] Thus the government budget identity, for example, is explicitly respected. Bonds issued to finance a government deficit must be absorbed into savers' portfolios. The same is true of bonds or equities issued to finance private capital formation.

In this way the solution of a discrete-time Keynesian IS/LM model accounts for some phenomena that the instantaneous model does not. The discrete-time IS and LM curves include effects that in the continuous-time approach are displayed by shifting the curves as stocks change and tracking the moving solutions. The discrete-time solution also is only a temporary equilibrium; the new stocks will generally lead to different solutions in the next period.

Taken literally, both approaches are implausible. If it strains credulity to imagine simultaneous market clearings repeated every instant, it is certainly arbitrary to require the famous Auctioneer to clear every market on the same periodic schedule. Both treatments of time are imperfect and unrealistic representations of simultaneous and intertemporal interdependence. Theorists had better avoid dogmatism in favor of either method.

Deficit Financing and Crowding Out

The previous section is a prelude to my main subject, reconsidering the issue of financial crowding out, the effectiveness of expansionary fiscal policy unaccompanied by monetary expansion. *Financial* crowding out refers to an underemployment situation, in which displacement is not necessary to release resources for the use of the government or its transferees.

The standard IS/LM analysis says that complete crowding out will not occur unless (1) investment is perfectly interest-elastic (IS "curve" horizontal) or (2) demand for money is perfectly interest-inelastic (LM "curve" vertical). Condition (1) may be dismissed on the ground that adjustment costs and lags prevent investment from responding instantaneously or quickly to small deviations of the interest rate from the marginal efficiency of capital. Condition (2) may be dismissed, at least in principle, on the theoretical logic and empirical evidence of substitution between money and interest-bearing assets. Consequently the standard conclusion is that the impact of fiscal expansion will be expansionary, and crowding out will be only partial.

However, the force of the dismissal of condition (2) is weakened as longer time periods are considered. At the instant when government outlays are increased, wealth and its component asset stocks are given. The public can be reconciled to the existing money stock, even if its income-related transactions needs are greater, by higher interest rates. But wealth increases with the passage of time; the supply of government bonds is greater than it would have been less expansionary fiscal policy, while the money supply is unchanged. This is an additional source of upward pressure on interest rates. In continuous-time models, it would be represented by upward and leftward shifts of the LM curve. In a discrete-time model, part of this wealth effect would be included in the LM curve, which would for that reason be steeper than in the momentary model.

Do these wealth effects overcome the initial impact of expansionary fiscal policy? The monetarist answer is affirmative. This is, I believe, the rationale for Milton Friedman's assertion that no important proposition of monetary theory requires zero interest elasticity of the demand for money[9] (with respect to crowding out, I interpret him to mean that the instantaneous LM curve may be positively sloped but shifts backwards as deficits enlarge the stock of bonds relative to money); claims that Keynesian analysis of fiscal effects does not survive explicit recognition of the government budget identity;[10] and empirical findings, as in the St. Louis monetarist econometric model, that positive fiscal effects last only a few quarters.[11]

Figures 15.1 and 15.2 illustrate this monetarist scenario, carried to the extreme of more than 100 percent crowding out. In figure 15.1 the process is one of moving monetary equilibrium. In figure 15.2 it is telescoped into a single solution for a discrete time period, in which the increment of wealth is enough to make the LM locus negatively sloped. In figure 15.1, E_1 is the initial equilibrium at t_1, and, let us assume, one that would persist until t_2 in the absence of policy change. E_2 is the equilibrium at t_2 as a result of the new fiscal policy begun at t_1. In figure 15.2, E_1 and E_2 are alternative solutions for the period $t_2 - t_1$, E_2 with the more expansionary fiscal policy.

Within either of these frameworks, there are two necessary (but not sufficient) conditions for this scenario, or more precisely for output Y_2 at E_2 to be less than or equal to the output Y_1 at E_1. One is that the demand for money is positively related to wealth. The second is that the demand for wealth is positively related to the interest rate.

The argument is simple enough. At E_2 the demand for money must be the same as at E_1. But the interest rate is higher, and income is no higher. What keeps the demand for money up? It can only be that wealth is higher.

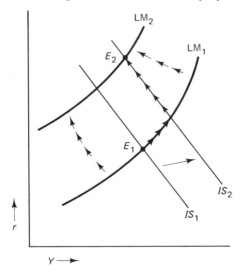

Figure 15.1 Crowding out more than 100 percent: continuous time version

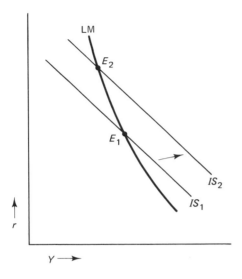

Figure 15.2 Crowding out more than 100 percent: discrete time version

Why do people want more wealth when their income is no higher? It can only be because the interest rate is higher.

Let the LM locus of figure 15.2 be defined by $M = L(r, Y, W)$ and suppose that $W = W(r, Y)$. The slope of the locus $\partial r/\partial Y$ is $-L_Y + L_W W_Y/L_r + L_W W_r$. Given that L_Y, W_Y, $L_W > 0$ and $L_r < 0$, this slope will be negative only if $L_W W_r > -L_r > 0$.

Is it plausible to expect this condition to be met? Money, in this context, is an asset on which the nominal interest rate is institutionally or legally fixed at zero or some other ceiling. As a constituent of public wealth, it is outside money, printed by the government to finance government deficits, an alternative to the issue for the same purpose of non-monetary liabilities bearing market-determined interest rates. The real world counterpart in the United States is the stock of high-powered money, defined as currency outside banks plus unborrowed bank reserves. The demand for this stock is derivative, via banks' reserve requirements and reserve behavior, from the public's demand for fixed-rate deposits.

In the scenario sketched above, interest rates on nonmonetary assets rise while those on monetary assets are unchanged; under this inducement, the public saves more and their wealth increases. Certainly they will hold more of the assets whose yields have risen. Will they also hold more money? On portfolio-theoretic grounds this seems unlikely; after all the motivation for the additional saving is the higher yield, which is lost to the extent that saving is diverted to money. The allocation of wealth accumulated in response to interest rate incentive will not be the same as of wealth accumulated at unchanged interest rates.

One possible rationalization is the transactions requirement for cash associated with portfolio management. Let α be the fraction of additional yield-induced wealth that goes into high-powered money to meet this transactions requirement. Let m be the ratio of high-powered money to wealth. Then the condition that $\partial L/\partial r$ be positive is $(Wr/W)/(-Lr/M) > m/\alpha$. Now m is very much larger than α, given the many purposes for which money is held other than portfolio transactions. So the elasticity of wealth with respect to the interest rate would have to be much larger than the substitution elasticity of demand for money.

Crowding Out in a Short-Run Discrete Time Model

I propose now to explore the issues raised in the previous section in two simple formal models. They are discrete-time models, and the government budget identity is explicitly respected. They are short-run models not in the sense that stocks are fixed but in the sense that stocks and other state variables are not stationary. I shall consider first an economy without capital and show that a positive total interest elasticity of money demand, derived from a positive interest-elasticity of saving, is necessary (but not sufficient) for the monetarist result. I shall turn then to an economy with an endogenous capital stock and show the same proposition. A comparison of the two models will indicate that the condition is both less likely to be fulfilled and less likely to be sufficient when capital accumulation is recognized.

A Model without Capital
The national product identities are:

$$Y = C + G = C + S + T - B_{-1}. \tag{15.1}$$

Here Y is national product, C private expenditure on goods and services, G government purchases, S saving, T tax payments, and B_{-1} government interest payments (equal to bonds outstanding at the beginning of the period). All variables refer to a time period of finite duration. Within the period the price level is taken as fixed, determined by events in previous periods. It may be different next period because of events in this one, but within the one-period model it is not endogenous. The same is true of price expectations. Thus the variables can be considered both real and nominal.

Taxes, net of transfers other than interest, will be taken throughout as a function of income $T(Y)$, with $T_Y > 0$. The points about fiscal policy can be made by regarding G as the policy variable. Accordingly S may be taken as a function of two endogenous variables. Y and the interest rate r, and of lagged variables like B_{-1}. The implications of the sign of S_r is a matter of central interest; the previous discussion suggests that $S_r > 0$ is necessary, though not sufficient, for complete or more than complete crowding out. Of course C can be derived from S. Thus $C_Y = 1 - T_Y - S_Y$ and $C_r = -S_r$. Although C connotes consumption, it could be interpreted to include investment expenditure in hybrid models of this genre, which allow investment but hold the capital stock constant. Indeed one way in which the important assumption $S_r > 0$ slips into such models is the natural assumption that investment is inversely related to the interest rate, $C_r < 0$.

The government deficit for the period is

$$D = G + B_{-1} - T. \tag{15.2}$$

The deficit is financed in proportion γ_B by selling bonds and in proportion $\gamma_M = 1 - \gamma_B$ by printing high-powered money. Unless otherwise noted, I consider only nonnegative values of both γ_B and γ_M. The fraction γ_B is a policy parameter; I shall be particularly interested in the case $\gamma_B = 1$. Bonds are assumed to be consols paying $1 net of tax per period. Their quantity B is measured by the coupon liability. During the period the increase in quantity of bonds is $\Delta B = B - B_{-1}$. The price of bonds is q_B.

Similarly the increase in the stock of money is $\Delta M = M - M_{-1}$. Thus:

$$q_B \Delta B = \gamma_B D$$
$$\Delta M = \gamma_M D. \tag{15.3}$$

In this model all private saving is absorbed by the government deficit, as implied in (15.1):

$$S = D = q_B \Delta B + \Delta M. \tag{15.4}$$

The public's wealth changes not only by saving but by capital gain or loss on their initial bond holdings B_{-1}. The capital gain, positive or negative, is $(q_B - q_{B,-1})B_{-1} = \Delta q_B B_{-1}$. The relevant interest rate is the one period rate on bonds r_B, which depends on the expected price of bonds next period q_B^e. A bond costing q_B held until next period will yield the holder $(1 + q_B^e)/q_B - 1 = r_B$. Thus $q_B = (1 + q_B^e)/(1 + r_B)$. Now q_B^e may depend on q_B, but I assume some regressivity in this dependence, so that $\partial q_B^e/\partial q_B < 1 + r_B$. This insures that $\partial q_B/\partial r_B$, which is equal to $-q_B/(1 + r_B) - \partial q_B^e/\partial q_B$, is negative. This derivative also describes the relation of Δq_B to r_B. I shall represent it as q_B' below.

Wealth owners decide the values of the two assets they will hold at the end of the period, or equivalently the increments in these values during the period. $F^B(\ )$ and $F^M(\ )$ represent these increments for bonds and money respectively. The targets F^B and F^M are achieved by saving and, in the case of bonds, by capital gain. They are both functions of within-period endogenous variables, r_B and Y, of predetermined initial stocks q_B, $_{-1}B_{-1}$ and M_{-1}, and of other lagged or exogenous variables. Their relation to saving is

$$S(\ ) = F^B(\ ) - \Delta q_B B_{-1} + F^M(\ ). \tag{15.5}$$

This identity may be regarded as a definition of saving in terms of asset accumulations, and I will dispense with the saving function in the formal model below. The marginal propensity to save S_Y is the sum $F_Y^B + F_Y^M$, which will be assumed, as is traditional, to be positive but less than $1 - T_Y$. Note that the capital gains term in (15.5) may make $S_{r_B} > 0$ even if $F_{r_B}^B + F_{r_B}^M \leq 0$, because the public will save to recoup the capital losses due to an increase in the bond interest rate. In order to concentrate on the monetarist issue, I shall assume that $S_{r_B} > 0$.

Here is the model, relating three within-period endogenous variables (r_B, Y, D) to the policy parameters (G, γ_B):

$$\begin{cases} F^B(\ ) - \Delta q_B B_{-1} - \gamma_B D = 0 \\ F^H(\ ) \qquad\qquad - \gamma_M D = 0 \\ \qquad T(Y) + D \quad = G + B_{-1}. \end{cases} \tag{15.6}$$

The principal interest is in the effects of variation of G on the solution of (15.6).

$$\begin{bmatrix} F_{r_B}^B - q_s' B_{-1} & F_Y^B & -\gamma_B \\ F_{r_B}^M & F_Y^M & -\gamma_M \\ 0 & T_Y & 1 \end{bmatrix} \begin{bmatrix} \partial_r/\partial G \\ \partial Y/\partial G \\ \partial D/\partial G \end{bmatrix} = \begin{bmatrix} 0 \\ 0 \\ 1 \end{bmatrix}. \tag{15.7}$$

Let Δ be the determinant of the Jacobian and Δ_{ij} its minor with respect to the element in row i, column j. Then:

$$\Delta = \Delta_{33} - T_Y \Delta_{32}$$
$$\frac{\partial r_B}{\partial G} = \frac{\Delta_{31}}{\Delta}, \quad \frac{\partial Y}{\partial G} = -\frac{\Delta_{32}}{\Delta}, \quad \frac{\partial D}{\partial G} = \frac{\Delta_{33}}{\Delta} \tag{15.8}$$

The two principal cases to consider are $F_{r_B}^M < 0$ and $F_{r_B}^M \geq 0$. In the first case, the substitution effect is dominant, as in conventional short-run Keynesian analysis. In the second case, the wealth effect dominates the substitution effect; an increase in interest rate induces additional saving, and some of it goes into money.

Case 1

The sign pattern of the determinant is

$$\begin{bmatrix} + & ? & -\gamma_B \\ - & + & -\gamma_M \\ 0 & +T_Y & +1 \end{bmatrix}. \tag{15.9}$$

Δ_{33} is positive, even if F_Y^B, the ? in (15.9), is negative. (If the second row of Δ_{33} is added to the first, Δ_{33} becomes $[\pm \; \ddagger]$ on the assumption that $S_Y = F_Y^B + F_Y^M > 0$.)

Δ_{32} is negative. Hence Δ, $\partial Y/\partial G$, and $\partial D/\partial G$ are all positive. Δ_{31} is $F_Y^B(\gamma_B - 1) + F_Y^M\gamma_B$. If F_Y^B is negative, $\partial r_B/\partial G$ is certainly positive, however the deficit is financed. (It would be possible to reduce the interest rate while increasing G if not only the deficit but part of the preexisting debt were monetized, that is, if γ_B were sufficiently negative. This is true because $F_Y^B + F_Y^M$ is positive.) If F_Y^B is positive, $\partial r_B/\partial G$ will be positive for high values of γ_B, notably 1, but negative for low values, notably 0.

These are standard Keynesian results and here serve only to show that they are altered neither by explicit respect for the government budget equation nor by the assumption that saving responds positively to interest rate.

Case 2

The sign pattern of the Jacobian is

$$\begin{bmatrix} + & ? & -\gamma_B \\ + & + & -\gamma_M \\ 0 & +T_Y & +1 \end{bmatrix}. \tag{15.10}$$

The sign of $F_{r_B}^M$ in the second row, first column, is positive instead of negative. Here it is convenient to consider first $\gamma_B = 1$, and $F_Y^B < 0$. Then Δ_{33} is positive, but Δ_{32} is also positive. So Δ may have either sign. It will be positive if and only if $F_{r_B}^B/F_{r_B}^M > (F_Y^B + T_Y)/F_Y^M$. Roughly and allegorically speaking, the condition is that a rise in interest rate has a comparative advantage in absorbing bonds, a rise in income in absorbing money. (Taxes generated by income increases arc a way of absorbing bonds when the deficit is bond financed, hence the term T_Y on the right-hand side of the inequality.)

If this condition is met, then the monetarist configuration of figure 15.2 results: $\partial r_B/\partial G > 0$, $\partial Y/\partial G < 0$, $\partial D/\partial G > 0$. Letting F_Y^B, the ? in (15.10), become positive does not change this outcome as long as the condition for positive Δ is fulfilled. However a rise in F_Y^B relative to F_Y^M makes the condition less likely. A priori portfolio substitution effects justify the assumption that $F_{r_B}^B$ exceeds $F_{r_B}^M$, and transactions balances the assumption that F_Y^M exceeds F_Y^B. This is enough to make Δ_{33} positive but guarantees positive Δ only if T_Y is zero.

If the condition is not met and Δ is negative, then the counterintuitive conclusions are: $\partial r_B/\partial G < 0$, $\partial Y/\partial G > 0$, $\partial D/\partial G < 0$. Figure 15.3 shows this outcome in IS/LM terms. Both IS and IM are negatively sloped, but IS is steeper. It is tempting to dismiss this solution as unstable. But if system (15.6) really describes the equations that the economy somehow solves simultaneously within the period, we have no right to do so. There is no shorter run, no dynamic process in real time of which this solution is an equilibrium. To say any solution is unstable is just to impugn gratuitously the iterative computer program of the Walrasian auctioneer who simultaneously clears the markets.

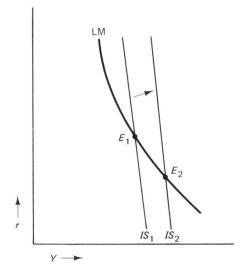

Figure 15.3 Fiscal expansion lowers interest and raises income?

In any event, there is always a positive value of γ_B, less than or equal to 1, below which $\partial Y/\partial G$ is positive. $\partial r_B/\partial G$ will also be positive if F_Y^B is negative. But if F_Y^B is positive, $\partial r_B/\partial G$ will be negative. Still excluding the possibility that Δ_{33} is negative, $\partial D/\partial G$ will always be positive.

A Model with Capital

In this model, part of each period's production is added to the capital stock available for use in subsequent periods. A unit of capital stock in use earns an aftertax return of R per period. The public owns equity titles to the whole stock, and the market value of equity per unit of capital is q_K. The yield to the equity holder for the period is r_K. This depends, of course, on q_K^e. Analogously to the relation between the valuation and one-period yield of bonds, $q_K = (R + q_K^e)/(1 + r_K)$. I assume, as in the bond case, sufficient regressivity of expectations so that q_K is negatively related to r_K. However equity valuation is also a function of another within-period endogenous variable, Y, for two reasons. One is that the contemporary earnings rate R varies directly with Y. The other is that expected future earnings R and interest rates r_K, summarized in q_K^e, are affected by current business activity. This calculation may go either way. As daily stock market reports remind us, we cannot generalize about the effect of current economic news on equity values, the relation between q_K and Y. Taking $q_K = q(r_K, Y)$, I will denote the partial derivatives as q_{r_x}, q_Y.

As previously assumed for other assets, savers have a demand for accretion of the value of their holdings of equity during the period $F^K(\ )$. This demand is met in two ways. One is the capital gain $\Delta q_K K_{-1}$ on the stock of capital at the beginning of the period. This capital gain depends indirectly on r_K and Y via the valuation function $q(r_K, Y)$ The other source of supply is by new net investment $q_K \Delta K$. This is taken to be $I = \varphi(q_K)K_{-1}$ where φ is an increasing function of q_K and thus related to r_K (negatively) and to Y. The quantity I serves the same role for capital as $\gamma_B D$ and $\gamma_M D$ serve for bonds and money.

The accounting identities (15.1), (15.4), and (15.5) are extended in obvious ways:

$$Y = C + I + G = C + S + T - B_{-1}. \tag{15.11}$$

$$S = D + I = q_B \Delta B + \Delta M + q_K \Delta K. \tag{15.12}$$

$$S(\ ) = F^B(\ ) - \Delta q_B B_{-1} + F^M(\ ) + F^K(\ ) - \Delta q_K Y_{-1}. \tag{15.13}$$

The model, relating four within-period endogenous variables (r_K, r_B, Y, D) to the policy parameters (G, γ_B), is the following:

$$
\begin{cases}
F^K(\ ) - \Delta q_K K_{-1} - \varphi(q_K)K_{-1} = 0 \\
F_B(\ ) - \Delta q_B B_{-1} - \gamma_B D \quad\quad = 0 \\
F_M(\ ) \quad\quad\quad - \partial_M D \quad\quad = 0 \\
\quad\quad\quad T(y) + D \quad\quad\quad = G + B_{-1},
\end{cases} \tag{15.14}
$$

$$
\begin{vmatrix}
F^K_{r_K} - q_{r_K}K_{-1} & F^K_{r_B} & F^K_Y - q_Y K_{-1} & 0 \\
\quad - \varphi' q_{r_K}K_{-1} & & - \varphi' q_Y K_{-1} & \\
F^B_{r_K} & F^B_{r_B} - q'_B B_{-1} & F^B_Y & -\gamma_B \\
F^M_{r_K} & F^M_{r_B} & F^M_Y & -\gamma_M \\
0 & 0 & T_Y & 1
\end{vmatrix}
\begin{bmatrix}
\dfrac{\partial r_K}{\partial G} \\[4pt]
\dfrac{\partial r_B}{\partial G} \\[4pt]
\dfrac{\partial K}{\partial G} \\[4pt]
\dfrac{\partial D}{\partial G}
\end{bmatrix}
=
\begin{bmatrix}
0 \\ 0 \\ 0 \\ 1
\end{bmatrix},
$$

$$\tag{15.15}$$

$$
\begin{cases}
\Delta = \Delta_{44} - T_Y \Delta_{43} \\
\dfrac{\partial r_K}{\partial G} = -\dfrac{\Delta_{41}}{\Delta}, \quad \dfrac{\partial r_B}{\partial G} = \dfrac{\Delta_{42}}{\Delta}, \quad \dfrac{\partial y}{\partial G} = \dfrac{-\Delta_{43}}{\Delta}, \quad \dfrac{\partial D}{\partial G} = \dfrac{\Delta_{44}}{\Delta}.
\end{cases} \tag{15.16}
$$

Like the previous model, there are two principal cases to consider: $F^M_{r_K}$, $F^M_{r_B} < 0$ and $F^M_{r_K}$, $F^M_{r_B} > 0$.

Case 1

The sign pattern of the determinant of the Jacobian is

$$
\begin{bmatrix}
+ & - & ? & 0 \\
- & + & ? & -\gamma_B \\
- & - & + & -\gamma_M \\
0 & 0 & +T_Y & +1
\end{bmatrix} \tag{15.17}
$$

The standard Keynesian results apply once again. For 100 percent bond finance, ($\gamma_B = 1$), Y, D, and r_B all rise with G. (As in the first model, these conclusions do not depend on the signs of the ? terms, provided every column in Δ_{44} has a positive sum.) But r_K might possibly fall if the top ? is positive (for example, if prosperity tends to lower expected equity values).

Case 2

The sign pattern is

$$\begin{bmatrix} + & - & ? & 0 \\ - & + & ? & -\gamma_B \\ + & + & + & -\gamma_M \\ 0 & 0 & T_Y & 1 \end{bmatrix}.$$

(15.18)

To avoid a tedious catalog, I consider solely $\gamma_B = 1$ and confine myself to the plausible assumption that $\varDelta_{44}$ is positive. As in the first model, positive interest responses in the money row make $\varDelta_{43}$ positive. The monetarist configuration then arises when $\varDelta = \varDelta_{44} - T_Y \varDelta_{43}$ is also positive.

However, a high T_Y can make $\varDelta$ negative, particularly if the ? entries in (15.18) are strongly positive. This gives rise to the same type of counter-intuitive results as in the simpler model: $\partial r_K/\partial G < 0, \partial Y/\partial G > 0, \partial D/\partial G < 0$. However the bond interest rate may go either way.

Finally consider a case intermediate between cases 1 and 2, with $F_{r_K}^M$ positive, and $F_{r_B}^M$ negative. An increase in wealth induced by higher equity yields raises the demand for money. But bonds and money are strong substitutes. With positive entries in the third (Y) column, and with a pattern of signs indicating that bonds are a closer substitute for money than for capital, $\partial Y/\partial G$ will be positive.

Long-Run Stationary Equilibrium

The long-run equilibria of models of this type, and the comparative statics of these stationary states, have been examined in the Blinder-Solow and Tobin-Buiter studies cited in note 1. The latter looks at the stability of those states, using a continuous-time model, but does not consider the implications of interest-responsive demand for wealth.

Here I shall confine myself to a cursory look at the long-run equilibrium of the second model of the previous section. The purpose is not realism. It is not realistic to imagine that policy never changes or that output is demand-determined over so long a run. The purpose is rather to pursue the pure logic of the issue. For example the persistence of the "Keynesian" conclusions cited earlier would be called into question if under the same behavioral assumptions the stationary state value of Y turned out to be inversely related to G.

In the long run, there are steady-state stock demands K^D, B^D, M^D, summing to desired wealth. These are functions of Y and of the interest rate r_B and r_K. Actual and expected q's are equal: $r_K = R$ and $q_K = 1$;

$q_B = 1/r_B$. The supply of capital is endogenous, $K(Y, r_K)$, with $K_Y > 0$, $K_{r_K} < 0$. This relationship is technological. For example, a Cobb-Douglas CRS production function implies $K = \alpha Y/r_K$. Taking the supply of money M as exogenous, then the outstanding stock of bonds B is endogenous. (Alternatively one could specify the fractions of money and bonds in the total value of debt and let that total be the endogenous variable.) The budget is balanced in long-run equilibrium. The equations, in the four endogenous variables (r_K, r_B, Y, B) are:

$$\begin{cases} K^D(\ ) - K(Y, r_K) = 0 \\ B^D(\ ) - B/r_B = 0 \\ M^D(\ ) = M \\ \quad T(Y) - B = G, \end{cases} \tag{15.19}$$

$$\begin{bmatrix} K^D_{r_K} - K_{r_K} & K^D_{r_K} & K^D_Y - K_Y & 0 \\ B^D_{r_K} & B^D_{r_B} + \dfrac{B}{r_B^2} & B^D_Y & -\dfrac{1}{r_B} \\ M^D_{r_K} & M^D_{r_B} & M^D_Y & 0 \\ 0 & 0 & T_Y & -1 \end{bmatrix} \begin{bmatrix} \dfrac{\partial r_K}{\partial G} \\ \dfrac{\partial B}{\partial G} \\ \dfrac{\partial Y}{\partial G} \\ \dfrac{\partial B}{\partial G} \end{bmatrix} = \begin{bmatrix} 0 \\ 0 \\ 0 \\ 1 \end{bmatrix} \tag{15.20}$$

The Jacobian has the same structure as (15.15), except that the bottom diagonal element is -1 instead of $+1$. Thus $\Delta = -\Delta_{44} - T_Y\Delta_{43}$. A Keynesian sign pattern insures $\Delta_{43} < \Delta_{44} > 0$, $0 < T_Y < 1$. So Δ may have either sign. Positive Δ implies positive $\partial Y/\partial G$, $\partial B/\partial G$, and $\partial r_B/\partial G$ and ambiguous $\partial r_K/\partial G$. Note that because of the increase in bond interest B, $\partial Y/\partial G$ exceeds $1/T_Y$, the amount necessary to collect taxes enough to cover the increase in G. Figure 15.4 is illustrative. LLM is the long-run balance of money demand and supply, and GT is the balanced budget locus. Both curves carry with each point the value of B that maintains portfolio balance. The rightward shift in GT represents an increase in G.

It is also possible that Δ is negative—if T_Y is low, for example. This means that the LLM curve is steeper than GT, and the comparative statics give perverse results. In the Tobin-Buiter paper, it is shown—though for a continuous-time model of somewhat different structure—that this equilibrium is unstable. An increase in government purchases starts the economy off on a track of increasing income and interest rates, which, left to itself, never converges to a balanced budget equilibrium.

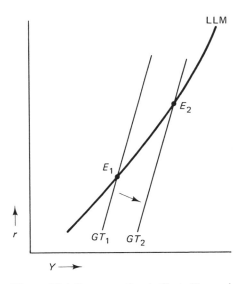

Figure 15.4 Long run fiscal effect: Keynesian case

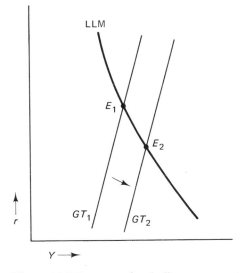

Figure 15.5 Long run fiscal effect: monetarist case 1

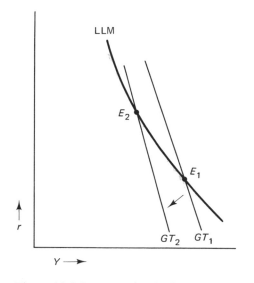

Figure 15.6 Long run fiscal effect: monetarist case 2

With the monetarist sign pattern, the two possibilities are illustrated by figures 15.5 and 15.6. In formal terms Δ_{43} is now positive. If Δ_{44} is positive, then Δ is negative and $\partial Y/\partial G = -\Delta_{43}/\Delta$ is positive, while $\partial r_B/\partial G$ and $\partial B/\partial G$ are negative. Figure 15.5 (monetarist case 1) applies. But in the analogous short-run case, Y is moving in the other direction. This suggests that the equilibria displayed in figure 15.5 are unstable and irrelevant. A monetarist nightmare comes true. Deficit spending feeds on itself in an ever weaker economy afflicted with high and rising interest rates. Figure 15.6 (monetarist case 2) represents a Δ_{44} so negative that Δ becomes positive. The budget balance line GT slopes the wrong way; moving northeast along it, the demand for bonds declines, and taxes fall to match. Expansionary fiscal policy is represented by a downward shift of GT. This long-run configuration is possibly a stable version of the monetarist scenario.

Concluding Remarks

I have tried to rationalize the monetarist claim that fiscal policy is ineffective or worse in its effects on aggregate demand, even though the instantaneous demand for money is inversely sensitive to interest rates. I found a rationalization in interest-induced saving, provided greater wealth, whatever motivated its accumulation, entails greater transactions balances. I doubt the empirical importance of such behavior, but that is another question.

At the same time, I have shown that the standard Keynesian results can, in theory, apply for long periods of time. They do not violate the government budget constraint.

What difference does it make? After all no one need advocate or practice the use of fiscal stabilization policies without the active help of monetary policies. Yet if money is not all that matters, monetary policy itself must take account of the macroeconomic effects of fiscal measures. With two major tools we can aim not only at domestic stabilization but at some other target too—growth or external balance. The moral is embarrassingly obvious, but it is frequently denied or ignored.

Notes

1. See Alan S. Blinder and Robert M. Solow, *The Economics of Public Finance* (Washington, D.C.: Brookings Institution, 1974), pp. 48–57 and literature there cited. See also their article "Does Fiscal Policy Matter?" *Journal of Public Economics* (November 1973): 318–37. My own contribution, with Willem Buiter, is "Long-run Effects of Fiscal and Monetary Policy on Aggregate Demand," in J. Stein, ed., *Monetarism: Studies in Monetary Economics* (Amsterdam: North-Holland, 1976), 1: 273–336.

2. J. M. Keynes, *General Theory of Employment, Interest, and Money* (New York: Harcourt Brace, 1936), p. 245. He goes on to say, "This does not mean that we assume these factors to be constant; but merely that, in this place and context, we are not considering or taking into account the effects and consequences of changes in them."

3. Ibid., p. 246.

4. Writing before Harrod inaugurated modern growth macroeconomics, Keynes embedded his model in a stationary setting: constant labor force, technology, and so forth. Thus the only steady state would be one with constant capital stock. But it is easy to embed it instead in a setting with a nonzero natural rate of growth. The same problem of interpretation arises when solution of the Keynesian equations gives a rate of net investment relative to the capital stock different from the natural growth rate.

5. A. Lerner, *Economics of Control* (New York: Macmillan, 1944), pp. 330–345. Lerner had previously presented the ideas in a 1937 paper of which a summary was published in Manchester Statistical Society *Report of Group Meetings*, 1936–1937.

6. Keynes, *General Theory*, p. 247.

7. P. A. Samuelson, *Foundations of Economic Analysis* (Cambridge: Harvard University Press, 1945), pp. 276–283. J. R. Hicks, *The Trade Cycle* (New York: Oxford University Press, 1950), pp. 136–154.

8. Some authors consider a beginning-of-period stock equilibrium, in which existing asset supplies are priced, followed by a within-period "flow equilibrium" in which asset accumulations, among other variables, are determined. This construction makes no sense to me.

9. M. Friedman, "Interest Rates and the Demand for Money," *Journal of Law and Economics* (October 1966), 71–85.

10. W. L. Silber, "Fiscal Policy in IS-LM Analysis: A correction *Journal of Money, Credit and Banking* 2 (November 1970), 461–72.

11. L. C. Anderson and K. M. Carlson, "A Monetarist Model of Economic Stabilization," *Federal Reserve Bank of St. Louis Review* 54 (April 1970).

A Selected Bibliography: Abba P. Lerner

Abba Lerner's publications cover a time span of more than forty-five years and encompass more than two hundred books, monographs, and articles. Space limitations preclude a full listing of the bibliography, but the editors agreed that a partial listing of Lerner's works would be both appropriate and useful.

Books and Monographs

The Economics of Control. New York: Macmillan, 1944. Reprinted New York: Augustus M. Kelley, 1971.

Planning and Paying for Full Employment (edited with Frank D. Graham). Princeton: Princeton University Press, 1946.

The Economics of Employment. New York: McGraw-Hill, 1951.

Essays in Economic Analysis. London: Macmillan, 1953, and New York: St. Martin's Press, 1953.

Everybody's Business. East Lansing: Michigan State University Press, 1962.

Flation. New York: Quadrangle Press, 1972. Baltimore: Penguin, 1973.

Economic Efficiency (with Ben Shachar; in Hebrew). Tel Aviv: Amikam, 1970.

Contributions to Books

"Economic Liberalism in the Postwar World." In *Postwar Economic Problems*, ed. Seymour E. Harris. New York: pp. 127–139. McGraw-Hill, 1943.

"Money." In *Encyclopaedia Britannica*, pp. 693–699, 1946.

"Investment, Economic Aspects." In *Encyclopaedia Britannica*. 1947. Revised July 1961.

"Foreign Economic Relations of the United States." In *Saving American Capitalism*, ed. Seymour Harris, pp. 275–284. New York: Knopf, 1948.

"The Burden of the National Debt." In *Income, Employment and Public Debt: Essays in Honor of Alvin H. Hansen, Hoyd A. Metzler*, ed., pp. 255–275. New York: Norton, 1948.

"Immigration, Capital Formation and Inflationary Pressure." In *The Economics of International Migration*, ed. Brimley Thomas, pp. 52–62. London: Macmillan, 1958.

"Macro-economics and Mirco-economics." In *Logic, Methodology & Philosophy of Science*, Proceedings of the 1960 International Congress, ed. Ernest Nagel, Patrick Suppes and Alfred Tarski. Stanford: Stanford University Press, 1961.

"Meta Economics." In *Study of Soviet Economy*, ed. N. Spulber pp. 105–109, 124–125. Indiana University Publications, February 1961.

"Consumer's Surplus." In *Encyclopaedia Britannica*, 1962.

"Keynesian Economics in the Sixties." In Keynes's *General Theory: Reports of Three Decades*, pp. 222–234. New York: St. Martin's Press, 1964.

"Capital." *International Encyclopaedia of the Social Sciences*. May 1968.

"Micro-Economic Theory." In Alan A. Brown et al., *Perspectives in Economics*, pp. 29–43. New York: McGraw-Hill, 1968.

"The Big Powers and Economic Development in the Middle East." In *The Big Powers and Present in the Middle East*, ed. S. Merlin. pp. 76–83. Rutherford: Fairleigh Dickinson University Press, 1968.

"On Instrumental Analysis." In *Economic Means and Social Ends*, ed. Robert Heilbroner, pp. 131–136. Englewood Cliffs, N. J.: Prentice-Hall, 1969.

"Price Flexibility and the International Money Market." In *Understanding Economics: Essays in Public Policy*, ed. Yung-Ping Chen, pp. 55–65. Boston: Little, Brown, 1974.

Articles and Review Articles

"The Diagrammatical Representation of Cost Conditions in International Trade." *Economica* (August 1932): 346–356.

"The Diagrammatical Representation of Elasticity of Demand." *Review of Economic Studies* (October 1933): 39–44.

"Notes on Elasticity of Substitution. II. The Diagrammatical Representation." *Review of Economic Studies* (October 1933): 68–71.

"A Note on the Elasticity of Substitution." *Review of Economic Studies* (February 1934): 147–148.

"The Concept of Monopoly and the Measurement of Monopoly Power." *Review of Economic Studies* (June 1943): 157–175.

"The Concept of Arc Elasticity of Demand. II." *Review of Economic Studies* (June 1934): 226–230.

"The Diagrammatical Representation of Demand Conditions in International Trade." *Economica* (August 1943): 319–334.

"Economic Theory and Socialist Economy." *Review of Economic Studies* (October 1934): 51–61.

"Economic Theory and Socialist Economy. A Rejoinder." *Review of Economic Studies* (February 1935): 154–156.

"A Note on the Theory of Price Index Numbers." *Review of Economic Studies* (October 1935): 50–56.

"Further Notes on Index Numbers. III. A Reply." *Review of Economic Studies* (February 1936): 157–158.

"Further Notes on Elasticity of Substitution. III. The Question of Symmetry." *Review of Economic Studies* (February 1936): 150–151.

"The Symmetry Between Import and Export Taxes." *Economica* (August 1936): 306–313.

"Mr. Keynes' 'General Thory of Employment, Interest and Money.'" *International Labour Review* (October 1936): 1–20.

"A Note on Socialist Economics." *Review of Economic Studies* (October 1936): 72–76.

"Capital, Investment and Interest." *Proceedings of the Manchester Statistical Society, 1936–37*, pp. 26–31.

"Some Notes on Duopoly and Spatial Competition" (with H. W. Singer). *Journal of Political Economy* (April 1937): 145–186.

"Statics and Dynamics in Socialist Economics." *Economic Journal* (June 1937): 253–270.

"International Trade and Transfer." *Econometrica* (October 1937): 371–372.

"A Rejoinder to Professor Cassel." *International Labour Review* (1937): 23–26.

"Saving Equals Investment." *Quarterly Journal of Economics* (February 1938): 297–309.

"An Undialectical Account of Dialectics." *Science and Society* (Spring 1938): 232–239.

"Alternative Formulations of the Theory of Interest." *Economic Journal* (June 1938): 211–230.

"Theory and Practice in Socialist Economics." *Review of Economic Studies* (October 1938): 71–75.

"The Relation of Wage Policies and Price Policies." *American Economic Association Papers and Proceedings* (March 1939): 158–169.

"Equilibrium and Dynamic Concepts in the Theory of Employment." *Econometrica* (April 1939): 186–187.

"Budgetary Principles." *Cowles Commission Conference* (report) (July 1939).

"Saving and Investment: Definitions, Assumptions Objectives." *Quarterly Journal of Economics* (August 1939): 611–619.

"From Vulgar Political Economy to Vulgar Marxism"(review). *Journal of Political Economy* (August 1939): 557–567.

"Ex-Ante Analysis and the Wage Theory." *Economica* (November 1939): 436–439.

"Professor Hicks' Dynamics" (review). *Quarterly Journal of Economics* (February 1940): 298–306.

"Some Swedish Stepping Stones in Economic Theory" (review). *Canadian Journal of Economics and Political Science* (November 1940): 574–591.

"The Economic Steering Wheel." *University Review* (University of Kansas City) (June 1941): 2–8.

"Functional Finance and the Federal Debt." *Social Research* (February 1943): 38–51. Reprinted in *International Postwar Problems* (October 1945).

"User Cost and Prime User Cost." *American Economic Review* (March 1943): 131–132.

"Interest Theory—Supply and Demand for Loans or Supply and Demand for Cash." *Review of Economic Statistics* (May 1944): 88–91.

"Government Spending, Public Debt, and Postwar Taxation." *International Postwar Problems* (January 1945): 92.

"Marxism and Economics: Sweezy and Robinson" (review). *Journal of Political Economy* (March 1945): 79–87.

"Planning and Freedom." *International Postwar Problems* (July 1945): 308–319.

"Monetary and Fiscal Policy." *Review of Economic Statistics* (May 1946): 77–81.

"The Problem of Full Employment—Discussion." *American Economic Review Supplement* (May 1946): 330–335.

"Geometrical Comparison of Elasticities." *American Economic Review* (March 1947): 662–663.

"Money as a Creature of the State." *American Economic Association Papers and Proceedings* (May 1947): 312–317.

"A Note Suggested by Samuelson's 'Market Mechanism and Maximization.'" RAND mimeographed LPC2 (June 16, 1949).

"The Inflationary Process: Some Theoretical Aspects." *The Review of Economics and Statistics* (August 1949): 193–200.

"Wage Policy in Full Employment," *Report of the Varese Meeting of the Econometric Society* (September 1950): 6–8.

"Fighting Inflation." *Review of Economics and Statistics* (August 1951): 194–196.

"Factor Prices and International Trade." *Economica* (February 1952): 194–196.

"The Essential Properties of Interest and Money." *Quarterly Journal of Economics* (May 1952): 192–193.

"On the Marginal Product of Capital and the Marginal Efficiency of Investment." *Journal of Political Economy* (February 1953): 1–13.

"Discussion on Social Choice Functions." *Econometrica* (September 1953): 482.

"Inflationary Depression and the Regulation of Administered Prices."

Joint Economic Committee, Conference on Economic Stability and Growth (March 31, 1958), pp. 257–268.

"Planning For Israel's Solvency" *Midstream* (Summer 1958): 47–57.

"Statement to Joint Economic Committee of the Senate for the Study of Employment, Growth and Price Levels" (September 24, 1959).

"Consumption-Loan Interest and Money." *Journal of Political Economy* 67 (October 1959): 512–518.

"On Generalizing the General Theory." *The American Economic Review* 50 (March 1960): 121–143.

"Economics and the Control of Man—The Case of the Economist." *American Scholar* (Summer 1960): 377–385.

"The Burden of Debt." *Review of Economics and Statistics* (May 1961): 139–141.

"Depresion Administrada." *Revista de Economica Latinoamericana*, no. 3 (Julio–Septembre 1961).

"A Note on the Rate of Interest and the Value of Assets." *Economic Journal* (September 1961): 539–543.

Review of Milton Friedman's "A Program for Monetary Stability." *Journal of the American Statistical Association* (March 1962): 211–220.

"Own Rates and the Liquidity Trap." *Economic Journal* (June 1962): 449–452.

"The Analysis of Demand." *American Economic Review* (September 1962): 783–797.

"Comments on Modigliani and Johnson, 'Debt, Exchange rates, Inflation vs. Employment'." *Review of Economics and Statistics*, 45 (February): S144–146.

"Consumers' Surplus and Micro-Macro." *Journal of Political Economy* (February 1963): 76–81.

Review of Milton Friedman's "Capitalism and Freedom." *American Economic Review* (June 1963): 458–460.

Testimony before House Banking & Currency Committee, Hearings, Subcommittee on Domestic Finance, *The Federal Reserve after 50 years*, vol. 2, pp. 1398–1431.

"On Some Recent Developments in Capital Theory." *American Economic Review* (May 1965): 284–295.

"Conflicting Principles of Public Utility Price Regulations," *Journal of Law and Economics* (June 1966): 61–70.

"Distributional Equality and Aggregate Utility: Reply." *American Economic Review* (June 1970): 442–443.

"On Optimal Taxes with an Untaxable Sector." *American Economic Review* (June 1970): 284–294.

"Understanding the Marxian Notion of Exploitation." *Journal of Economic Literature* (March 1972): 50–51.

"From the Treatise on Money to the General Theory." *Journal of Economic Literature* (March 1974): 38–42.

"From Pre-Keynes to Post-Keynes." *Social Research* (Autumn 1977): 387–415.